THE SHOWMAN AND THE SLAVE

THE SHOWMAN AND THE SLAVE

RACE, DEATH, AND MEMORY
IN BARNUM'S AMERICA

BENJAMIN REISS

HARVARD UNIVERSITY PRESS
Cambridge, Massachusetts, and London, England 2001

Copyright © 2001 by the President and Fellows of Harvard College
All rights reserved
Printed in the United States of America

Library of Congress Cataloging-in-Publication Data

Reiss, Benjamin.
  The showman and the slave : race, death, and memory in Barnum's America / Benjamin Reiss.
    p. cm.
  Includes bibliographical references and index.
  ISBN 0–674–00636–4
  1. Popular culture—United States—History—19th century. 2. Barnum, P. T. (Phineas Taylor), 1810–1891. 3. Heth, Joice, d. 1836. 4. Women slaves—United States—Biography. 5. Freak shows—Social aspects—United States—History—19th century. 6. Whites—United States—Race identity. 7. African Americans in popular culture—United States—History—19th century. 8. Racisim in popular culture—United States—History—19th century. 9. Death in popular culture—United States—History—19th century. 10. Northeastern States—Race relations. I. Title.

E165 .R36 2001
306'.0973'09034—dc21   2001024173

CONTENTS

FIGURES

ACKNOWLEDGMENTS

My thanks go first to Aida Donald, whose faith in this project and steady hand at the tiller saw me through the publication process.

I also owe special thanks to Mitchell Breitwieser at the University of California, Berkeley, for his wise suggestions and for helping me see the potential in what I had found. Also of profound help to me at Berkeley was Sam Otter, whose encyclopedic knowledge of antebellum culture was both an inspiration and a great resource. Alexander Saxton generously agreed to read an early version of this project and gave me terrific feedback. Janet Adelman provided me encouragement just when I needed it most, and Frederick Crews offered what turned out to be excellent advice on publishing. In that regard, Rick Balkin also deserves thanks. David Zimmerman let me bend his ear out of shape and gave me countless suggestions and offerings of moral support. Josh Sens and Andy Cameron read an early draft of the first few chapters, and helped me find a voice. The rest of my Bay Area friends are all over the margins of this book, having given me such a rich life in the present to balance my generally solitary meditations on the past.

Along the way I had many generous respondents and correspondents who sent me their manuscripts, pointed me to valuable documents, and offered thoughtful perspectives on my work. An incomplete list includes Bluford Adams, Rachel Adams, Robin Bernstein, Russ Castronovo, Jay Cook, Lucinda MacKethan, Fred Pfening III, Michael Sappol, A. H.

Saxon, and Rosemarie Garland Thomson. Lucy Maddox and the editorial board at *American Quarterly* helped me shape an earlier article related to this project. At Tulane, I've been fortunate to have a supportive network of faculty colleagues; I especially thank Teresa Toulouse, Geoffrey Harpham, and Lawrence Powell for their insights, encouragement, and company. At Harvard University Press, I had the benefit of two thoughtful, constructive reader's reports. The first reader was anonymous; the second started out that way and then turned into Bryan Wolf. I also thank Elizabeth Suttell for all her help at the Press, and Elizabeth Gilbert for her excellent copyediting.

This work could not have been completed—or even begun—without financial support from a Mellon Fellowship in the Humanities. Two additional dissertation-year fellowships and two research travel grants from the University of California, Berkeley, and summer research fellowships from both UC Berkeley and the Tulane University Committee on Research, allowed me to follow through. Thanks also to librarians and archivists Dorothy Koenig and Michaelyn Burnette at UC Berkeley, Jim Prichard of the Kentucky State Archives in Frankfort, and Mary V. Thompson of the Mount Vernon Ladies' Association. As I retraced some of Barnum and Heth's path, I had many excellent hosts: Stuart and Marcella Bernstein, Jeffrey Gordon and Alice Oldfather, Rick Heyman and Maria Vanoni, Andrea and Patrick Page-McCaw. My parents, David and JoAnn Reiss, contributed both the genes and a good bit of the environment that enabled me to write this book; I'm not sure which to thank them for most.

This book is for Devora, who has given me love, trust, laughter, and the best gift of all: Isaac.

THE SHOWMAN AND THE SLAVE

INTRODUCTION:
THE DARK SUBJECT

It was not a story to pass on.
—Toni Morrison, *Beloved*

IN THE SUMMER OF 1835, a twenty-five-year-old dry goods salesman named P. T. Barnum quit his day job to go on the road with "The Greatest Natural and National Curiosity in the World," thus launching one of the most remarkable careers in American show business. This curiosity was an old and infirm black slave woman named Joice Heth, who had supposedly "arrived at the astonishing age of 161 years" and been the former nurse of the infant George Washington. On the strength of these claims, she had been exhibited in towns and cities across Kentucky, Ohio, Virginia, and Pennsylvania by a hapless itinerant showman from Kentucky named R. W. Lindsay. When Lindsay couldn't turn a profit, he sold his interest in the exhibit to Barnum, who after a brief but tumultuous reign as a newspaper editor in his native Connecticut had held a variety of odd jobs in New York. As Heth's new manager and virtual owner, he found fortune and fame; but Heth became, after a life of slavery, the butt of a long-running practical joke that would outlive her by decades. In fact, wrote one commentator, "the funniest part came when the old wench died."[1]

Barnum's display of Heth started with a two-and-a-half-week stay at the fashionable Niblo's Garden in New York, where thousands came to marvel at this living historical relic. Similar engagements followed in Providence, Boston, Hingham, Lowell, Worcester, Springfield, Hartford, New Haven, Bridgeport, Newark, Paterson, Albany, and many towns in between, with several return visits to the city of New York. Newspapers reported Heth's comings and goings avidly, and crowds flocked to hear her tell stories about how she had witnessed the birth of "dear little George" and been the first to clothe and even breast-feed him; to ask her questions about the upbringing of the Father of the Nation; to join in with her as she sang the hymns she had supposedly taught him; and to laugh at her impertinent stories about the redcoats and at her haughty pretensions to be "Lady Washington." Her debility was a draw, too, and many came to gaze on— even to touch—her amazingly decrepit body. Joice Heth was advertised as weighing only forty-six pounds; she was blind and toothless and had deeply wrinkled skin; she was paralyzed in one arm and both legs (apparently the result of a stroke); and her nails were said to curl out like talons. "Indeed," wrote one observer, "she is a mere skeleton covered with skin, and her whole appearance very much resembles a mummy of the days of the Pharaohs, taken entire from the catacombs of Egypt."[2]

In the course of Heth's northern tour, several controversies arose over her identity, most of them either planted or manipulated by Barnum. Was she still a slave? If so, who owned her, and who profited from her exhibit? How had she achieved her extraordinary longevity, and what, if anything, did this achievement reveal about the nature of the different races and the propriety of slavery? Were blacks somehow more hardy than whites, or did they simply flourish under the permanent custody of whites? Was she the real thing? In one of the more absurd attempts to drum up publicity, she was said to be not just a fraud but not even a human being at all: a story planted in a New Haven newspaper—and taken seriously by more than one visitor and at least one editor—asserted that Heth was in fact an automaton made of India rubber, whalebone, and metal springs, whose voice was ventriloquized by an offstage puppeteer.

Her death on February 19, 1836, occasioned the greatest controversy of all and provided the opportunity for spectacle that helped turn Barnum into a cultural icon. And as a few upstart New York commercial newspapers covered the story, they found novel ways to increase their circulation and visibility. Heth had become one of the first true American media celebrities, but ultimately—as a corpse and then as a memory—she became an advertisement for Barnum and this new mass media even more than they advertised her. In order to gratify public curiosity about Heth's longevity, Barnum arranged to have an autopsy performed in public (charging 50 cents admission, of course). Over a thousand spectators gathered around a surgical table in a makeshift operating theater in New York's City Saloon and watched as the respected surgeon David L. Rogers carved into her body. Tens of thousands more followed the story as it was covered in clinical detail and debated in the local papers. Rogers's surprising conclusion was that Heth could not have been more than eighty years old and that every aspect of her story was therefore a hoax. A surreal journalistic war erupted in the wake of these findings, as papers outdid themselves trying to discover the "real" story. Barnum and his associate, a quick-witted lawyer named Levi Lyman, fed the flames for months, planting more hoaxes and bogus exposures, playing off journalistic rivals who were only too ready to expose each other's gullibility while neglecting the possibility of their own. Barnum and Lyman claimed that Heth was alive and well and living in Connecticut and that the body on the operating table had belonged to someone else; they claimed that Heth's remains were to be embalmed and sent on tour in Europe; they claimed to have invented Heth's story; they claimed to have been taken in like everyone else.

What eventually emerged from this series of improvisations on the corpse's identity was the celebrity of Barnum, who, through his pioneering interventions in the development of commercial culture, practically invented the modern notion of fame and—not surprisingly—became the most famous of all nineteenth-century Americans.[3] Barnum's fame mounted steadily after his orchestration of the Heth affair: he toured with the Fejee Mermaid (actually half a skeleton of a fish ingeniously melded to half a skeleton of a monkey), Tom Thumb (the amusing "little General" Charles Stratton, who famously charmed the queen of England), and Jenny Lind (the Swedish Nightingale, whose rapturous voice enthralled millions of Americans); he became the wildly successful proprietor of the American Museum (which housed an eclectic assortment of human "freaks," savages, exotic curiosities from the natural realm, works of art, and dramatic performances); he embarked on political campaigns (he became mayor of Bridgeport and ran an unsuccessful campaign for Congress after the Civil War); and finally, he collaborated with James A. Bailey in "The Greatest Show on Earth." He promoted his own name and image tirelessly by means of publicity stunts such as having an elephant plow his Connecticut farm every time a train passed, or loudly broadcasting his offer to buy the house in which Shakespeare was born and have it removed in sections to his museum in New York.

But who was Joice Heth? In his many autobiographical writings (the final version of which was perhaps the second most widely read book of the nineteenth century, after the Bible),[4] Barnum revisited the question many times, but ultimately he concealed as much as he revealed. In the earliest version (a lightly fictionalized series of newspaper sketches in 1841), she is entirely Barnum's invention, a "worthless" old slave whom he discovers languishing on a Kentucky plantation and who inspires his first great money-making enterprise. Despite the fact that this narrative was written after the emancipation of slaves in all northern states and in it Barnum's self-styled narrator refers to himself as a "Yankee," he speaks casually of "owning" Heth. As if in proof, she is portrayed as little more than a puppet whose words, actions, and even appearance are controlled by her "master." He delights in contriving ingenious methods to compel her to work when she resists his control; he even pulls out all her teeth to make her look older (a claim he would later deny). His absolute mastery of her—his negation of her will, and his ability to fashion her into whatever audiences would pay him to see—is virtually the entire point of his story.[5] But by the 1869 edition of his autobiography, *Struggles and Triumphs*, Barnum was telling an entirely different story about his relation to Heth. Although the book includes an account of the exhibit in a chapter called "My Start as a Showman," Barnum tries to distance himself from responsibility for it, claiming even to have believed in the genuineness of her claims. It was "a scheme in no sense of my own devising; one which . . . I honestly believed . . . to be genuine; something, too, which, as I have said, I did not seek, but which by accident came in my way and seemed almost to compel my agency." As for the results of the autopsy, whose utter mystification Barnum spent seven months laboring to produce, all he could say was that "the doctors disagreed, and this 'dark subject' will probably always continue to be shrouded in mystery."[6] Whose agency was compelled by whom? Joice Heth had become not a marionette but a "dark subject," a controlling phantasm who "seemed almost to compel my agency."

I have spent the last few years recovering the lost story of Heth and Barnum from a Babel of newspaper and journal accounts, from diaries, court records, and state archives, from letters and short stories, pamphlets, drawings, advertisements, poems, memoirs, jokes, histories, genealogies, and biographies. From this swirling collection of voices, though, the mystery of her identity has often only taken new shapes. For all her fame, Heth led a life that was doubly erased—once through slavery and once through imposture. Because slaves were not citizens and indeed were considered less than fully human, they have little autonomous presence in the records that historians and genealogists use to resuscitate the dead. Unlike most slaves, though, she went on, in old age, to lead a public life, an exhaustive record of which needed only to be unearthed. But that record is little more than a thorough account of who Joice Heth was not. This book is mainly an attempt to reconstruct Heth's public persona as the nurse of Washington and the oldest living human, partly an attempt to track down the private Joice Heth, and throughout an effort to explore the cultural significance of both.

How does one read the fragmentary, perplexing, often even deliberately mystifying traces of Heth's career? Carlo Ginzburg has written that historical evidence is not like a window onto another world, but neither is it like a wall; instead, it is like bits of distorted glass. "Without a thorough analysis of its inherent distortions (the codes according to which it has been constructed and/or it must be perceived), a sound historical reconstruction is impossible."[7] The peculiar difficulty in this case is that we have records of a public responding to deliberate distortions of a woman's life, and so behind the distorted bits of glass are more bits of glass—and behind these, a woman acting. And yet when the distorted and obscurely referential fragments are viewed from a certain angle, the bits of glass mirror those who would look through them. To piece them together, then, is to catch a slice of mid-nineteenth-century America off guard. Visitors who left responses to Heth's exhibit are informants on a state of collective fantasy, in which Heth became practically whatever her observers wanted her to be. That fantasy, though, was never more than a distorted vision of her visitors' everyday social lives. In the way that a dream tells us about an individual's unconscious, these records can tell us about a society's unspoken assumptions, its underlying and competing fictions of national, racial, regional, class- and gender-based, religious, and individual identities.

It is often the clash of representations that I will focus on here—the ways in which dissonance and even open argument over Heth symbolized and sometimes deflected wider issues of power, possession, and publicity in the antebellum period.[8] Heth's exhibit received many readings that bolstered dominant cultural assumptions, others that shored up a weak point, and yet others that posed problems or signified dissent—at least in a minor key. The conflicts that arose were inevitable because the claims surrounding the exhibit almost deliberately provoked disbelief, skepticism, or argument. They also arose because of the liminal status of the exhibited woman herself: at times Heth conformed to the classifications of human identity underlying her audience's sense of themselves and the world around them, and just as often she unsettled those classifications. Heth belonged to a degraded race, but was exalted for her role in history; she was paralytic and half dead but curiously animated; she was a human but was viewed as a trained animal; she was a slave in the "free" North. These ambiguities pressed on the boundaries of the normal and, in so doing, helped bring those boundaries into sharper focus. As recent scholars on the history of wonders and curiosities have written, "no one was ever indifferent to wonder," for to contemplate the singular, the odd, or the unnatural was "to challenge the assumptions that ruled ordinary life."[9] Indeed, to make sense of this singular curiosity was also to make sense of normality, to wrestle with the meanings of ordinary life that stood in implicit contrast to the vision of her extraordinariness.

To take a tour with Barnum and Heth is also to take a tour of antebellum cultural history. The story of who Joice Heth was not—the story of Barnum's Heth in the eyes of her publics—appears in retrospect not just as distorting and reflecting glass but as a wondrous magnet, attracting and reworking many of the most potent cultural forces of the period: the new role of medical science in understanding the human body; the importance for a divided nation of sustaining (or inventing) memories of revolutionary unity; shifting attitudes toward death and religion; the changing roles of women in public life; the effects of urbanization on culture and social life; competition between classes for control of the political and cultural spheres; and the emergence of the mass media and a genuinely capitalist culture. Most telling, though, and connected to each of the above, are matters of race and slavery. The Barnum-Heth tour was a traveling, shapeshifting, improvised forum for public discussion—and, just as often, public avoidance—of the racial issues that were coming to dominate political and cultural discourse, and which were newly shaping nineteenth-century Americans' self-perceptions. In particular, studying the exhibit and what was made of it illuminates disturbing aspects of northerners' psychological and even material involvement in southern slavery. Even as Heth was recounting the birth of the Father of the Nation, the man considered responsible for the freedoms northern whites enjoyed, she was at all times doing a slave's work. This work entailed not only literal servitude to a white man but a figurative public servitude to the northern whites who visited her and followed her story. Audiences reacted to her in ways that reveal much about their own conceptions of what it meant to be white, to be black, to own oneself, to own another, and to be owned.

The political meanings of race were particularly contentious in 1835, and they helped make the summer in which Heth, Barnum, and their crew wandered across the Northeast the most violent season in the history of the young Republic. Between July and October at least 109 riots broke out, more than half of which were related to debates over race and slavery.[10] This outbreak had been brewing for some time. After American participation in the international slave trade was outlawed in 1808, debates over the propriety of slavery died down for a time, only to be reignited when tensions over slavery's place in an expanding nation prompted the Missouri Compromise of 1819–20. In the following years abolitionists grew more assertive in their activities, and slave owners in the South became equally adamant about protecting their interests, often threatening and periodically practicing violence upon any who dared question their beloved institution.[11] With Nat Turner's insurrection in 1831 and the founding of William Lloyd Garrison's *Liberator* the same year, the rhetoric and behavior on both sides grew more volatile than ever, especially on the antiabolition side. Adding to this were the economic tensions between white workers and the growing free black communities in the North, both of whom were trying to adapt to new labor conditions and new urban living arrangements. Despite the fact that slavery had been outlawed in all northern states, some of the most intense rioting was in the North: Philadelphia had five major race riots between 1832 and 1849, and there were sporadic outbursts in Boston, Dayton, and New York, including a major riot in New York in 1834.[12] On this night, thousands of whites attacked the abolitionist Lewis Tappan's home, mobs brought homemade weapons to black churches, homes, and businesses, and they beat up blacks on city streets. One witness wrote, "Throughout the night the screams of tortured Negroes could be heard."[13] And on through the summer of 1835, across the country, and across Joice Heth's path, abolition meetings were violently disrupted, black churches were assaulted, fires blazed, and black and white abolitionists were dragged through the streets.

The Joice Heth exhibit itself never prompted a riot, a rather surprising fact given that theatrical displays often touched off the worst violence, and that many of these disputes took the shape—as, in a way, the Joice Heth exhibit did—of debates over the meaning of the revolutionary past.[14] But in tracing Heth's itinerant course, one feels the flames of the summer of 1835 licking at the edges of the canvas. The show was for whites an occasion to put down the stones and torches and puzzle over or laugh at—rather than fight about—the meanings of "race," a concept that was undergoing a profound change in American society. From the late eighteenth through the early nineteenth century, the Enlightenment tradition and the revolutionary ethos combined to create an egalitarian view of race among intellectuals: because all men were created equal, racial difference was subordinated to a broad commonality between the races. Race was a "problem"—but it was generally solved with reference to environmental causes; in the case of blacks, it was thought that exposure to the sun, or to disease, or to corrupting social forces created dark skin, "peculiar" facial features, and the "uncivilized" behavior that went with blackness. Implicit—and sometimes explicit—in these formulations was the idea that with time, exposure to a new climate, and proper nurturance and training, blacks would become, as nature's God intended them to be, equal to whites. (Some learned scholars even believed that blacks would *become* white.) This egalitarianism was often undercut by laws and popular opinions that treated blacks as profoundly unequal, but even in the strongest slaveholding states, few whites publicly challenged the idea of a common origin and a common humanity for all the races.[15]

By the 1830s, however, countervailing forces in law, science, and politics were beginning to change all that, by emphasizing the common bonds of European groups at the expense of blacks and Indians. Thus were created the supposedly natural categories of "whiteness" and "blackness." As of 1825, virtually all men of European descent could vote, as the property qualification for enfranchisement had been eliminated in most states and was scaled back in others. And by the time of Andrew Jackson's reign, African Americans and Native Americans were formally excluded from voting in most of the "free" states; Native Americans remaining on eastern lands were forcibly removed to the West; and free blacks in the South were subject to novel types of legal harassment.[16] Scientists during the period helped make the deepening of white privilege seem rational, even natural. As opposed to the environmental theories propounded in the previous generation, the new racial anatomists elaborated theories of separate evolutionary tracks, different mental capacities, and affinities between the "lower" races and the animal world. These efforts were, in the 1830s, rather disorganized and improvisatory; we can see in scientific reaction to the Heth exhibit some early and at times nearly accidental application of the emerging discourses of racial science to the problem of reading her identity.[17]

It was in the realm of popular culture that the lessons of racial solidarity were brought home to a mass of white Americans. During the 1830s and 1840s the cultural guardianship of the elite was explicitly challenged by increasingly rowdy working-class forms of entertainment, which rapidly became highly commodified and nearly ubiquitous. As these popular entertainments became more varied and voluble in the growing cities, they actively broke down some of the distinctions between whites, in part by depicting race as the one truly impassable boundary. In this emerging urban commercial culture—the realm of the penny paper, the blackface minstrel show, the museum, and the freak show—blacks and Indians were usually represented as savage, grotesque, freakish, comical, exotic, and profoundly uncivilized. The implication was that to be white was to be clean about the body, physically and mentally able, polite, and otherwise "normal."[18] Coverage of Heth's exhibit—and particularly of her dissection—became a commercially driven pseudo-event lodged within a growing capitalist cultural enterprise, one that drew on the energies of a potentially unruly urban crowd and turned those energies to profit. As such it was an early episode in the history of mass culture, one in which various meanings were tried out, some embraced, some discarded, some merely laughed at. In this way her story, and especially its grisly end, helped shape the world we still inhabit; but reimagining it can also lead us down some of the roads not taken, those that end in the obscure cul-de-sacs of history.

By looking in detail at the strange career of Joice Heth, this book will examine the marks left by slavery on the culture of the modernizing North and, by implication, some of the marks left by that culture on our own. Parts I and II follow Heth's career on stage, both as a living performer and posthumously, as a figure in the writings of Barnum and others. These sections show how the various ways of interpreting Heth—both her body and her act of imposture—constituted for white audiences and readers a series of indirect readings of and fantasies about their own positions in society. Part III briefly reverses the looking glass by asking how Heth generated her story. How did her act of imposture resonate with the culture of slavery from which it emerged? And how, after eighty years of life as a slave, could she have been prepared for her improbable second career as a celebrity in the North? The focus is not on what white audiences made of her, but on what she might have made of them.

I
DEATH AND DYING

POSSESSION

PHINEAS TAYLOR BARNUM was in August 1835 a young man of some accomplishment but no real calling. Born on July 5, 1810, in the thriving hat- and comb-manufacturing town of Bethel, Connecticut, he was named for his maternal grandfather, a Revolutionary War veteran and one of Bethel's largest landowners. Phineas Taylor had bequeathed to his daughter Irena sixty-three acres of land upon her marriage to Philo Barnum, who made a comfortable living as a tailor, farmer, tavern keeper, store owner, and operator of a freight service between Danbury and Norwalk. Despite the material comforts of his upbringing, Barnum would habitually refer to himself in later life as a "tailor's son," and his autobiographies would present him in the classic rags-to-riches mode of the American self-made man. His father, it is true, died in 1828 amid some financial difficulties, but Barnum greatly exaggerated the effects of this loss on his circumstances: "The world looked dark indeed, when I realized that I was for ever deprived of my paternal protector! I felt that I was a poor inexperienced boy, thrown out on the wide world to shift for myself, and a sense of forlornness completely overcame me."[1] Barnum's most recent biographer, A. H. Saxon, has pointed out that not only did Barnum still have, in his grandfather, one of Bethel's wealthiest citizens to care for him, but he consistently portrayed himself as a fifteen-year-old at the time of his father's death, when in fact he was seventeen.[2] This self-mythologization was broadly accepted, as a *New York Times* review of his 1854 autobiography attests: "From being poor and obscure, he has rapidly made himself very rich and famous."[3]

Bethel was not a likely site for the birth of the greatest showman of the century. Its politics and culture were dominated by the Congregationalist church, whose stern moralism and elitism sprang from its Puritan heritage. The influence of the church made theatrical displays and commercial amusements of any kind rare. But the Barnums—a family of great practical jokers—belonged to the relatively new and much more liberal Universalist church. Barnum thus perceived himself as something of an outsider in Connecticut, and he would forever after see his career as a crusade against prudery and high seriousness. After his father's death, he made his way to the city of New York, where he took a job as a clerk in a grocery store. New York, with its relatively tolerant Dutch-influenced culture, had had a viable theater since the 1730s, whereas Connecticut, Rhode Island, New Hampshire, and Massachusetts were still subject to laws suppressing stage plays and other theatrical amusements.[4] In his off-hours Barnum went to the theater, which he had had no opportunity to do as a child. Much as this suited him, he was unhappy working for a salary, and he moved back to Bethel a year later to be with his grandfather and to open a fruit and confectionery store. He also took up with a young tailoress named Charity Hallett, a "fair, rosy-cheeked, buxom-looking girl with beautiful white teeth" whom he had met two years earlier.[5] Charity was apparently attracted to his exuberance, cleverness, and drive for success, but in the years after their marriage in 1829 these qualities would take their toll on her. Her life with Barnum was marked by numerous episodes of "nervous illness," which periodically incapacitated her and which Saxon interprets as a desire for escape. (It was her husband, though, who would make the escape: three months after Charity died in 1873, he secretly married a twenty-two-year-old English actress, Nancy Fish. Barnum's second wife, too, would become a "semi-invalid" who found she benefited greatly from stays in the sanitarium; she recovered from her mysterious condition after Barnum's death.)[6]

Barnum's restlessness is apparent in his résumé of the next few years. While running the store, he became a successful agent for a lottery business, and with his new funds he opened a larger country store and began dealing in real estate. Eventually, though, his indignation at what he perceived as the Congregationalists' stranglehold on power led him to involve himself in politics. Connecticut was one of the last states in New England to retain a tax on its citizens in support of churches—giving even more power to the Congregationalists—and its blue laws were the harshest in the nation. Barnum wrote several letters to local papers protesting these archaisms, and when they were rejected, he decided, at the age of twenty-one, to open his own paper, while maintaining a hand in his other business ventures.

Few issues of the *Herald of Freedom* survive, but those that do display a lively writing style, a commitment to Jacksonian egalitarianism, a fierce disdain for the social elite, and an eagerness to expose the editor's enemies as hypocrites or even conspirators against freedom. In railing against *"purse-proud overbearing lordlings"* and the *"disgraceful aristocratical party"* that ruled the state's General Assembly, Barnum made enemies easily and was sued by several readers, including his own uncle. The most spectacular scrape stemmed from his charge that Seth Seelye, a deacon of the church and rival Bethel store owner, had "been guilty of taking *usury* from an orphan boy."[7] Exactly what this means and why it would be so explosive a charge is not clear. Was the Bethel-Danbury area paralyzed by fear of those who sought to squeeze profits from orphan boys? The charge seems more expressive of the values of seventeenth-century England than those of an America on the verge of its most rapid period of capitalist expansion, but then again, so does Bethel itself. To protect his honor, Seelye sued, and the twenty-three-year-old Barnum was fined one hundred dollars and sentenced to sixty days in jail. This setback ultimately provided Barnum his first moment in the spotlight. His cause was taken up by the Reverend Theophilus Fisk, a Universalist minister who edited a liberal religious paper in New Haven and who, like Barnum, frequently berated the ruling classes.[8] "Is it possible," wrote Fisk, that "an American, a Freeman—a Husband—has been torn from his family hearthstone and by the strong arm of oppression has been incarcerated within the gloomy walls of a Common Jail!!! An American Citizen!!! by the iron hand of power shut out from the glorious sunlight—and that too for no crime!!!"[9] By the end of his jail term, Barnum found himself a local hero. At the courtroom where he had been convicted, a throng of sympathizers and curious onlookers gathered for a celebration. A choir sang an ode written in his honor, and

Fisk gave a rousing speech on the freedom of the press. The party then moved on to a local hotel for a grand banquet, and at the evening's end Barnum was driven home in a six-horse carriage, with sixty more carriages in procession, to the accompaniment of a military band and booming cannons.[10] This event whetted Barnum's taste for outrageous display and scenes of self-aggrandizement. Because Bethel could promise few such moments (and because the lottery was now outlawed), within a year he was off to New York again.

It is worth lingering over one scene from his childhood in Bethel. There were few African Americans living in the area, but as in most of New England, those few were overwhelmingly poor, and they constituted a disproportionate percentage of the region's convicted criminals.[11] On November 13, 1817, when Barnum was seven, the Danbury court sentenced one such man, a former slave known as "Black Amos" Adams, to death for a "heinous" criminal assault on a white woman. As Adams's was only the second execution in town history (the other had also involved a black man), the event caused a public sensation. This was a local instance of a wave that was sweeping across the country. Popular interest in public executions was so high that one writer speculated on the existence of an organ of destructiveness in the human brain that led people to seek out scenes of bodily punishment.[12] The 1830s would usher in an era of penal reform that outlawed such spectacles in favor of arguably more terrifying hidden forms of punishment; but until then public executions—especially those of blacks—were a popular form of street theater.[13] As an old man, Barnum recalled the carnival atmosphere surrounding Black Amos's death. People had walked or ridden as far as twenty-five miles to see the hanging, many arriving in town the night before. First the prisoner was led up to the Congregational church, where the minister preached a lengthy sermon, and then a parade—with fife and drums—continued on to the place of execution. Refreshment booths were set up in the square, and so many onlookers climbed into trees to get a better view of the gallows that branches came crashing down. "When he dropped and my mother groaned," Barnum wrote in a letter nearly seventy years later, "I was too young to realize that there was any occasion for sorrow."[14] By the time of this writing, Barnum had remade himself as a Republican politician and had become a firm opponent of capital punishment as well as a supporter of African American suffrage, and so the scene played back for him like echoes of a guilty conscience. But the spectacle of northern whites gaping at a dead black body, while enterprising souls turned a profit at the concession stands, eerily foreshadows the spectacle that was to inaugurate Barnum's extraordinary career as an entrepreneur of culture. Indeed, as one historian suggests, as the whipping post and gallows were withdrawn from the public eye, lurid commercial entertainments filled the void in popular taste.[15]

Two years after Barnum left Bethel for good, when he was working in a dry goods store in lower Manhattan and dreaming of something greater, a man named Coley Bartram approached him with a tantalizing proposal. As Bartram explained it, he and his partner had recently "owned an interest in a remarkable negro woman whom he believed to be one hundred and sixty-one years old, and whom he also believed to have been the nurse of General Washington." Bartram had then sold out his interest to his partner, R. W. Lindsay, of Jefferson County, Kentucky, who was still exhibiting the woman in Philadelphia's Masonic Hall. The exhibit had drawn the notice of the press in New York and Boston, who anticipated Heth's arrival in their cities. Lindsay, however, proved to have "very little tact as a showman" and was eager to get her off his hands; Bartram suggested to Barnum that he be the one to take her.

Why Barnum? His autobiographies—which together come to over a thousand pages—are for all their historical interest determinedly unrevealing psychologically. Bartram, described as merely "acquainted" with Barnum and the owner of the store, appears out of nowhere. And so does Barnum's decision to pursue the strange offer and a life in the field of amusements. To the extent that he speaks of his career change at all, it is in providential terms: it was "the business for which I was destined . . . I did not seek the position or the character. The business finally came in my way; I fell into the occupation."[16] All I can add to this insistently empty explanation is to record one episode in Barnum's life that goes unmentioned in any of his memoirs or in any biographies of him. In 1831, when he was working in New York for the first time, he fell in with a traveling comedian from Pennsylvania named Col. Hugh Lindsay. (I have been unable to determine whether Colonel Hugh was any relation of the R. W. Lindsay who first exhibited Heth.) Colonel Lindsay left behind a memoir, one of the more explicit portraits of popular amusements in the early nineteenth century. In it, he mentions employing "a young man by the name of Barnum, from New York," who performed legerdemain and owned an "educated goat."[17] Exactly what this goat did on stage is not clear, but we can probably place it in the long line of spin-offs of the famous "Learned Pig" that toured England in the late eighteenth century and inspired many imitators in America. This pig rearranged cards on the ground to spell names, solve arithmetical problems, and tell time.[18] Or Barnum and Lindsay's goat may have been an automaton like "le canard artificiel" of Jacques de Vaucanson—a mechanical creature that quacked, ate, drank, swam, and, as a final flourish, produced a small turd—or the mechanical elephant, which could produce the same effect (but which took twenty-four hours to do so).[19] Whatever the precise nature of their goat's identity and performance, Colonel Lindsay and Barnum were visited one day by a skeptical old lady, who pronounced her opinion that the goat was nothing more than "a show-actor dressed in a goatskin." When her daughter pointed out that the goat had just produced some "discharge," the old woman responded, "Pooh, they are nothing but dried cherries," and proceeded to chew on them. She shortly became nauseated and had to leave the room in haste. If this demonstrates anything, other than Colonel Lindsay and Barnum's outrageously bad taste, it is that Barnum as a young man was not much disposed to reflect on the direction his life was taking: a good laugh and the possibility of making a few dollars probably seemed like enough. And contrary to Barnum's self-representation, the episode shows that when Bartram approached him four years later with his odd proposal, Barnum was not a complete novice in the entertainment line.

At Bartram's suggestion, Barnum traveled to Philadelphia in July of 1835 to meet R. W. Lindsay and his charge. Heth had been described in the press as a "curiosity" and a "natural wonder," and Barnum drove south in a state of considerable excitement. In a back room of the Masonic Hall, he examined the woman, her story, and the documents attesting her authenticity. First he inspected her body. The following, taken from Barnum's 1854 autobiography, is the fullest description he ever gave of Joice Heth's appearance, but it is also unintentionally revealing about his own fascination.

I was favorably struck with the appearance of the old woman. So far as outward indications were concerned, she might almost as well have been called a thousand years old as any other age. She was lying upon a high lounge in the middle of the room; her lower extremities were drawn up, with her knees elevated some two feet above the top of the lounge. She was apparently in good health and spirits, but former disease or old age, or perhaps both combined, had rendered her unable to change her position; in fact, although she could move one of her arms at will, her lower limbs were fixed in their position, and could not be straightened. She was totally blind, and her eyes were so deeply sunken in their sockets that the eyeballs seemed to have disappeared altogether. She had no teeth, but possessed a head of thick bushy gray hair. Her left arm lay across her breast, and she had no power to remove it. The fingers of her left hand were drawn down so as nearly to close it, and remained fixed and immovable. The nails upon that hand were about four inches in length, and extended above her wrist. The nails upon her large toes also had grown to the thickness of nearly a quarter of an inch.[20]

Such scrutiny of the human commodity by the prospective owner was a normal feature of the slave trade, but here almost all of the usual terms were reversed. Compare Barnum's examination of Heth to the former slave John Brown's description of the slave pen:

The slaves are brought from all parts, are of all sorts, sizes, and ages, and arrive in various states of fatigue and condition; but they soon improve in their looks, as they are regularly fed, and have plenty to eat. As soon as we were roused in the morning, there was a general washing, and combing, and shaving, pulling out of grey hairs, and dyeing the hair of those who were too grey to be plucked without making them bald. When this was over—and it was no light business—we used to break-fast, getting bread, and bacon, and coffee, of which a sufficiency was given to us, and that we might plump up and become sleek. . . . The poor wretches who are about to be sold, are instructed to look "spry and smart": to hold themselves up, and put on a smiling, cheerful countenance. When spoken to, they must reply quickly, with a smile on their lips, though agony is in their heart, and the tear trembling in their eye. They must answer every question, and do as they are bid, to show themselves off; dance, jump, walk, leap, squat, tumble, and twist about, that the buyer may see they have no stiff joints, or other physical defect.[21]

The one constant in the two accounts is the focus on the slave's docility and happiness; immediately after his description of Heth's body, Barnum wrote that "she was very sociable, and would talk almost incessantly as long as visitors would converse with her." This apparent consent to her examination, of course, may well have been simulated under coercion as it was with the slaves Brown describes. But all the other terms of the inspection were reversed. In contrast to the plumping and preening, the jumping and tumbling that increased the value of the slave in the typical inspection, Lindsay clearly wanted to showcase Heth's hideousness and immobility. The marks of her decrepitude became the chief attraction for Barnum, who correctly surmised that they would also become authenticating marks as powerful as any documents attesting to her longevity. His graphic descriptions of her debility—cataloguing, even measuring, her grotesque features, down to the thickness of her toenails—would become a staple of journalistic representations of Heth.

The interest in the authenticity of the exhibit, however, cannot explain the intensity of Barnum's scrutiny. What would Barnum's position be, in his memory of this scene, as he witnessed Heth "lying upon a high lounge . . . her lower extremities . . . drawn up, with her knees elevated some two feet above the top of the lounge"? And why include this information? (He seems to have asked himself this in revising his autobiography in 1869, for his later description of his first meeting with Heth, otherwise identical to this one, omits the sentence in question.) Perhaps what readers of Barnum's account are being convinced of is not Barnum's belief in the story, but his recognition that he could translate his own disgusted attraction for her decayed sexuality into capital. Such attraction would also impel another, and far broader, northern market for black bodies that Barnum helped get off the ground: that of the blackface minstrel show.[22]

Barnum relinquished his focus on Heth's wondrously hideous body long enough to remark on her genial nature. In addition to noting Heth's "sociability," he reported that she laughed, sang, and told engrossing stories about "her protégé, 'dear little George,' as she termed the great father of our country . . . 'In fact,' said Joice, and it was a favourite expression of hers, 'I raised him.' " Supporting these assertions, Lindsay offered documents. Most prominent was a bill of sale, impressively yellowed and folded over so many times that the creases were nearly torn. The bill, dated February 5, 1727, transferred "from Augustine Washington [George's father], of the County of Westmoreland, Virginia, to Elizabeth Atwood [a sister-in-law and neighbor of Mr. Washington] . . . 'one negro woman, named Joice Heth, aged fifty-four years, for and in consideration of the sum of thirty-three pounds lawful money of Virginia.' " Because Mrs. Atwood lived near Mount Vernon, Lindsay explained, Aunt Joice was called in at the birth of George and "clothed the new-born infant." (Later versions of the story have her suckling him as well, although her age of fifty-four would have rendered this suspicious to anyone who took the trouble to do the math.) Barnum's account of the interview becomes at this point rather tangled and obscure. How could it be that no one had taken note of such an interesting personage as the nurse of Washington before? Lindsay's explanation, Barnum claims, was that Heth "had been lying in an out-house of John S. Bowling of Kentucky for many years, that no one knew or seemed to care how old she was, that she had been brought thither from Virginia a long time ago, and that the fact of her extreme age had been but recently brought to light by the discovery of this old bill of sale in the Record office in Virginia, by the son of Mr. Bowling." The young Bowling then made inquiries, took the paper home, and "became confirmed in regard to the identity of Joice with the slave described in the paper."[23]

This pseudo-response raises more questions than it answers. Who exactly was Bowling? How had he obtained Heth from Mrs. Atwood? What had his son been doing snooping around the Record Office in Virginia? Why had Heth herself not told anyone of her background, if she was now so garrulous about it? It seems likely that Lindsay gave this story to Barnum with an assortment of nods and winks. Or that Lindsay, in his apparent dimness, believed he was putting one over on Barnum, and that Barnum knew that Lindsay thought this and humored him, believing that the questions left unanswered could themselves turn out to be profitable. At any rate, Barnum simply concludes that "this whole account appeared to me satisfactory, and I inquired the price of the negress."

From 1854 on, Barnum reiterated this story about his meeting with Lindsay and consistently asserted that he had believed in Heth's authenticity. As he put it in an 1877 interview, "I believed the documents in her possession as much as I believe the declaration of independence."[24]

(Amazingly, his biographer Saxon concludes that Barnum probably did believe the documents, and only came to suspect that they were false later on in the tour.)[25] Prior to that date, however, Barnum had bragged of having invented the Washington's nurse story from whole cloth. Neither claim holds water. Granted, the increasingly broad array of natural wonders displayed before nineteenth-century audiences would have made the woman's preternatural old age plausible to many, but would not have been enough to convince her notoriously shrewd and calculating owner. Given Barnum's subsequent manipulations of the Heth exhibit, in which she would become everything from a freed slave advocating abolition to a human puppet absolutely bound by Barnum's will, from a cleverly constructed automaton to a performing corpse, we would have to posit a remarkably isolated naïveté to say that he actually believed from the outset that he was exhibiting the nurse of Washington. A more accurate claim might be that he saw no advantage in inquiring too deeply into the matter.

Nor could he have invented the story himself, since Heth was performing the role of Washington's nurse well before Barnum ever exhibited her. On January 17, 1835, the *Alexandria Gazette* ran the following article:

> Rather a Tough Story. A correspondent in one of the Cincinnati papers, states that a colored woman age 161 years is now exhibiting at one of their museums. She is said to have belonged to the father of Washington, and appears to have all her faculties except sight which she has been deprived of 60 years, before which time, however, she frequently had the pleasure of seeing our beloved Washington.—Her memory seems to be accurate. She recollects having joined the church about 140 years since and says she has received great happiness from having done so. It seems that she has had several very interesting visions; the relations of which are very interesting.

Six months later word had spread east and north, and newspapers in New York and New England began to anticipate her arrival.

> 161 YEARS OLD. The colored woman, who has been exhibited at Louisville, Ky., as being 161 years old, is travelling this way. We notice by the Wheeling Daily Gazette of the 20th, that she was then in that place attracting crowds of visitors, "as the greatest wonder now to be seen in the world." Her name is Joice Heth. The Gazette appears to entertain no doubt of the truth of her age as given to the public. In the description

of her it is said that "she was formerly the property of Augustine Washington, the father of Gen. George Washington, and purchased of him by E. Atwood, in 1727, as appears from the original bill of sale. She has been exhibited in various places and has elicited every where the wonder of those who have seen her; her appearance fully justifying the fact of her age. She has been blind about 75 years, and weighs only about 45 or 50 pounds; she retains her faculties in a wonderful degree, and relates many interesting incidents of time long since past."[26]

In these early notices, many of the features that would be central to Barnum's exhibit of Heth were already in place: a bogus bill of sale, the account of her transmission from Augustine Washington to Elizabeth Atwood, her blindness and general decrepitude, her religiosity, her lively anecdotes. While these records do not quite convince one that Barnum "honestly believed [the story] to be genuine," they do support his claim that the exhibit "was a scheme in no sense of my own devising."

Few recorded traces remain from Heth's tenure under Lindsay and Bartram as they traveled from Cincinnati through Kentucky and Virginia to Philadelphia. Whereas the subsequent northern exhibit generated an extensive record of reportage and commentary, the reactions of spectators along this more southerly trail can only be guessed. Of particular regret is that we have virtually no record of the response of whites in slave-owning states to this slave's performance. A large part of the problem is that Lindsay, possessing "little tact as a showman," was unable to generate widespread curiosity about and coverage of Heth's act.

Lindsay was asking $3,000 to take over the exhibit, but Barnum talked him down to $1,000. Even this amount, he later wrote, was beyond the means of a grocery store operator, and so, offering "glowing representations" of the "golden harvest" that was to be produced, he convinced a friend to loan him half. He sold out his interest in the store as well, and from that point on dedicated himself to the public exhibition of the remarkable, the curious, the specious, the spectacular, and the bizarre. It would be his great joke—and later his embarrassment—that he achieved his first triumph with an old, infirm, and quite possibly unwilling slave woman.

Barnum's biographers have been divided on the question of whether, in exhibiting Heth, Barnum became Heth's owner.[27] Barnum's own answers are typically contradictory. In 1854 he wrote that with his $1,000 payment, he "became the proprietor of the negress." But in his 1869 autobiography, he had become simply "the proprietor of this novel exhibition."[28] Not "the negress" but "the exhibition"—the difference is subtle but important. Slavery had been abolished in New York—which, along with New Jersey, was among the last northern slave-owning states—as of 1827, but free blacks were subject to limitations on their freedoms that made their separation from slavery precarious. Not only were they frequently kidnapped and sold in the South, but, under the Fugitive Slave Law of 1793, they could be tried as fugitives on the slightest pretext and were provided neither trial by jury nor counsel for the accused.[29] Barnum's claim to have owned Heth demonstrates yet another indignity attending black life in the "free" North. Even if it was not literally true, the fact that it could be uttered so casually shows that, under the right circumstances, the idea of a Yankee owning a slave in the North was not entirely preposterous.

So what is the truth? Two surviving documents will help. The first is a contract between Lindsay and John S. Bowling, Heth's apparent owner, dated June 10, 1835. In it, the two men from Jefferson County, Kentucky, "do agree for the term of twelve months, to equally participate in the gains and losses in exhibiting the African woman Joice Heth in and amongst the Cities of the United States." At the time of Heth's performances under Lindsay, then, she was still legally bound to Bowling; Lindsay owned only half of the exhibit, which was intended to last for twelve months. It follows that in addition to splitting the profits of the exhibit, they were bound to split some of the risks—if Heth were to expire during this time, then Lindsay was bound to "assist him Bowling, to Cincinati [*sic*] as he is infirm."[30] But a contract signed with Barnum on August 6 adds some confusion (Figure 1). In this agreement, Lindsay sells to Barnum and a man named William P. Saunders "the possession of the person of the African woman, JOICE HETH and the sole right of exhibiting her during the unexpired time of the twelve months" mentioned in the earlier agreement. Surpassing the more limited phrasing of the Bowling-Lindsay contract, the Lindsay-Barnum-Saunders agreement states repeatedly that "the possession of the *person* of . . . Joice Heth," as well as possession of her exhibit, is being transferred. It is not clear why Saunders backed out of the agreement (his name is consistently circled and crossed out in pencil) or

1. Portion of the bill of sale transferring possession of "the African woman Joice Heth" to Phineas T. Barnum. William P. Saunders is also listed as a purchaser, but his name—never mentioned in any other document pertaining to the exhibit—is circled and crossed out.

even who he is, nor is it clear what has happened to Bowling or his half of the claim. But what emerges is the sense that even if only Bowling is spoken of as the true "proprietor of the woman," Lindsay and Barnum both assumed broad powers over Heth. If they weren't exactly her owners, they were for a time certainly her masters: they could each be said to have leased her.

Barnum may later have sought to conceal his involvement in slavery, but his mastery over Heth reminds us that, well into the nineteenth century, slavery was truly an American institution, not just a southern one. As Joice Heth traveled north with Barnum, few questioned the propriety of his relationship with her, and even fewer latched onto the potential legal issues involved in a Yankee's participation in chattel slavery on free ground. This is all the more surprising given the explosiveness of the slavery debate during this period. No abolitionist paper seems to have commented on her exhibit, and no abolition society took her up as a cause célèbre. No doubt there was more pressing work to be done in defending the masses of slaves under the lash in the South and warding off the mob that was always at the door; commenting on the career of an old woman who—if publicity was to be believed—was milking her celebrity status for all it was worth might well have seemed trivial and possibly even counterproductive. And yet it may also have been a missed opportunity. Here, after all, was no faceless slave laboring in some distant field. Could not Heth's purported connections to Washington, her charming stories, and all that made her of such great interest to northern visitors and readers turn her exhibit into a touring opportunity for abolitionist comment—and one paid for by her owner? (The only person to whom this tactic occurred—unsurprisingly—was Barnum himself, as will be seen.)

Although Barnum might not have entirely "owned" his "dark subject," his subsequent actions left no doubt about his willingness to own slaves. In the winter of 1837–38, shortly after his triumph with the Joice Heth autopsy, Barnum made a tour of the South. The *New York Atlas* (which would become a mouthpiece for Barnum in the 1840s) published an article by Barnum that tells of his purchasing a slave on a trip through Mississippi and of his whipping the slave and selling him at auction when he suspected him of stealing.[31] From his roots in lily-white Bethel, Barnum had become a slave owner in the South, who participated fully in the dirty work of bondage: buying, selling, and whipping human beings. That this experience did nothing, for many years, to injure Barnum's growing reputation—that he could, on the contrary, brag about it—gives a sense of what the abolitionists were up against.

What of Heth's other masters? Whether Bowling made it back to Cincinnati, with or without the assistance of Lindsay or Barnum, is unclear. Bartram, too, slipped off into obscurity, apparently returning to his farm in Connecticut.[32] Lindsay's life appears at first to have returned to normal. Two weeks after he sold out to Barnum, he made an application to the Jefferson County Court to open a tavern in Louisville. While Barnum was glowing in his newfound wealth and celebrity, Lindsay was involved in more mundane matters, suing a man for nonpayment for "Forty half-Barrels of Buckwheat flour."[33] In 1841, living in Pittsburgh, he put in another suit, this one against Barnum for nonpayment of "a pipe of brandy" that he claimed was owed him in the Joice Heth transaction, and he succeeded in having Barnum thrown in jail overnight.[34] Barnum's success where Lindsay had failed rankled, and the showman's growing fame seems to have unnerved him. Twelve years later, visiting a friend in Boston, Lindsay became ill after an alcoholic binge. He began raving about money that Barnum owed him, and persuaded his friend to apply to Barnum for relief. In his return letter, Barnum revisited, not for the last time, his involvement with Heth:

> I never had anything to do with him [Lindsay] except to buy from him, in *perfect good faith* & pay him the money for, an old *negress* which he falsely represented as the "nurse of Washington" and which he imposed on me as such by aid of a *forged bill of sale* purporting to have been made by the *father* of George Washington. I honestly *believed* all this & exhibited accordingly, as Lindsay had done for months previous. Finally she died & the imposition became manifest, and *I* have ever since borne the stigma of *originating* that imposture. I never denied it before—but I might have done so truly. This is all the "obligation" I am under to Lindsay, but he is a poor devil, and I hope to see him recover.[35]

He sent Lindsay one hundred dollars, and wishing to wipe away the stigma of his dark subject's imposture, he began to distance himself from one set of lies by telling another.

THE CELEBRATED
CURIOSITY

THE TRAFFIC IN NOVELTY in the early Republic was largely cultivated through channels of itinerancy, what one scholar has called a collection of "hawkers and walkers." Those with rare talents, products, performances, or other cultural wares to display made their way across the eastern states and as much of the frontier as was opened. Puppeteers, peep-show artists, lecturers, medicine men, practical phrenologists (those who set their hands to their visitors' crania in order to analyze their character "scientifically"), and animal exhibitors all solicited audiences in taverns, inns, and barns. The itinerant showman generally traveled alone, though he was often preceded by an advance man to drum up publicity by taking out newspaper advertisements, posting bulletins, or spreading gossip. Through the mid-1830s, most exhibitors took only what they could manage themselves: a moving diorama, a kaleidoscope, healing herbs, an automaton piano player, a hot-air balloon, a lion, a couple of camels, an owl, orangutan, or ox, or a "great tunny-fish, found stranded." To gauge the cultural value of Heth in comparison with some of these other exhibits, it is interesting to note that in 1834 James R. and William Howe of Somers, New York, had an elephant valued at $9,000, a rhinoceros worth $10,000, and a zebra, a Bactrian camel, a gnu, two tigers, and a polar bear each worth between $2,000 and $3,000, whereas a year later, Barnum paid a mere $1,000 for his year's possession of Heth.[1]

In the loose network of itinerant shows and salesmanship in the nation's early years, a wide range of culture was available both in cities and on the frontier, and the lines of cultural hierarchy that would harden in mid-century were significantly blurred. Lecturers such as Washington Irving and Benjamin Rush relied on the same channels of publicity as a touring rope-walker, a bearded lady, a fire-eater, or a magician. As late as the mid-nineteenth century, a newspaper article reported that Ralph Waldo Emerson's lecture tour had to compete for attention in Cincinnati with "a *notable* fat boy [who] was exhibiting at the Museum."[2] Certainly not all of these itinerants drew the same audiences,[3] but what bound would-be purveyors of culture together was the necessity of face-to-face transactions, repeated across time and space. For the new American nation, this leveling and immediacy were often offered as a public enactment of its democratic principles; even the Declaration of Independence had to be read aloud over and over to crowds in towns throughout the colonies before it could be ratified.[4]

Barnum's tour with Heth largely conformed to the parameters of early modern itinerant culture, even as it probed some of the new possibilities brought on by the emergence of the modern city: by the mid-nineteenth century a rapid acceleration of technological innovation and techniques of publicity would make cities the center of cultural production and would present a much wider range of products and experiences for cultural consumption. Barnum was more shrewd in conducting his road show than Lindsay had been, but like his predecessor, he exhibited Heth as a free-standing act in towns and cities across the East (later, her exhibit might have been a part of a more heavily commercialized and urban spectacle like a circus or museum), and he relied mainly on newspaper advertisements and word of mouth to attract visitors. From Philadelphia, Barnum and Heth moved on to New York's Niblo's Garden via the railway that had recently been laid down. "As she was bundled up in the Rail Road Cars," the *New York Herald* wrote in its subsequent "exposé" of the Heth affair, "people gazed, wondered, looked and some laughed."[5] The railroad was a key development in the commercialization of leisure and the development of nineteenth-century capitalist culture, but Barnum's use of it shows that the transformative potential of the transportation revolution was not yet fully felt in the realm of entertainment. In contrast to the itinerancy that he practiced with Heth, the model that he pioneered later in the century was to use the railroads and new roads—as well as notices in a new mass-circulation press—to draw outsiders into the city, where they would pay to see enormous, flashy spectacles that could not be so easily bundled up and sent to a new town.

Niblo's Garden contained elements of both the old itinerant and the emerging urban cultures; it also marked some of the class tensions surrounding new urban cultural styles.[6] The most fashionable of New York's "pleasure gardens" (privately owned, European-style enclosed ornamental grounds that were open to the public as a resort or amusement area), it was known as a summer gathering spot for what one patron called "the aristocratic or at least the toffish Broadway set." Opened in 1828 by the jovial, moon-faced coffee-house owner and caterer William Niblo, it took up a full city block at the former site of the Columbian Gardens, on the corner of Broadway and Prince Street. This spot is now in the center of a swirling megalopolis but was then "remote from the dust and bustle of the city proper, quite a little walk from the densely populated quarters" of lower Manhattan, so special coaches were needed to transport customers from the city's center to his establishment (Figure 2). On the grounds, Niblo transplanted large trees and exotic flowers and plants to adorn the Columbian's flower beds and serpentine walks. Around the garden, he built a tall wooden enclosure, around the inside of which were a number of latticed boxes containing simple board seats and a rough table at the center. In these boxes a battalion of black waiters—the ultimate symbol of luxury—served the wealthy patrons and those affecting wealth, "belles and beaus" alike. Each waiter at Niblo's wore a white apron and blue belt with a circular badge, on which was inscribed a number, so that any patron who felt insulted by a waiter's behavior could report him to Mrs. Niblo. These were the only African Americans—other than "exhibits" like Joice Heth—allowed in Niblo's, or indeed in virtually any New York pleasure garden. (The exception was African Grove, which catered to "privileged" blacks—those who required genteel skills in their work and had daily contact with whites: servants, coachmen, waiters, barbers, dressmakers, and milliners.)[7]

After strolling along Niblo's famous promenade lined by arches of lamps on ornately carved pillars, peering into the wondrous hermit's cave and marine cavern which glittered with stalactites and opened onto a view

2. Corner of Broadway and Ann Street, New York, 1831. The stagecoach at the center, with "Niblo" on the door, is taking patrons to Niblo's Garden, where Joice Heth performed in 1835. On the far left is the American Museum, purchased by Barnum in 1845, advertising a "Great Antique Living Monster, a Native of Kentucky." The City Saloon, site of Heth's postmortem, was also in this neighborhood.

of the sea, marveling at the dioramas of London's Great Fire and of the Israelites leaving Egypt, or simply sitting under lovely parasols and enjoying such delicacies as lemonade and the finest of ice creams, visitors could pay an additional 25 cents to witness light entertainments in Niblo's Saloon. The Saloon had been converted from an old stable on the Columbian Gardens' grounds into "a handsome hall with a well-laid floor and a gallery, accessible by broad staircases on three of its sides." Itinerant acts who performed there included the great Ravel family of traveling gymnasts, dancers, pantomimes, and contortionists, the first polka dancers ever witnessed in New York, a famous opera baritone, and troupes of comic actors. Upon the arrival of the Joice Heth exhibit, then, Niblo's was still offering modest entertainments in the classic itinerant mode, but the venue proved so popular that Niblo opened a second, larger dramatic hall behind the Saloon, where more lavish and immobile spectacles were produced. New York itself was undergoing a parallel transformation in the 1830s, from a provincial town to a thriving commercial center.[8] The historian Peter Buckley concludes that Niblo, along with Barnum, helped bring into being a "new kind of leisured audience" that "took in" the theater and popular amusements as part of a business trip or family outing to the newly exciting city.[9]

In selecting Niblo's, Barnum was casting his exhibit as a respectable entertainment. Although New Yorkers were more tolerant of theater than were New Englanders, many still held powerful prejudices against it: prostitutes solicited openly along theater row in the Bowery and even inside many establishments, and theaters were suspected of appealing to the licentious sensibilities of patrons.[10] Niblo's was somehow exempt from suspicion, in part because it was so expensive that the rougher sort couldn't get in. As Barnum wrote, "Niblo's is the only place of amusement where the shining lights of righteousness will be seen. You may give them there the same entertainment that you have in a theatre, and they will see no offence in it, although they denounce theatrical performances in good set terms, and swear . . . that the audience that visits such abomination is on the high road to damnation."[11] The great antebellum chronicler of popular culture and low-life activity, George Foster, elaborated on this "righteousness" by explaining that Niblo had expressly forbidden prostitutes to solicit on the premises. "The secret was simple—no woman is admitted to this house, unless accompanied by a gentleman. The consequence is that rowdies avoid the house, or if they visit it, have no inducement for misbehaving—and respectable and quiet people freely come, with their wives and children, sure of being neither shocked by obscenity nor frightened by violence."[12]

Joice Heth arrived bundled up, carried on a sedan chair into an apartment in the dwelling house attached to Niblo's Saloon on August 10, 1835. At the beginning of her long northern trek, she was already suffering bouts of fatigue. One editor who had been to visit her at the Masonic Hall in Philadelphia reported that "she sings several religious hymns, and laughs at a good thing said and done. But these are only on occasional starts. When we saw her, she lay in bed quiet and noiseless."[13] William Niblo was familiar with both Heth and Barnum. Heth he had seen during her stay in Philadelphia; Barnum had applied a few months earlier to be a bartender at his establishment, and been rejected. Apparently more impressed with Heth than with her exhibitor, he quickly came to terms with Barnum. In exchange for half the proceeds, Niblo was to provide room and lighting, pay for advertising and printing, and sell tickets. Barnum arranged for lighted transparencies—a new technology at the time—to be hung, bearing the simple message

JOICE HETH

161

YEARS OLD.

In addition, he commissioned a woodcut with Heth's likeness, showing a woman with a deeply wrinkled face and nearly closed eyes wearing a lacy bonnet and a modest dress. Her left arm, the paralyzed one, lies across her breast, and her fingernails, which many observers compared to talons, double the length of her fingers. This woodcut became the basis for ubiquitous posters that were plastered over the city, as well as for ads in the leading newspapers (Figure 3).

Even before Heth arrived, anticipatory blurbs began to appear in the papers, at no charge to Barnum or Niblo:

> Niblo, whose prolific genius for the invention of novelty to please the public, never fails;—has now recourse to the antique, instead of modern discoveries—and has found a woman! Startle not reader—she is a woman of by-gone days! One hundred and sixty-one years of age! Niblo has engaged her for a few days only—and she will, no doubt, prove as great an object of attraction as the forthcoming comet itself. She will be a greater star than any other performer of the present day, and has no fear of a rival—and having been the slave of Washington's Father, renders her an object of intense interest—and will, no doubt, receive the congratulations of every individual in New York.[14]

Despite this favorable publicity, Barnum later wrote, he was concerned that some of New York's editors might have "an idea Joice was a humbug."[15] To manage this potential obstacle and to promote the Heth tour

THE GREATEST
Natural & National
CURIOSITY
IN THE WORLD.

Nurse to GEN. GEORGE WASHINGTON, (the Father of our Country,)
WILL BE SEEN AT

Barnum's Hotel, Bridgeport,
On FRIDAY, and SATURDAY, the 11th. & 12th days
of December, DAY and EVENING. *also Monday*

JOICE HETH is unquestionably the most astonishing and interesting curiosity in the World! She was the slave of Augustine Washington, (the father of Gen. Washington,) and was the first person who put clothes on the unconscious infant, who, in after days, led our heroic fathers on to glory, to victory, and freedom. To use her own language when speaking of the illustrious Father of his Country, "she raised him." JOICE HETH was born in the year 1674, and has, consequently, now arrived at the astonishing

AGE OF 161 YEARS.

She Weighs but FORTY-SIX POUNDS, and yet is very cheerful and interesting. She retains her faculties in an unparalleled degree, converses freely, sings numerous hymns, relates many interesting anecdotes of *the boy* Washington, and often laughs heartily at her own remarks, or those of the spectators. Her health is perfectly good, and her appearance very neat. She is a baptist and takes great pleasure in conversing with ministers and religious persons. The appearance of this marvellous relic of antiquity strikes the beholder with amazement, and convinces him that his eyes are resting on the oldest specimen of mortality they ever before beheld. Original, authentic, and indisputable documents accompanying her prove, however astonishing the fact may appear, that JOICE HETH is in every respect the person she is represented.

The most eminent physicians and intelligent men in Cincinnatti, Philadelphia, New-York, Boston, and other places, have examined this *living skeleton* and the documents accompanying her, and all, *invariably*, pronounce her to be, as represented, 161 *years of age!*

A female is in continual attendance, and will give every attention to the ladies who visit this relic of by-gone ages.

She has been visited in Philadelphia, New-York, Boston, &c., by more than TWENTY THOUSAND Ladies and Gentlemen, within the last three months.

Hours of Exhibition, from 9 A. M. to 1 P. M. and from 3 to 5, and 6½ to 10 P. M.

ADMITTANCE 25 Cents, CHILDREN HALF-PRICE.

Printed by J. BOOTH & SON, 147, Fulton-st N. Y.

3. Handbill advertising the Joice Heth exhibit.

generally, Barnum hired an advance man, who was to become an integral part of the exhibit. This was Levi Lyman, a fast-talking young lawyer from Penn Yan, New York, a town noted primarily for producing the strongest whiskey in the state. Bored by his job as a clerk in the courthouse of Yates County, Lyman had moved to the city of New York seeking thrills. Barnum later described him as "a shrewd, sociable, and somewhat indolent Yankee," who "possessed a good knowledge of human nature, was polite, agreeable, could converse on most subjects, and was admirably calculated to fill the position for which I engaged him."[16] No surviving record reveals the exact nature of the contract between them, but in a joking retrospective account of the Heth affair, Barnum wrote that to motivate Lyman, who was, after all a bit "indolent," he sold him "a share of my black beauty."[17]

Barnum and Lyman's first act was to invite the most important New York newspaper editors to a private interview with Heth before she was exhibited to the public. To grasp the nature of this meeting, it is necessary to understand some of the transformations that were taking place in antebellum journalism. (This subject will also be taken up at greater length in Chapter 7.) A central feature of New York's emergence as the first "modern" American city was the newspaper revolution of the 1830s, which had profound effects on popular culture. Most early nineteenth-century newspapers were supported by political parties or government contracts. With secondary revenues coming from wealthy subscribers and none from street sales, they were essentially organs of the early Republic's elite. But in the mid-1830s, a new crop of entrepreneurial editors arose from the class of artisans who had manufactured these "six-penny" papers. Fed up with the constraints of the genteel system and making use of innovations in printing and paper-making technology, they opened the first penny dailies: independent, inexpensive papers that survived on sales, advertising, and moxie. The originator of the penny press was Benjamin Day, previously a printing press operator, who began the *New York Sun* in 1833. By 1835 he was the first to use a steam press, which ran off 5,000 sheets an hour, as opposed to the old single-cylinder model that could manage only 2,000. (Later in the decade, the *Sun* would produce 40,000 sheets an hour.) He increased advertising space and marketed his paper aggressively, which helped bring the price down to a penny. In 1835 James

Gordon Bennett, the notorious "squint-eyed Scotsman" who had worked as a teacher, clerk, and proofreader before becoming a freelance writer, opened the *New York Herald*. Employing the Fourdrinier paper-making machine and new processes of bleaching, he began to manufacture paper from colored rags instead of the far more expensive wood pulp.[18] These two men, along with the editor of the short-lived *Transcript,* forged the brash new voice of commercial journalism, appealing largely to readers who had been deemed unworthy of the six-penny papers' attention. By "diffusing useful knowledge among the operative classes of society," Benjamin Day wrote in 1835, the *Sun* was "effecting the march of intelligence to a greater degree than any other mode of instruction." The papers were hawked aggressively by what one disapproving New Yorker called a "gang of troublesome ragged boys," and made their mark by peddling stories of crime, scandal, and sensation.[19] Because these editors used many of the same publicity techniques that Barnum himself was using to promote Heth—bold type, inventive forms of display, and manipulation of public spaces to advertise a private concern—a natural allegiance formed between the showman and these other entrepreneurs of culture.[20]

Barnum and Lyman could not have known how big a hit their exhibit would become in the penny press (especially after Heth died), but sensing that their exhibit could benefit from the newspaper wars, they arranged a special viewing of "Aunt Joice" for leaders of both the penny press and the traditional papers. The showmen were not particularly original in using newspapers as a way to attract attention to their exhibit—accounts of "monstrous births" and other human anomalies were among the first items circulated in French newsbooks and English broadsides of the seventeenth century. In addition to giving impetus to some of the earliest forms of Western journalism, accounts of these singular curiosities continued to be a staple of newspaper reporting up until Barnum's day.[21] In turning to the editors, Barnum and Lyman were exploiting a long-standing connection between "news" and "curiosity" as well as a newly vigorous competition among the press.

In an exclusive story that Lyman dictated to Bennett's *Herald* six months after Heth's autopsy, he described the meeting: "Aunt Joice was laid out in clean bib and tucker, for the inspection of the editors. She had been treated to a new dress, and had rehearsed all her parts, about Washington—how she was converted—how she was baptized—together with some new pieces, such as, how she was a princess in Africa—how she was sold in slavery . . . [The editors] all hurried to Niblo's to get the first peep at the new wonder of the world. Niblo received them with great politeness, as he always does, but let them make the best of their way into the affair to examine which they had come." At the end, according to Lyman, "they were firm believers," but "the expense of making these sudden conversions was . . . considerable." He provided the *Herald* a table of expenses:

Convincing the Courier and Enquirer, $49,50
" Evening Star,   31,46
" penny Sun,   42,00
" Transcript,   21,75
" Journal of Commerce,   17,25
" Gazette,   5,67
" Daily Advertiser,   7,56
" Commercial Advertiser,   30,00[22]

Conspicuously absent from this list is the *Herald* itself. We might suspect Lyman of buttering up his publisher but for the fact that the *Herald* was in coming months one of the only papers in the city to voice skepticism about Heth's authenticity—so presumably Bennett either was not offered or refused to accept the bribes doled out to the other papers. (Indeed, a future biographer of Bennett would claim that the *Herald* "did not sell *puffs*," or advertisements posing as news.)[23] In any case, Barnum's failure to "convert" Bennett was not a problem for Barnum initially, because on the very day that Heth was first exhibited in New York, the building housing the *Herald*'s offices went up in flames in the great Ann Street fire, and Bennett remained out of business until the day after Heth, Barnum, and Lyman left town.[24]

Bribes and fires notwithstanding, the rush of publicity for Heth was like a flood—"Victoria herself would hardly have made a greater sensation," Barnum wrote. He assiduously promoted Heth's name through private and public means. "I had great leisure, now that my companion attended to the old woman, and I employed it in various ways to my own advantage. In particular, I took good care to mix as much in society as I could, and raise the curiosity of my hearers in regard to Joyce [*sic*], by little anecdotes, which I knew, would be repeated every where."[25] And of course there were advertisements. Billed as "the most astonishing and interesting exhibit in the world," Heth was originally scheduled to be seen from 8 A.M. to 10 P.M., but she proved unable to stand the strain. Visitors came to her private chambers singly or in groups, most shook her hand, a few took her pulse, many talked with her and perused the documents supporting her story, some sang or prayed with her, and all stared as she took food, smoked a pipe, or simply lay on her cot. A few days later, as a result of the "fatigue attending her conversing, shaking hands, &c. with her numerous visitors," her workday was reduced from fourteen hours to eight hours (six days a week). The exhibit ran from 9 A.M. to 1 P.M. and from 6 to 10 P.M. Despite her fatigue and the reduced hours, she proved a big draw, and though she was originally slated to stay only a few days, she remained on at Niblo's from the twelfth to the twenty-eighth of August. According to Barnum, he and Niblo were pulling in $1,500 a week.[26]

What, other than a few greased palms and some dinner-party gossip, made Joice Heth such an attraction? Was she a wonder, one of nature's prodigies like the Virginia dwarfs or the Siamese twins, whose paths she often crossed on the touring circuit? An exotic alien like Afong Moy, the "tiny-footed stranger" whose "disgustingly bound feet" made her such a prized attraction? Was it Heth's scientific value as an embodiment of the different aging processes of the different races that merited her display? Or her patriotic value as a living repository of memories of a glorious past? Because she was a storehouse of ancient religious practices? Or simply because she was an interesting performer? Barnum placed hundreds of newspaper ads for her exhibit at Niblo's, one of which suggests all of these possibilities:

GREAT ATTRACTION AT NIBLO'S—UNPARALLELED LONGEVITY—FOR TWO DAYS LONGER.—In consequence of the immense crowds of visitors to the exhibition of JOICE HETH, the NURSE OF WASHINGTON, at Niblo's Garden, during the last weeks and the unpleasant weather which has deprived thousands of ladies and gentlemen from visiting her, who are anxious to behold this greatest of all curiosities, Mr. Niblo . . . has affected a further engagement with JOICE HETH . . . Joice Heth is unquestionably the most astonishing and interesting curiosity in the world! She was the slave of Augustine Washington (the father of Gen. Washington,) and was the first person who put cloths [*sic*] on the unconscious infant who was destined to lead our heroic fathers on to glory, to victory, and to freedom. To use her own language when speaking of her young master, George Washington, "*SHE RAISED HIM!*" Joice Heth was born in the island of Madagascar, on the coast of Africa, in the year 1674, and has consequently now arrived at the astonishing age of ONE HUNDRED & SIXTY-ONE YEARS!!! She weighs but FORTY-SIX POUNDS, and yet is very cheerful and interesting. She retains her faculties in an unparalleled degree, converses freely, sings numerous hymns, relates many interesting anecdotes of the *boy* Washington, *the red coats,* &c., and often laughs heartily at her own remarks, or those of the spectators. Her health is perfectly good, and her appearance very neat. She was baptized in the river Potomac, and received into the Baptist Church *one hundred and sixteen years ago,* and takes great pleasure in conversing with ministers and religious persons. The appearance of this marvellous relic of antiquity strikes the beholder with amazement, and convinces him that his eyes are resting on the oldest specimen of mortality they ever before beheld. Original, authentic, and indisputable documents prove, that however astonishing the fact may appear, Joice Heth is in every respect the person she is represented.[27]

Different observers stressed different aspects of the exhibit, but most early reports favored grotesque images of her body over accounts of her life story. Heth's body fascinated a reporter for the *Commercial Advertiser,* who, while drawn by her claims to be Washington's nurse, came away with a different interest. Expressing a certain skepticism about the authenticity of her story, he still wrote that "our curiosity has been much gratified" (after all, the thirty dollars paid to his paper must have been good for something). Describing her shrunken limbs and "long attenuated fingers" that "more resemble the claws of a bird of prey, than human appendages," her shriveled frame, paralysis, and blindness, he concluded that "she comes up exactly to one's idea of an animated mummy," and therefore "amply compensates the time and cost of a visit."[28] The *Transcript*'s reporter was fascinated to find that her eyes were "entirely run out and closed."[29] The *Evening Star* reported that "her nails are near an inch long, and the great toes horny and thick like bone and incurvated, looking like the claws of a bird of prey. One long tusk is seen in her mouth. She enjoys her food with gusto, and what is astonishing, hears perfectly. She is nothing but skin and bones; lies constantly in bed, eating or smoking her pipe."[30] The reporter for the *Family Magazine* elaborated more fully on the condition of her toenails, describing them as resembling "blue horn." And in a paroxysm of grotesque fascination, he saw fit to include the information that while "food is administered to her regularly three times a day, with a little whiskey . . . evacuations occur but once in a fortnight!"[31]

In most of these accounts, Heth's exhibit was viewed in the tradition of human curiosities, or what would later become known as the freak show. As Rosemarie Garland Thomson has shown, human curiosities had been exhibited frequently and interpreted variously since antiquity. Whereas the Romans and Greeks generally saw in anomalous human forms wondrous signs of the plenitude of the universe and evidence of God's presence, "monstrosity" was in the medieval period typically taken as a portent of great or terrible events.[32] This conception of the monster as "prodigy" developed alongside a "natural" view of the causes of anomaly, but these interpretations were not incompatible. One sixteenth-century Alsatian scholar wrote that a "natural" explanation of monsters was possible, but "we know that nature is God's minister in matters both favorable and unfavorable, and that through her agency he aides the pious and punishes the impious, according to their different conditions." By the end of the seventeenth century, as science began to replace religious frameworks for understanding human forms and functions, the intellectual elite began to reject the divine readings of monstrosity, and by the time of the Enlightenment, the monsters and marvels of earlier periods came under the province of medical science. Accordingly, medical explanations for bodily anomaly supplemented the sense of religious wonder that attended the exhibits of human oddities. Supplemented, rather than replaced: the new ways of measuring, diagnosing, and explaining did not entirely supplant the old ways of looking, marveling, and interpreting; the exhibits of human oddities from the eighteenth century through the early twentieth smuggled the premodern sense of wonder into a scientific frame.[33] Thus the words most frequently used to describe Heth were "curiosity," "wonder," and "marvel," and her display was often viewed as a religious event, even as it was interpreted through a scientific lens.

Displays of human curiosities, or *lusus naturae*—freaks of nature—were among the most popular traveling entertainments of the late eighteenth and early nineteenth centuries, although the "golden age of the freak" did not begin until the 1840s, when the opening of Barnum's American Museum ushered the freak show into the era of mass culture.[34] In 1813 the Boston Museum exhibited as a "wonderful production of Nature" a man named Lambert, weighing 839 pounds, and his wife, who weighed only 89. Also exhibited was Mrs. Anna Moore, who was said to have lived six years without eating or drinking. Over the next few years, the trio moved on to Hartford, New York, Philadelphia, and several other cities, providing a moving theater of the extraordinary human body.[35]

Such exhibits typically highlighted the physical anomaly, grotesque features, extreme disability, or exotic racial or cultural difference of the displayed human object, and often more than one such quality at a time: racial and/or sexual exoticism (in the case of hermaphrodites or bearded ladies, for instance) was exaggerated, intermingled, and made to seem coextensive with bodily abnormality. For example, toward the end of the eighteenth century Henry Moss, a black man afflicted with a disease that gave him white hair and spotted skin, exhibited himself in Philadelphia and attracted the attention not only of the general populace but of the noted scientist Benjamin Rush. Rush, a leading voice of Enlightenment egalitarianism, viewed blackness as nothing more than the product of disease—a strand of leprosy, to be precise—and believed that nature was effecting a spontaneous cure. Like the black boy whose skin reportedly whitened upon contact with the juice of unripe peaches, Moss was for Rush evidence of the possibility of such a transformation.[36]

Half a century later, Barnum helped commercialize scientific interest in racial anomaly in his American Museum, where he exhibited African

Americans with vitiligo, albinism, and microcephaly, proposing that they were the "missing links" in an evolutionary chain extending upward from monkey to black man to white. The difference between the earlier and later scientific explanations of racial ambiguity is telling. Whereas Rush read Moss's exhibit as evidence of the environmentally produced divisions between black and white, Barnum's later displays tended to reinforce racial boundaries as ineradicable: the "missing links" were presented as evidence for evolving racial science, which stressed the natural hierarchies of the races.[37] During an era in which the social and biological meanings of racial identity were hotly debated, the freak show became an avenue for displaced discussion of those meanings. By holding bodies that were supposed to be abnormal and deviant up for display, freak shows asked their audiences to dwell implicitly on the normative meanings of the body: particularly, what it meant to be "white" or "black."

Discussions of Heth's longevity almost inevitably raised questions about the biological differences between the races—and these supposed differences, no matter in what form, could be used to promote the idea of the superiority of the white race. Many observers meditated on the causes behind Heth's longevity. "The most remarkable circumstance," the *Evening Star*'s reporter wrote, "is that her pulse is full, strong, and perfectly regular, and near 80 in a minute, without the slightest ossification of the artery."[38] Invariably, this extraordinary fact of her body came to be interpreted through her audiences' racial ideology. Some commentators began to worry, for instance, that Heth would not be able to manage a winter in the North, as her black blood could not tolerate the extreme cold. "Joice Heth goes South in about two or three weeks," the *Herald* announced when she made a return visit to New York in early December. "She says she cannot spend the winter in the North, where the cold is so severe and the nights so long. The South is her native element."[39] The comparative adaptability to different climates had been for centuries a central question concerning the meaning of race. The discussion extends as far back as the ancient Greek philosopher Ptolemy, who speculated that the dark complexion and woolly hair of Africans were a result of their exposure to the hot sun; but this idea faltered in Renaissance thought when it was shown repeatedly that many people living along the equator had straight hair and brown rather than black skin. In the Enlightenment period, egalitarian thinkers like Rush returned to the climate to help them explain one of the most puzzling perceived features of blackness: the behavioral differences that seemingly made Europeans so industrious and Africans so indolent and uncivilized. It was the sun, Rush argued, that depraved blacks, and the tropical abundance that made them lazy. His contemporary Samuel Stanhope Smith brought the environment back to the causation of physical appearance itself, arguing that if it was the sun and heat that released the bile that caused the blackness (and associated behaviors) of Africans, it was the vapors of stagnant waters, the condition of poverty, and social disorganization that caused black color to "stick," as it apparently did not with other natives of the tropics. Blackness, therefore, could be cured, but for the masses of blacks this would be a much longer process than the apparently speedy recovery of Henry Moss.[40]

The *Herald*'s notion that Heth's illness was a result of improper exposure to the northern climate looks, in this light, like the least egalitarian position considered yet, for it contravenes the Enlightenment proposition that, as Rush put it, "human nature is the same in all Ages and Countries." Instead, the implication was that different races had inherently different physical constitutions. This was an idea with growing currency in the 1830s. One physician commented: "The African races are very susceptible of cold, and are as incapable of enduring a northern climate, as a white population are of supporting the torrid sun of Africa."[41] This notion—most lucidly formulated by the English anatomist Robert Knox—took on an explicitly racist meaning in the United States, as advocates of slavery argued that the South, with its semitropical climate, was as much a "natural" environment for blacks as Africa was. When the southern ethnologist Josiah Nott, for instance, wrote (in 1844) that "the white man cannot live in tropical Africa, or the African in the frigid zone," he supported this argument by pointing to the unequal mortality rates for blacks in the North and South.[42]

The *Evening Star* similarly used Heth's old age to support this theory. "Since public attention has been drawn to that antidiluvian [*sic*] personage, Joice Heth," the paper reported, "the subject of the comparative longevity in different states is frequently alluded to." Quoting an unnamed study, the article went on to reveal that North Carolina had, "over the age of 100 years, 58 white and 297 colored; and in Virginia 54 white, 328 colored . . . and all the slave-holding states" had similar proportions. By contrast, New York had only 115 centenarians, few of whom were black. In conclusion, the *Evening Star* asked, "Do not these facts prove that the calumniated climate of the South, which has been so decried for its marshes, stagnant streams, and pine barrens, is at least admirably adapted for the African race?"[43] The explanation for the reported old age of Heth (and for her northern demise) as well as the alleged longevity of so many other slaves was that they were naturally well suited for the southern terrain and the southern way of life, which supported the paper's pro-slavery stance. Heth's body was an exaggeration of a typical phenomenon, not so much an anomaly as an entry in the emerging field of statistics—a field that used scientific measurements to give political calculations an air of authority and objectivity.[44]

One odd early record of the Heth exhibit in New York shows how a casually scientific frame of mind could turn the freak's body into an occasion for a related sort of political comment. Grant Thorburn, a popular Scottish-born travel writer who had made a fortune in the seed business, made one of the most thorough early records of a visit to Heth. This Thorburn— known as "Lawrie Todd" ever since the British writer John Galt had created a fictional character of that name based on Thorburn—was himself seen as something of a freak.[45] Another writer described him as "an extraordinary genius, with a personal identity seldom encountered in the common walks of life. His shuffling gait, the result of a malformation, made him always conspicuous even in a crowded thoroughfare, while his strict Quaker garb . . . added to the grotesque outline of his short, unprepossessing figure."[46] Thorburn's writings covered a vast array of subjects, from politics to the natural sciences to the theater, and he saw in Heth a combination of all three. "I have been to see Joice Heath [*sic*] today," he wrote the editor of the *Evening Star.* "I find that, with all her other rare qualities, she is a *profound smoker* . . . I asked her how long she had used the pipe; she answered, one hundred and twenty years. So if smoking be a poison, it is, in her case at least, a very slow one."

At the time of Thorburn's visit to Heth, northern reform societies were condemning the smoking of southern tobacco as an immoral act. One

Boston newspaper, for instance, lauded a recent statute banning tobacco smoking in public places and disparaged Philadelphians for being "the most inveterate street smokers this side of the Mason Dixon line." Thorburn, however, was an unusually strong northern propagandist for the weed, resulting from his business connections with southern tobacco planters (he may have exported tobacco seeds from his shop in New York). Complementing his frequently stated idea that tobacco was a natural agent promoting longevity, he also thought that the economic system undergirding most tobacco production was part of the natural order. Through his business contacts south of the Mason-Dixon line, Thorburn had a vested interest in promoting the southern slave system, which—like tobacco—was beginning to come under organized attack in the North. Thorburn reported that, in addition to smoking, Heth sang cheerfully throughout his visit. The northern tour of Joice Heth, which featured a pipe-smoking slave in apparently good health and spirits at age 161, thus served for Thorburn as a perfect advertisement for a product and, by implication, for an entire way of life.[47]

The myriad descriptions of Heth's body as a grotesque wonder or as a medical specimen support Rosemarie Garland Thomson's view that Heth was the "quintessential American freak."[48] Unlike the typical "freak," however, Heth's fame rested on her supposed personal history as much as on her physical singularity. Whereas a focus on her body degraded her, the connection to Washington exalted her. She was not simply a curiosity, but what Robert Bogdan, the pioneering historian of the freak show, has called an "aggrandized" freak.[49] In the same articles that described Heth's bowel movements, blue toenails and curling "talons," emaciated frame, ravaged face, and general immobility, she was also portrayed as a living piece of Washingtoniana, whose memories were as valuable as her body itself. In contrast to the disgust inspired by her appearance, her personal history inspired awe.

The contradictions in Heth's symbolism—as freak and as exalted icon—recall the distinctions made by Mikhail Bakhtin in his discussion of "carnivalesque" displays of the human body. In such folk celebrations, according to Bakhtin, the "grotesque body" emphasizes "those parts . . . that are open to the outside world, that is, the parts through which the world enters the body or emerges from it, or through which the body itself goes out to meet the world . . . This is the ever unfinished, ever creating body," a fusion of two bodies in one, "the one giving birth and dying, the other conceived, generated, and born."[50] To celebrate the "open" grotesque body through carnival inversion, in Bakhtin's utopian view, is to oppose official culture.[51]

Joice Heth's grotesque body, in contrast to the "official" body of Washington, created a carnivalesque juxtaposition, especially when we consider the role of physical images of George Washington's body in antebellum culture. In many ways, the physical image of Joice Heth was the precise, almost systematic opposite of Washington's iconic form. Washington's image—the most popular being Gilbert Stuart's *Athenaeum* head (1796) and perhaps the most dramatic being Rembrandt Peale's *George Washington, Patriae Pater* (Figure 4)—was held up for antebellum America as the perfect image of classicism. As Bakhtin has written, the classical body, as opposed to the grotesque, "was a strictly completed, finished product . . . isolated, alone, fenced off from all other bodies. All signs of its unfinished character, of its growth and proliferation were eliminated; its protuberances and offshoots were removed, its convexities (signs of new sprouts and buds) smoothed out, its apertures closed."[52] That Washington's body did indeed possess "protuberances," "offshoots," and "convexities" is made clear by other, less frequently copied images of Washingtoniana than the dignified, classically proportioned (and titled) offerings of Stuart and Peale (Figure 5), but the popularity of images such as theirs attests to the need of the early Republic to fashion the republican image as one of order, balance, and harmony.

Beginning in the 1820s, phrenologists and artists who were interested in phrenology began to take a great interest in Washington's head, stressing it as a model of proportion and overall strength of character. Peale, for instance, wrote of his own paintings of Washington that his aim was to show "how far his [Washington's] corporeal features corresponded with his acknowledged moral and mental greatness." Looking at Peale's Washington, the great phrenologist George Combe meditated on the physical harmony of Washington's figure, and especially his high development in the cranial region that produced "benevolence." And as Charles Colbert

4. Rembrandt Peale, *George Washington, Patriae Pater,* oil painting, c. 1824.

shows in his study of phrenology and the fine arts, there was a tendency in portraiture for Washington's head through the 1840s to expand in order to emphasize it as a phrenological—and classical—ideal of harmony.[53] Indeed, a popular text on the principles of phrenology included a Washington head as the model of "Well-Balanced Organization."[54] Colbert argues that Washington's phrenological and artistic image was that of a "natural

5. Christian Gullager, *George Washington,* oil painting, 1789.

national" type—that is, a model of the perfection of the Anglo-Saxon head. In contrast, African Americans were often depicted as the counterimage of this ideal: the same popular phrenology book that analyzes Washington's extraordinarily balanced head analyzes the "African Head" to show its deficiency in "reasoning capacities" (Figure 6). In this sense, the grotesquely rendered African American form helped define the national ideal by providing its negation.

In popular culture, however, the image of a misshapen, nonideal, grotesque human form could just as often invert the classical ideal as define it; Joice Heth's freakish body, in contrast to the "official" image of George Washington, presented antebellum readers and spectators opportunities for such a Bakhtinian cultural inversion. (If George Washington was a

A WELL-BALANCED ORGANIZATION.

No. 13.   WASHINGTON

6. Heads of George Washington and an "African" in a popular handbook on the principles of phrenology.

PERCEPTIVES LARGER THAN REFLECTIVES.

THE VARIOUS RACES also accord with phrenological science. Thus, Africans generally have full perceptives, and large Tune and Language, but retiring Causality, and accordingly are deficient in reasoning capacity, yet have excellent memories and lingual and musical powers.

No. 38.   AFRICAN HEAD.

"natural national" type, what could the "GREATEST NATURAL AND NATIONAL CURIOSITY IN THE WORLD" represent?) This inversion involved primarily a degradation or topographical lowering—"to concern oneself with the lower stratum of the body, the life of the belly and the reproductive organs . . . , acts of defecation and copulation, conception, pregnancy, and birth." Journalists emphasized her toothless mouth and "deeply sunken" eyes as they opened blindly onto the world. A figure both of decay and of childbirth, she was represented as "ever unfinished, open to the outside world." And the performance was itself open, unfinished, dependent on audience involvement, as opposed to the classical ideal of fully realized structures. Barnum wrote: "We would . . . question her in relation to the birth and youth of General Washington, and she always gave satisfactory answers in every particular. Individuals among the audience would also frequently ask her questions, and put her to the severest cross-examinations, without ever finding her to deviate from what had every evidence of being a plain unvarnished statement of facts."[55] In some ways, her performance provided a provocative set of reversals of antebellum social hierarchies even as the image of her body reinforced them: in a white bourgeois culture that emphasized manliness and virility, it placed a decrepit female black body on center stage; it presented the Father as an infant and a slave as the authority. It was not often, after all, that a slave woman was asked questions about sacred national history in public.

How can we reconcile this paradoxical overturning and reinforcing of the lines between high and low, classical and grotesque, power and submission? The Heth exhibit was neither simply a carnivalesque inversion of power nor an act of simple degradation; rather, it was what Peter Stallybrass and Allon White call a "hybrid" event, a "more complex form of the grotesque" in which "new combinations and strange instabilities in a given semiotic system" arise. Part of this instability rests in the fact that the exhibit produced an inversion not so much for the performer as for the spectators, for whom Heth stood, in Stallybrass and White's term, as the "low-Other." This is a figure who is simultaneously socially excluded and the object of intense nostalgia and fascination, and whose body elicits both disgust and longing, produced by a bourgeois "psychological dependence upon precisely those Others which are being rigorously opposed and excluded at the social level." It is through images of the body that one can read this process—for the body is the site of "transcoding" for competing social meanings.[56] The *Family Magazine,* for example, saw no contradiction between the two ways of transcoding Heth's body—as a constipated, blue-toenailed human grotesque or as an exalted "object of nostalgia, longing, and fascination." But in many accounts, the symbolism of her grotesque body was in tension with her audiences' nostalgia for the age of revolutionary heroism. In a culture that idealized George Washington above all others, she was celebrated and reviled as a monstrous perturbation of that ideal.

PRIVATE ACTS,
PUBLIC MEMORIES

THE LIFE OF JOICE HETH, the newspapers and magazines frequently pointed out, spanned an extraordinary range of world events. "All the landmarks on the great stream of time, for nearly two centuries, have been visible to Joice Heth," wrote one reporter (who momentarily forgot her blindness), "and thousands of events, of which we are barely cognisant, have whirled before her like the shifting scenes of a play." In what became a ritual of reportage, the more notable of these events were listed: she was born in the reign of Charles II of England and Louis XIV of France; her contemporaries included Newton, Locke, Tillotson, Bolingbroke, Addison, Steele, and eight English sovereigns; since her birth, the world had seen the Habeus Corpus act, King Philip's War with the Massachusetts colonists, the Revolutionary War, the first European explorations of the land beyond the Mississippi, the Northwest Territory, and the South Pacific—and, of course, the birth of George Washington.[1] The opportunity to dwell on the significance not only of these events, but of passing time itself, was clearly a draw in the exhibit. Heth's anecdotes and the wondrous agedness of her body put many visitors in a reflective, even nostalgic frame of mind. Part of the wonder was not just her reports of what she had witnessed, but the way in which those memories underscored all that had happened, all that was happening, in the world of her visitors. As one famous English visitor to the States put it: "At present all is energy and enterprise; every thing is in a state of transition, but of rapid improve-

ment—so rapid, indeed, that those who would describe America now
would have to correct all in the short space of ten years; for ten years in
America is almost equal to a century in the old continent."[2] Amid this flux,
Joice Heth represented symbolic—and actual—continuity, an anomalous
point of stasis in an ever-changing landscape. When visitors juxtaposed
Heth with the shifting grounds beneath her, the inevitable result was not a
simple nostalgia, but a sense of time speeding up, the past becoming more
past than ever and the present taking on a wondrous instability:

> When the *father* of the United States was born, Joice Heth was fifty-
> nine years old—since which time we have fought our battles of inde-
> pendence, established our government, and peopled our country with
> twelve millions of freemen. In her youthful days, history informs us,
> people were wont to travel on foot or with horses; now, with the speed
> of the wind, steam propels us over land and water, and balloons trans-
> port us through the air! Indeed, it is not extravagant to believe, that the
> time is close at hand, when the period comprised in the first 100 years of
> Joice Heth's life, will be linked on to the *dark ages!*[3]

What sustains a sense of identity through physical and environmental
change is memory.[4] Heth's memories of swaddling Washington, of the future general's favorite gray horse, of the menacing presence of the redcoats, were valued in part because they helped create an aura of stable
identity, set off against a backdrop of social and political transformation:
she connected the age of Newton to the age of railroads; Charles II to Andrew Jackson. What was even more remarkable about the exhibit, though,
was how little any of those transformations had affected her. Of "all the
landmarks on the great stream of time," Heth could hardly be said to have
noticed a single one, with the exception of the events surrounding Washington's childhood. And even in connection with Washington, she exhibited a striking ignorance. This seemed to some the sign of her authenticity
not only as a human anomaly but as a living token of the cherished past:
how could her story be faked if she wasn't even aware of its importance? A
Rip Van Winkle without the sleeping fit, she had leapfrogged over a century in her memories. While she remembered minutely the incidents in
Washington's infancy, and while "the 'red coats' . . . seem to have made a
very vivid and lasting impression upon her mind, and she still appears to

harbour an inveterate antipathy towards them," the *Family Magazine* reported, "as to all subsequent events, her memory seems to be almost *tabula rasa.*" She remembered, too, that "when George Washington was considerably advanced in boyhood, he left his paternal roof, and that she, a short time afterwards, was sent into Kentucky"; amazingly, though, "Joice recollects nothing more of George Washington! She knows not that the infant boy she nursed, had no sooner grown to manhood, than he became the 'first in war, first in peace, and the first in the hearts of his countrymen'—she remembers not that he died the adoration of his country, and claimed by the whole world as the boon of providence to the human race!"[5]

Paul Fraisse and Jacques Le Goff have written that individual memory is, in a sense, socially constructed. We tend to treat our memories as if they were some private reserve, connecting ourselves only to our past selves, but in fact "the history of our childhood . . . is composed not only of our own first memories, but also of our parents' memories." The process of socialization, likewise, is an extension of individual memory, for to constitute a society is to create an illusion of "a collective memory preceding and extending beyond the individual memory."[6] None but a very few old-timers in 1835 could be said to "remember" Washington's rise, but all Americans were assumed to have a sense of the past that Heth lacked. This hypostatized public or collective memory is what united people in a sense of national identity. Paradoxically, these public memories were precisely what Heth "remembers not"—and it was these gaps that made audiences cherish the merely private ones she supposedly did have. Her lack of historical awareness meant that her memory was a preserve, self-sufficient and blissfully uncontaminated by the prosthetic memorial devices provided by pedagogy, folklore, and elementary civic culture. It is only through socialization that one comes to know of Washington's universal adoration, and only by social exclusion that one can avoid knowing of it.

Most of the particular memories Heth offered were so well known as to be banal, which suggests that it was a place in memory itself—rather than any specific memories—that her audience craved: a psychic and social space promising an intimate, unmediated connection to the past.[7] Joice Heth the "living relic," then, was less a popular historian than what Joseph Roach has referred to as a human "effigy": someone who performs "a set of actions that hold open a place in memory into which many different people may step . . . Performed effigies—those fabricated from human bodies and the associations they evoke—provide communities with a method of perpetuating themselves through specially nominated mediums or surrogates: among them, actors, dancers, priests, street maskers, statesmen, celebrities, freaks, children, and especially, by virtue of an intense but unsurprising paradox, corpses."[8] Heth as effigy provided something that books—which depend on a gulf between reader, speaker, and event—could not convey but that popular performance in all its immediacy could: a memory grounded and reproduced in bodies and places, a memory that was born of and re-created a social bond, a memory that reinforced a sense of identity and community.

From the vantage of 1835, however, there was no neutral "place of memory" in which to stand: to imagine the past was always to find oneself right back in the present, with all its swirling confusions. Despite the lack of overt political content in the exhibit, its circulation of memories puts it squarely in the realm of antebellum politics. "Memories and identities," John Gillis has written, "are not fixed things, but representations or constructions of reality, subjective rather than objective phenomena."[9] As such, they are connected to politics and struggle. "Remembering" Washington and the revolutionary past ostensibly marked one's inclusion in the civic life of the nation, but Heth's performance, curiously, highlighted her exclusion as an African American and as a woman. Similarly, in the wider culture the cast of such memories and the uses to which they were put indicated division as often as unity.

For a man who was thirty-six years dead, George Washington was in the news a good deal in 1835. "Somebody is raising money to build a monument to the memory of Washington," ran an item in the *New York Herald* on November 25, 1835. "What profanation! A monument has long since been built to the memory of Washington. Where is its foundation? In the breasts of free men in both Europe and America. Where is its highest pinnacle? Far beyond the brightest star in the heaven itself—in the bosom of Him who liveth for ever and ever."[10] From the time of Washington's death in 1799 to the outbreak of the Civil War, the mythic Father of the Nation was by far the most venerated figure in American history; as this article made clear, he had passed beyond history into the realm of myth. Skirting the line between nationalist hero worship and religious veneration, the writer suggested that to memorialize Washington was akin to breaking the Old Testament injunction against making a graven image of God. Such fears of profanation notwithstanding, production of Washingtoniana became a highly profitable cottage industry. Between 1800 and 1860 over four hundred books, essays, and articles on Washington appeared in print (most of them outrageously flattering), and artists by the dozen painted his portrait, so that his face invested countless trinkets, walls, and mantelpieces with a touch of republican nobility. So prevalent did the idealized image of Washington become that Walt Whitman wrote in 1858, "His portrait hangs on every wall, and he is almost canonized in the affections of our people."[11] Indeed, the wall over the fireplace in the most famous domicile of nineteenth-century America, Uncle Tom's cabin, would not have been complete without being adorned by "a portrait of General Washington, drawn and colored in a manner which would certainly have astonished that hero, if ever he happened to meet with its like."[12] And even Chingachgook, otherwise known as Indian John, or the Last of the Mohicans, makes his first appearance in James Fenimore Cooper's 1823 novel *The Pioneers* wearing only a loincloth and "a silver medallion of Washington that was suspended from his neck by a thong of buckskin."[13]

The function of such iconography was ostensibly to establish a connection between strangers in the name of national identity, a connection that was imperative to a sense of belonging in a republic. At the same time, as Benedict Anderson has written, the slippage between nationalist enthusiasm and religious veneration was something of a threat to the republican idea of the nation. The imperative to police this line arises from the need of the modern nation-state to replicate itself through a series of interchangeable leaders, a process that would be threatened by undue exaltation of any one figure.[14] This tension helps clarify why, for all the lionization of Washington, a public memorial was not begun until 1848 and not completed until 1885, which Michael Kammen explains by citing the widespread view of such official conferral of monumental status as undemocratic.[15] Nonetheless, the cult of Washington gathered steam through the early national and antebellum periods, and it threatened—in the eyes of some—a smooth passing on of the torch of republicanism. A jealous John Adams wrote of the "idolatrous worship" accorded his more famous colleague; Washington was deified "by all classes and nearly all parties of our citizens, manifested in the impious applications of names and epithets to him which are ascribed in scripture only to God and to Jesus Christ. The following is a part of them: 'our Savior,' 'our Redeemer,' 'our cloud by day and our pillar of fire by night,' 'our star in the east,' 'to us a Son is born,' and 'our guide on earth, our advocate in heaven.' "[16]

This deification grew more intense through the antebellum period, a circumstance that George Forgie has attributed to three causes. First, as the old Revolutionary War heroes died off in the early and mid-nineteenth century, many Americans began to ask—in an occasionally paralyzing way—whether their society was living up to its earlier heroic deeds. In politics, popular culture, and pedagogy, the image of Washington stood alternately as a model of virtue and as a scolding Father or angry God, and invoking his name was often a prelude to a jeremiad. Furthering this was a widespread anxiety about the loss of tradition in urbanizing America and the political and social instability that followed from that loss. In an era when so many sons found themselves cast adrift in bewildering cities with no familial structures to guide them, "society began to concern itself with child nurture as a political matter . . . At a time when expanding economic opportunity meant that boys were beginning to need a wider range of models than their surroundings were likely to provide, history stepped in to supply them in the form of the founding heroes." And finally, just as actual families were losing their cohesiveness, disunion on a broader scale was threatening the national "family": it began to look as though the North and the South could not live together as one nation. Amid these anxieties, George Washington, as the Father of all fathers, stood as a figure of authority among squabbling sons, attracting all the deference and resentment authority elicits.[17]

This widespread veneration, though, does not imply any sort of agreement over the meaning of Washington's life, or his relevance to the present. A graphic example is the sectional debate over the fate of his corpse that arose in Congress in 1832 (four years before the corpse of his supposed nurse would touch off another, even more sensational debate). The Senate and House had established a joint committee to plan a commemoration of the one hundredth anniversary of Washington's birth, and a proposal emerged to have his remains removed from Mount Vernon and placed in a tomb below the center of the U.S. Capitol rotunda. Edward Everett, then a senator from Massachusetts, spoke for many northerners when he proclaimed that the procession of pallbearers would be a spectacle "unexampled in the history of the world . . . The Sacred remains are . . . a treasure beyond all price, but it is a treasure of which every part of this blood-cemented Union has a right to claim its share."[18] Blood-cemented partners or no, southerners resisted this northerner's appeal to the "right" to move the body north; the plan faltered as southern congressmen lined up to keep the body in Mount Vernon, where it would emphasize Washington's southern roots.

The legacy of Washington and other figures from the revolutionary past was hotly contested among numerous other political groups; at stake was the direction of the Republic itself. One of the key issues was whether the Revolution was a finished event or an ongoing process, whether America had achieved democracy or was still forging it.[19] The first interpretation, not surprisingly, was stressed by elites, and the second by those seeking political representation and social status. Memory was both the battleground and a weapon. Through the 1820s, for instance, official Fourth of July celebrations in major cities stressed order and hierarchy. These were generally tightly focused on the heroism of Washington, and featured civic and political leaders in the front ranks of the parades, with heavy doses of self-congratulatory rhetoric emanating from the speakers.[20] To use Eric Hobsbawm's phrase, this "invented tradition" served to solidify power by representing to the populace the proper relationship between people, government, and history.[21] At the same time an undercurrent of unofficial, popular celebrations of the event provided opportunities to engage in carnivalesque upheaval of those officially sanctioned representations, those safe public memories. Featuring mockery, masking, drinking, brawling, and generally frolicsome behavior, these events became an expression of growing radical republicanism and the reclamation of an alternative revolutionary history among workers who in the 1830s found their standard of living slipping while the capitalist classes were accumulating vast reserves of wealth.[22] The day became an enactment of what Alfred Young has called the "contest for public memory of the Revolution."[23] The elites wanted images of a glorious past to secure an orderly present; those below often saw revolutionary mobbing, rioting, effigy-hanging, tarring and feathering, and dumping of tea as models for the only sort of action that would reverse their declining fortunes in the present.

One might suppose that Barnum, given his radical Jacksonian background, would have used the Joice Heth exhibit to open the doors to a feisty artisanal countermemory of the Revolution. Heth's lowly social status and her decidedly grotesque appearance might have touched a chord with the revelers of Philadelphia, New York, and Boston, who turned the revolutionary past into a vehicle for asserting their rights in the present. (One labor organizer, in typical fashion, reworked the Declaration of Independence to assert the "inalienable right" of workers "to affix a price on the only property we have to dispose of: our labor.")[24] The closest the exhibit ever came to this sort of carnivalesque deployment of history was in Boston, where the Jacksonian *Morning Post* reported that "a match is expected between Joice Heth and the '76 veteran who is here in full uniform—the old soldier was seen near Concert Hall on Saturday."[25] This soldier was probably one of the old veterans who had gained sudden celebrity in the wake of an 1832 law that required all survivors of the Revolutionary War to submit a written narrative of their war years in order to receive a pension. Over twenty thousand veterans applied, many of them protesting vigorously and publicly if their claims were denied, others becoming minor celebrities when their stories were circulated. An unintended result of this law was to highlight the stories of numerous impoverished old veterans, and to provide fodder for the Jacksonian claim to a populist reclamation of history.[26] Heth's "marriage" to such a man is an instance of the wild fun that resulted from the old, conservative stories of Great Men giving way to more democratic stories celebrating the Revolution's presence in contemporary life.

This, though, was an isolated incident, generated from the pen of a clever partisan editor and apparently not an intentional ploy on the part of Heth's exhibitors. Barnum's failure to pursue an edgy, populist reworking of revolutionary themes doubtless owed something to the "shining lights of righteousness" at Niblo's, which would have made any unseemly political insinuations dangerous. It also would have been out of keeping with certain aspects of the exhibit itself (in which, again, Barnum innovated little in these first few weeks): Heth served up rather "safe" memories of

Washington's mythic childhood and seemed, conveniently to elite patrons of the pleasure gardens, to know nothing of the violent acts of commoners that helped win national independence. Heth's gender would have posed an additional problem for her in making a claim to the unfinished business of the revolutionary past. Despite the fact that many subordinate groups used the heroic legacy of the Founding Fathers to support their own calls for independence, women in the 1830s were generally not among them. In 1776 Abigail Adams had warned her husband of a female rebellion if the male revolutionaries did not "Remember the Ladies" who are held by "Laws in which we have no voice, or Representation"; nonetheless, women's concerns were generally excluded from the rhetoric of the Revolution through the first half of the nineteenth century. Fourth of July celebrations typically had space for women only as passive spectators (or as harlots), and it was not until 1848 that Elizabeth Cady Stanton introduced her "Declaration of Sentiments" to the women's convention in Seneca Falls: "We hold these truths to be self-evident: that all men and women are created equal."[27]

More than these factors, though, it was her race that placed a limit on Heth's usefulness for postrevolutionary protest. There was, to be sure, a context for viewing racial oppression through the lens of the revolutionary past. During the antebellum period, newly assertive abolitionists—both white and black—began to look at the origins of the nation for inspiration in the struggle to end slavery. In 1833 William Lloyd Garrison opened his "Declaration" to the American Anti-Slavery Society in Philadelphia by reminding his listeners that "more than fifty-seven years have elapsed since a band of patriots convened in this place, to devise measure for the deliverance of this country from a foreign yoke"; he then urged that "in purity of motive, in earnestness of zeal, in decision of purpose, in intrepidity of action, in steadfastness of faith, in sincerity of spirit, we would not be inferior to them."[28] Garrison may have eschewed the violence of the earlier patriots in the present case, but four years earlier, the African American writer and activist David Walker had no such reservations. Referring ominously to the "first Revolution," he implied that a slave revolt could be based on the very principles on which the nation was founded: "See your Declaration, Americans!!! Do you understand your own language?"[29] As an entertainer, one with solid Jacksonian credentials who was playing to a largely refined audience, Barnum was more shrewd than to allow his exhibit to be associated with this type of explosive sentiment. As she mouthed the words of the young Washington, Joice Heth was never allowed to apply the political lessons of his greatness to herself; in fact, she was shown not to have the faintest clue as to what those lessons were. The place in memory that Heth opened up was, after all, for her visitors, not for herself.

For all that, the Heth exhibit seems to have been largely inoffensive to whites struggling for recognition from below, and it did symbolically turn some tables. But although it featured the voice of the dispossessed revising the central image of cultural authority, it did not seem—to this point—offensive to the elite. In fact, it was put to remarkably conservative uses: it stressed the happiness of a slave and her subordination to a great man; it stressed a woman's defining role in domestic child rearing; it stressed the comedy, rusticity, and even exoticism of the dispossessed, rather than their anger and privation.

Along with this was a heartwarming appreciation for young Washington's honesty and strength of character that was straight out of Mason Weems. In his notorious 1809 "biography," *The Life of Washington*—a production that shares many qualities, including brazen fraudulence, with the exhibit of Joice Heth—Weems made the most successful attempt to fashion an image of Washington that would symbolize national unity rather than the clamor of politics. Whereas Barnum made his profits exhibiting George Washington's mythical childhood through the body and words of a "curiosity," Weems capitalized on the image of the child Washington as a curiosity in itself. This little book, written by a sometime preacher and oft-time itinerant salesman and public ranter, contains equal parts legitimate anecdote, sermon, patriotic narrative of a vaguely inspirational character, and pure hokum. Weems's stories, the most famous of which, of course, is the one about the cherry tree, were read in countless primary and Sunday school classrooms. As we all know, when Augustine Washington finds his favorite tree chopped down and asks his son if he knows what has happened, the boy's "sweet face brightened with the inexpressible charm of all conquering truth, [and] he bravely cried out: 'I can't tell a lie, Pa; you know I can't tell a lie. I did cut it with my hatchet.'" This famously wins his father's pronouncement that "such an act of heroism in

my son, is more worth than a thousand trees, though blossomed with silver, and their fruits of purest gold."[30] The young Washington's heroic
truthfulness, supposedly a beacon for American youth, is in direct contrast
to Weems's whole-cloth invention of the anecdote itself. Nor was the
author above reaping the golden fruit of his own little lies. Urging his publisher to issue an expanded edition of the book, Weems wrote: "You have a
great deal of money in the bones of old George, if you will but exert yourself to extract it"; and a year later he was pushing for the issuance of an "elegant edition" priced at three or four dollars.[31] More respectable writers
frequently denounced Weems's mercenary abuse of the memory of Washington, and the author—like Barnum after him—became known as something of a confidence man.

Despite Weems's notoriety, his bogus image of the naturally honest Father in his youth stuck in nineteenth-century readers' minds, and it became the subject of paintings and etchings and of countless retellings. At
least one of these versions reworks the story so that Washington's truthfulness emerges in his relationship to the slaves on his father's plantation. In
an 1864 tale by Uncle Juvinell (Morrison Heady), the hatchet has become
an Indian tomahawk and Augustine Washington initially suspects a little
slave boy, Jerry, of cutting down the tree. George protests: "O papa, papa!
. . . Don't whip poor Jerry: if somebody must be whipped, let it be me; for
it was I and not Jerry, that cut the cherry tree."[32] This nostalgic view of the
natural beneficence of the slave-owning Father, published and distributed
in Boston, tells us something about the power of Washington's image as an
emblem of unity, which could, for a moment, gloss over even the cause of
the horrific violence of the Civil War. But it also reveals cracks in the
edifice of what Russ Castronovo has called the period's "monumental culture." Most biographies of Washington during the antebellum period
touch on his slave owning, but as Castronovo notes, these representations
are markedly apolitical, serving as reminders of Washington's wealth, authority, or kindness. The idea of Washington as a unifying figure can cover
so much divided ground only if it is stretched to the point of snapping, a
process Castronovo calls "the breakdown of Washington as national
signifier."[33]

Barnum and Heth offered their own version of Weems's tall tale, one
that placed Heth herself in the garden as a witness. Several newspaper re-

ports mention that "she relates many anecdotes of Washington's early days, among them that of cutting the tree, and confessing to his father." The *Herald* included a conversation between Heth and a patron, in which she was quizzed about the famous story.

> "Joice, do you remember about the peach tree?"
> "Yes, dat I do, very well."
> "Well, tell it."
> "Wy, de boys be playing in de garden—de garden be away up by Missy Atwood's—de boys play, and George be dere."
> "Well, what did they do?"
> "Dey damage de peach tree very much—break de branches."
> "Well, what said master to that?"
> "Old Massa Wassington be very angry—de boys deny dey did 'em—young Massa George stood up like a man—'Fadda, I do 'um,'—old Massa den not whup 'um."
> "Why did he not whip him?"
> "Wy?—'cause he tell de truth, dear boy,—'cause he tell de truth."[34]

What did Heth's blackness and her status as a slave add to this reiteration of the Washington story? Nothing, in terms of the narrative itself. As with Uncle Juvinell's Jerry and other slaves enlisted in the ritual recounting of the heroism of the Founding Fathers (such as one "Isaac," a former slave at Monticello whose memoirs recounted the beneficence of Washington and the brilliance of Jefferson),[35] her race was ostensibly secondary to her duty to remember. But that secondariness was itself a crucial aspect of the performance, in that it suggested that in the time of the Fathers, race was not a divisive issue and did not detract from national greatness; only the sight of a worshipful black slave could testify so forcefully to this point.

The Barnum-and-Heth version of the cherry tree scene (here a peach tree) also reveals the curious mixture of degradation and exaltation that characterized responses to Heth. Her story itself takes place on mythic terrain, but her reported dialect recalls the many stage representations of African Americans in which they are made to parody—unintentionally—great moments in Anglo-American literature and history: all that constitutes the official memory of the nation. The English actor Charles Mathews, for example, won over American audiences in the 1820s by imitating a black American actor he claimed to have seen butchering the part of Hamlet.[36] And in George Stevens's 1834 drama *The Patriot*, Sambo, a black character (also portrayed by a white actor in blackface) who claims he is descended from a trusted servant of Washington, makes a similar hash of Washington's memory. When his master asks Sambo to take out the bust of Washington and dust it for the Fourth of July celebration, Sambo replies: "Yes Massa—de big Washington, me lub him massa! were he 'live, me would hug him massa, as him Sambo do—*dis!*" and then broke into the wildly popular "Jim Crow" dance routine.[37]

William Andrews has argued that this antebellum trope of the ridiculous black patriot took shape in part because blacks were presumed incapable of progress (unless aided by whites) and therefore stood outside of history. In the words of Hegel, "Africa is a land of perpetual childhood" whose natives are "capable of no development or culture . . . As we see them at this day, such have they always been."[38] Stuck in the past, oblivious to the changes around them, Heth and Sambo were portrayed as developmentally stunted, but they were also shielded from the anxieties of change. (One version of the Heth story has her blissfully ignorant of the identity of Andrew Jackson: "General Jackson! who de plague be he?—neber heard ob sich a man—neber heard young George speak ob sich a person.")[39] These stagings of nostalgia and regression—coming shortly after the final emancipation of slaves in the northern states—thus expressed a conservative longing for a place and time in which blacks were perfectly in their place. But they also created a fantasy in which white audiences could escape change, progress, and even linear time itself. Both the remembrance of Washington and its voicing in black (or blackface) dialect stood as a counterbalance to the changes wrought by modernization and those advocated by abolitionists: all those steam-powered engines, hot-air balloons, piecework jobs, and revised declarations of independence. History books and biographies strove to recapture what was lost, and monuments were erected to solidify those absences as a presence on the landscape—but these attempts only signify, as Pierre Nora has written, the pastness of the past, its separation from the present. True memory, in contrast, "takes refuge in gestures and habits . . . in the body's inherent self-knowledge, in unstudied reflexes and ingrained memories."[40] A visit with Heth promised a face-to-face encounter with such a body, an encounter made all the more pure by Heth's inability to distance herself from the past, to move with the stream of time and view historically the birth of the man who gave birth to the nation.

In performing their memories of Washington, both Sambo and Heth were made to call attention to their own debased condition—through a comically broken patois in Heth's case, through an inability to express himself in any other mode than dancing in Sambo's. The newspapers that reported Heth's dialect were in a sense like actors greasing and corking up their faces to look black: one can sense the editorial delight in impersonating her voice—or, more precisely, making her voice fit the contours of an agreed-upon shorthand for black inarticulateness ("Fadda, I do 'um"). Symbolizing a more general lowliness or unfitness for participation in the exalted realm of Washington (or Shakespeare), this inarticulateness paradoxically underscored that exalted realm, setting it off against its implied negative. Heth's case was more complicated, though, than either Mathews's or Stevens's stagings of black characters, most obviously because Heth's visitors—and those who met her at second hand, through press coverage of her tour—believed (with a few notable exceptions) that they were getting the real thing: an *actual* black woman who had actually coddled, if not suckled, the great Washington. But still, her act was made palatable to the public by its adherence to a "code" of blackness developed on the stage. In the eighteenth and nineteenth centuries, black characters in stage dramas were almost invariably portrayed by whites in blackface; self-contained blackface entertainments served as entr'actes to otherwise unrelated dramas; and eventually the blackface minstrel show became its own, wildly popular, genre.[41] Throughout this history, certain conventions were nearly always operative. In blackface entertainments, blacks were characterized by childishness, ignorance loudly masquerading as knowledge, fast dancing, grotesque sexuality, and a misplaced dandyism; in the more "respectable" theater, black characters were still generally figures of fun—typically servants or slaves who never questioned their lowly status.

Blackface performance in America was an enormously complex development, with a genesis in European minstrel shows as well as in the creolized urban world of New York and along the canals built by poor whites and blacks. Recent studies have shown that minstrelsy had a vigorous and often antiracist life on the streets, where songs, steps, and gestures were exchanged between whites and blacks.[42] As it evolved into a dominant American cultural form, however, it held little promise for interracial dialogue. According to one critic, the "code" of blackface dialect and gesture that made it onto "legitimate" stages stunted the development of a legitimate African American theatrical tradition well into the twentieth century.[43] More germane here, though, is the way in which African American entertainers of the nineteenth century were compelled to conform to the code if they were to appear before white audiences. The history of blackface entertainment includes several instances in which African Americans performed songs and dances usually associated with whites in blackface.

Barnum's career in the early 1840s included managing some of the leading blackface dancers and singers, including one black man whose face he rubbed over with cork, whose lips he painted with vermilion, and on whose head he placed a "woolly wig." All this was done, one observer noted, to appease whites who might resent being "asked to look at a real . . . negro."[44] This dancer did later emerge from behind the veil of blackface to dance before whites under the name of Juba, and he achieved widespread recognition dancing as a black man rather than as a simulacrum of a white man dancing as a black man. Despite his astounding talents (noted by Charles Dickens in his *American Notes*),[45] Juba's license to perform before white audiences came from his (possibly coerced) conformity with the stage codes of blackness. Similarly, although Joice Heth found her place in public because of her physical anomaly and her socially significant memories (or invented memories), it was her conformity to the stage conventions of "blackness" that made the performance acceptable. She was a physical oddity, a servant, deferential to white authority figures, and an illiterate woman whose speech was, or could easily be made to seem, rough and comical—all characteristics that would help her escape the resentment of whites who were "asked to look at a real . . . negro." Like Juba, however, her stage presence was strong enough that she occasionally seemed to pierce those codes, startling observers with an unexpected display of wit, a moving hymn or anecdote, or simply the force of her unique association with Washington.

Despite Heth's conformity to unwritten stage conventions governing the performances of antebellum blacks, there was a genuine frisson of newness to the exhibit, which resulted from its highly original mixture of elements common to early- and mid-nineteenth-century popular culture. In an uneasy but endlessly fascinating way, it mixed the racist denigrations of the freak show and the dizzying inversions of the minstrel show with the nostalgic images of the cult of Washington. This ambivalence gave the act an open-ended quality that allowed for quite different and often competing meanings to be read onto her body and into her act. In particular, the exaltation and denigration of Heth sometimes clashed. Her racial identity and decrepitude fit her to be a freak, but her connection to Washington unfitted her. If she was truly whom she claimed to be, then her value was so high as almost to erase the degrading social fact of her blackness and to dress her up in a sort of whiteface.

This perspective occasionally made her marketing and display appear obscene. In an indignant letter to the editor of the *Sun,* one of Niblo's patrons, Henry Cole, asked "why SHE who nursed the 'father of our country,' the man to whom we owe our present happy and prosperous condition, should at the close of her life be exhibited as 'our rarer monsters are.' Is there not philanthropy enough in the American people to take care of her, although her skin be black?"[46] The connection to Washington led Cole to an interesting moment of racial confusion. His remarkable display of sympathy for Heth and her suffering body stretched but did not break the bounds of racist thinking: he urged readers to respect Heth *despite* her black skin. The fact that Cole believed in Heth's unique claim to historical importance did not, however, exempt her from all the humiliations associated with blackness, for he could still speak of her as a piece of property. He concluded by reminding the *Sun's* readers that Joice Heth "is the common property of our country—she is identified with the history of the foundation, rise and progress of our government—she is the sole remaining tie of mortality which connects us to him who was 'first in war, first in peace, first in the hearts of his countrymen'—and as such, we should protect and honor her, and not suffer her to be kept for a show, like a wild beast, to fill the coffers of mercenary men."

Cole saw in the display not so much Heth's grotesque body or even her historical importance; instead he saw her as what Roach calls a "human effigy," a performer through whose body collective memory passes like breath. This memory seemed to have little to do with Heth herself, as its

main function was to "connect us to him"—that is, viewers to their symbolic Father. Washington's status in popular phrenology as exemplar of
the Anglo-Saxon race cues us in to Cole's racial longing: could the "us"
who are connected to Washington through contact with Heth include
nonwhites?[47] Cole looked past Heth's body and saw in her story his own
race's mythological kinship to Washington. In contrast, Heth's status as a
freak made her act an exaggerated display of the conditions all blacks
faced: the facts of her race and decrepitude degraded her, justified her
captivity, even called into question her own human status (she had a
"tusk," "claws," and so on).

This pattern did not always hold, for it was her body that had elevated
her to the realm of mythic ideal. Her breasts, for instance, were represented as grotesquely shriveled dugs, and yet they were the very organs
that were said to have nourished the infant Father. Heth herself did not
apparently claim to have breast-fed Washington—Grant Thorburn reported that when he asked her how, at age fifty-four, she could have suckled Washington, she claimed only to have been a dry nurse—but the per-
sistence of such questions points to the widespread assumption that she
did so. For instance, a French visitor described Heth as "an old, black, id-
iot mummy, whose hideous black teats suckled the great Washington."[48]
And a New York newspaper reporter lamented, after her death, that "all
her stories of suckling General Washington" were proved false by the autopsy.[49] So if Heth was a conduit to the mythic past, then it was presumed
to be her body—and not just her story—that exalted her, even as it was an
object of derision.

The heavily gendered image of her body's past and present was the root
of another of the exhibit's paradoxes. At a time when women were rigorously excluded from major roles in public life, one loophole was beginning
to emerge: the woman whose private, domestic acts were somehow of
public significance. Best-selling women writers of the mid-nineteenth
century famously exploited this loophole, trumpeting women's hidden,
domestic virtues to great public acclaim; public ceremonies also featured
women most often when they symbolized the social significance of such
"private" virtues as domesticity, motherhood, and purity.[50] Barnum's later
writing about Heth suggests his self-conscious manipulation of this dynamic. After congratulating himself for the brilliant advertisement about

Heth's "having been the first person to put clothes on the unconscious infant," he described the effect of her recounting this domestic act to her audience: "The sentiment of putting clothes on the unconscious infant told well, and many fine ladies in their national enthusiasm, envied the black paws of old Joyce [sic], for the office they had performed."[51] In this remembered incident we have a fascinating glimpse of a most unusual encounter between different sorts of women in public, or at least Barnum's representation of such an encounter: the "fine ladies," relegated to the status of observers peering in, with some jealousy, on the life of a black woman who found the public eye through the significance of her private (and feminine) actions. The circulation of Heth's "memories"—if Barnum is to be believed—not only performed an inversion of race and class, but sparked a small moment of gendered bafflement, even resentment. His prose hints at the way in which that resentment was managed: it was not Heth's hands but her "black paws" that had clothed Washington. One does not have to read too deeply into this account to hear echoes of the racist utterances of Niblo's white female patrons putting this famous black woman back in her place.

Images of Joice Heth's "paws" are frequent indications of the dissonance of her grotesque body and its elevated memorial symbolism. The woodcut of her claw-like black appendages typified one set of responses to her body—emphasizing the grotesque, the barely human, the repulsive. At the same time, shaking her hand was the most direct route of contact imaginable to Washington and the glorious past he represented, and it was for some visitors worth the price of admission. (Her hours were curtailed, after all, because of the "fatigue attending her conversing, shaking hands, &c. with her numerous visitors.") This handshaking cannot be construed in a way that accords with Heth's status as a freak—in fact, most freaks were separated from their audiences by a pit, a cage, or a platform, emphasizing the audience's commonality and the freak's unbridgeable difference from them.[52] Shaking hands, in contrast, was a tacit acknowledgment of at least momentary social equivalence between the participants; it was for nineteenth-century Americans a fleshy gesture of republicanism. (Foreigners noted the American custom of handshaking with distaste. In his 1839 *Diary in America*, Frederick Marryat wrote, "you go on shaking hands here, there, and everywhere, and with everybody, for it is impossi-

ble to know who is who, in this land of equality.")[53] The equalizing effect
of handshaking was in the case of Heth a complex process. Shaking hands
with Heth perhaps did not so much elevate her to the ground of civility as
it elevated her white visitors: it ennobled them by means of a second-
degree contact with Washington, who had been dressed and caressed by
those very same black hands. Seen one way, the infant Father, his nurse,
and the spectators all met in this most egalitarian salute; in another way,
the handshake was part of Heth's ordeal, her subjection to bodily and even
scatological scrutiny.

To return to Stallybrass and White's formulation of the carnivalesque:
"Points of antagonism, overlap and intersection between the high and the
low, the classical and its 'Other', provide some of the richest and most
powerful symbolic dissonances in the culture."[54] The ritual handshake
with Heth was such a point of antagonism. It signifies the overlap, the
overdetermination of Heth by simultaneous yet often incompatible codes
of interpretation, that makes her exhibit register so many clashing historical forces in the antebellum period. How did constructed memories and
shared fantasies about the past hold the nation together, and how were al-
ternate memories used either to frame dissent or to shore up the dominant narrative? Could a gloriously imagined past ever be properly signified
by the broken vessels of the present? What was the relation between the
mythic past and the rapidly changing present? What role could women,
thought to be exiled to the private spaces of the home, have in telling the
public story of the nation? To what extent were blacks—and especially
slaves—a part of the stories that composed "official nationalism" or mythic
history? And what were blacks—people with souls, or pure bodies? No
single view of Heth ever held in this exhibit. Instead, as she traversed the
spaces of premodern and modern culture, half-alive and half-dead, shaking hands and being stared at, telling a story of a freedom that excluded
her, she elicited an unsettling mixture of disgust and envy, degradation
and exaltation, objectification and wonder.

SACRED AND
PROFANE

WHEN GRANT THORBURN asked Joice Heth if she belonged to a church, she responded that she was a Baptist and had been dipped in the Potomac River over a hundred years earlier. The answer touched the religious sensibilities of her visitors that day. "Some ladies, old and young, stood round her bed," Thorburn wrote. "They began to chaunt a hymn to a beautiful tune. The music seemed to electrify her frame—she joined in the chorus."[1] Sensing another opening, Barnum and Lyman began to stress Heth's love of church music in advertisements, and they arranged for ministers to make frequent visits.

Just before Heth left New York, the Reverend Luther Crawford of the Baptist Home Mission Society called on her at Niblo's and administered the sacrament to her. One observer was deeply touched: "No one could have witnessed the ceremony, and have heard her repeat and sing hymns without a firm conviction of the fervor of her piety."[2] The *New York Baptist*—one of a growing number of American religious journals—covered the event in some detail: "The last Lord's day she was desirous of commemorating the death of our Lord and savior; accordingly a few Christian friends, with a clergyman of the Baptist church, were convened by request, and this interesting ordinance was administered . . . At the close of the service, the old lady commenced an antiquated hymn, and waving her time-withered hand with great animation, sung—

> There is a land of pleasure,
> Where joy and peace forever roll, &c."[3]

Observers with a religious orientation were often most interested in what seemed to them the antiquarian aspects of her praying, several commenting that she "lined" her hymns in the style of a century earlier.[4] Yet what was perceived as "lining"—a method of hymn singing in which the audience responded to the leader's chanted lines—may have had a particularly poignant meaning for Heth. Slave spirituals were often performed in an antiphonal style that was derived from an African call-and-response pattern that whites perceived as similar to lining; this antiphonal style offered the singer a chance at once to express individual sorrows and hopes and to connect those feelings with the wider slave community.[5]

The lyrics Heth chose reinforce this interpretation. The "land of pleasure" refers at once to Israel and to heaven, the "promised land" beyond the broken world of the living. Taken from the book of Exodus, Heth's hymn suggests a longing for release that was frequent in both slave spirituality and the Euro-American tradition, but with different resonances in each. Moses' sojourn from Egypt into Israel was a frequent symbol of freedom for slaves: Israel became, in the symbolism of bonded African Americans, the North. Frederick Douglass wrote that when he and his fellow slaves sang "I am bound for the land of Canaan," they expressed "more than a hope of reaching heaven. We meant to reach the *North* and the North was our Canaan."[6] Eugene Genovese has argued that slave spirituality was profoundly "this-worldly at the very moment of its most apparently other-worldly pronouncements," and Heth's silent conflation of heaven with the North—like Douglass's—bore this out.[7] But the irony for Heth is that on tour in the North, singing to white audiences, she had found not Canaan but a different kind of Egypt, as she remained in the service of her enterprising masters. The fervor of the old woman's singing redoubled the song's ironies: whereas slaves in the South often sang to and with one another songs picturing the North as heaven, Heth had failed to find salvation in the North and apparently clung to a literal notion of heaven. Another account of the exhibit testified that she "converses freely about death, and is willing to meet it, often saying, 'Oh! that the Lord would in his mercy and goodness receive me home quickly.'"[8] The only "home," the only "land of pleasure" she could have imagined was the land she hoped to enter on her own death.

Or perhaps she imagined nothing of the sort. Barnum and Lyman would later claim to have invented her religious identity—forging documents attesting to her baptism and teaching her the hymns and religious anecdotes with which she charmed audiences—as thoroughly as they would claim to have manufactured her story of Washington. The question of Heth's interiority in this, as in so many other aspects of her exhibit, is practically unanswerable. What were her beliefs, her perceptions, her motivations? Was she forced to sing these hymns, or were they an authentic expression of spiritual longing and world-weariness? Several commentators wrote of the "joy" she injected into her singing, but was this, too, simulated? Or was it a comforting projection made by white onlookers, who wanted to imagine her happiness so that they wouldn't have to explore their own complicity in her misery? Would a failure to sing happily have brought punishment? Or was Heth complicit in the hoax, mimicking ancient religious practices in order to gull her visitors and increase her own sense of prestige? We have only "white" sources to turn to in reconstructing the story—much less the inner life—of this illiterate slave woman, and those sources are tainted heavily by racism, patronizing attitudes, and self-serving interests.[9]

On one score, though, we can speak with relative certitude. Heth's display of religiosity may well have been more than a touch theatrical, but Barnum and Lyman's later claims to have entirely invented her spirituality are manifestly implausible. Newspaper reports of Heth's exhibit from the R. W. Lindsay era noted aspects of her religious identity that were consistent with the northern press's later stories. "She recollects having joined the church about 140 years since and says she has received great happiness from having done so," ran a report from Cincinnati in January 1835, a full six months before Barnum met Heth in Philadelphia; and a Philadelphia paper reported in July that "she sings several religious hymns."[10] It could be that it was R. W. Lindsay who "taught" her religion or, more likely, that he encouraged her public displays of piety, although it is hard to imagine this inept showman coming up with such a compelling nuance.

Whatever the case may be, her songs of religious longing felt authentic enough to many visitors to transport them to a state of wonder, and at times her exhibit took on the feeling of a religious revival.

As she sang in New York of reaching her final rest in the land of plea-sure, Heth still had many northern cities to visit. On August 27, she and her exhibitors boarded a steamboat from New York bound for Providence, Rhode Island, and opened their exhibit the next day at the Masonic Hall over the main marketplace. The papers in Providence had been announc-ing her impending arrival for weeks, and when the exhibit began, most pronounced themselves satisfied: "To say we were astonished would be but a feeble expression of our feelings. We look on this extraordinary spec-imen of humanity, with something bordering on awe and veneration, and when we heard her converse on subject or circumstance which must have occurred more than a century since, and especially those connected with the birth, the infancy, and childhood of the immortal Washington—the mind was carried away by an intensity of interest, which no other object of curiosity has ever created in our breast."[11] "Awe and veneration": whether her hymn singing was part of a sham display of piety or not, the religious tone of her performance augmented her audience's sense that they were in the presence of sacred as well as national history, and it attracted pub-licity in Providence's religious circles. This attention led to one of the greatest challenges for Barnum and Lyman, as the ministers of Providence saw fit to look into the matter.

Compared with New York, Providence was a morally rigid, socially con-servative city, situated in the last northern state to maintain a property re-striction on the vote. It was dominated by a Protestant church and a social elite who had little tolerance for rowdy popular amusements. The only theater in town had closed in 1832, in the wake of religious attacks on it as a "nursery of vice" that was associated with brothels, grog shops, and gam-bling dens.[12] The moralizing church leaders preached to their congregants not just about the evils of northern city life and its immoral entertain-ments, but—as Providence was an early abolitionist stronghold—about those of the southern plantation. Because local traditions of deference to religious authority were still strong, the word of these ministers carried enormous weight with their audiences.[13] In the face of the ministers' abo-litionist and antitheatrical stances, Barnum ran into what he called "a

difficulty I had not foreseen." The promotional material for the Heth exhibit never stated clearly whether Heth was a slave or not. "This was a
great point for the priests," he later wrote: "They had not had an original
subject for a long time. They preached most fervently against the abomination of citizens giving their money to a creature whose family were
slaves. My attendance fell off. The priest-ridden people, under the anathe-
mas of the clergy, came no more. Curiosity itself was damped."[14]

To defuse the effects of the ministers' protest, Barnum turned their
own abolitionist rhetoric against them. A story planted in the *Providence
Daily Journal* and elaborated in handbills for the exhibit announced that
Heth's performance was in reality an antislavery benefit—the implication
being that Heth herself was no longer enslaved and was performing good
works of her own volition. "She has been the mother of fifteen children,"
the article ran, "the youngest of whom died two years ago at 116 years of
age. She has five great grand children, now the slaves of William Bowling,
Esq. of Paris, Kentucky, to the purchase of whose freedom the proceeds
of this exhibition are to be appropriated."[15] The ploy was effective: the
same paper later announced that "in consequence of immense crowds of
persons who have visited Joice," her exhibit at the Masonic Hall would be
extended for a week. In Barnum's more triumphal prose "a sudden revolution followed. The ministers repented then in sackcloth and ashes. More
fervently than they had preached against the exhibition they now
preached in favor of it. They exhorted their congregations to go . . .
Enough to say, a reaction took place. My exhibition room was crowded.
Emancipation and blarney carried all before them, and I pocketed the
rhino. 'Vive la humbug!'"[16] Related in such self-aggrandizing language,
Barnum's story may again seem of dubious authenticity. But surrounding
events—such as the sudden fascination of northern newspapers with
Heth's life in slavery and her exhibitors' loving care of her—do fit with
Barnum's account of the successful Providence abolitionist hoax, if they
don't quite support his statement of its magnitude.

Still, the ruse of turning abolitionist protesters into a cheering section
for Heth marked a high point of Barnum's duplicity in the management of
the Heth tour, and a new phase in Barnum's marketing savvy. In fashion-
ing a version of the Heth story that would win the approval of Providence's
abolition-leaning ministers, Barnum displayed an uncanny ability to adapt

to conflict, accident, and contingency—even to draw on such potential disruptions as a new source of energy and publicity. Barnum's "Joice Heth" was hardly a stable persona, but rather an improvised, shape-shifting construction that presented several possibilities for audience response, and then changed form depending on the nature of that response. In the course of the exhibit, protests, doubts, and even charges of fraud were enfolded into the performance; later, when Barnum had taken credit for the exhibit and begun to reveal some of his Wizard-of-Oz-like manipulations (while plotting others), his stature as the ultimate confidence man only increased. Over time, however, certain aspects of this operation became distasteful, even shameful, to him; the Providence abolitionist scheme was one of several incidents trumpeted in early versions of his life story and edited out of the later ones. Why was this so?

Heth's sojourn in Providence contributed, in its minor way, to the climate of hostility toward and ridicule of blacks in their new public positions as abolitionism gained steam in the North. By blurring the line separating public displays of African American piety and political activism from the racist grotesqueries of freak show culture, Barnum's hoax did violence to the abolitionist cause. Not only did it present a ludicrous image of black public figures at a time when a few blacks were just beginning to enter the public sphere, but, as Bluford Adams has written, the bogus abolition story seems to have been "calculated to undermine the efforts by free African Americans to solicit funds publicly for the purchase of their bonded friends and relatives."[17] Antiabolitionists' repeated attempts in following years to "expose" the fraudulence of former slaves who made their stories public make Barnum's joke on abolitionists seem not quite so innocent—especially to himself, as he presented himself, in retrospect, as a pious and fervent abolitionist.

When the Providence hoax was exposed in later years, it played like a parody not only of the stuffed-shirt abolitionist preachers of Providence but of some of the transformative religious developments of the day. Cast as a mock-religious revival, the Heth exhibit became a travesty of the religious movements collectively known as the Second Great Awakening that were sweeping across the North. Led by Baptists and Methodists but also growing to include new sects like the church of Mormon, the Second Great Awakening radically democratized the face of American Christianity. Rejecting the trickle-down notion that religious authority flowed downward from God through his ordained ministers until it finally reached the souls of sinners, the new evangelists believed that spiritual truth was something accessible to all, without intermediaries and without the necessity of official institutional structures.[18] Especially as America entered a phase of rapid capitalist and technological development in the early nineteenth century, evangelism drew on powerful new forces. Although traditional ministers railed against the sinfulness of the secular world, the more flexible new movements allied themselves with popular culture, staging hugely entertaining revival meetings and developing commercial forums for spreading the gospel.[19] Exploiting and even developing new printing technologies in urban centers, the newcomers published thousands of tracts, pamphlets, and newspapers (like the *Baptist,* which ran an awe-struck story of Heth's life)—as well as Bibles by the million. By 1830, there were 605 religious journals in the United States, whereas only 14 were in existence before 1790.[20] In addition, missionaries now were sent not solely to convert the heathen in places like Africa and India but to the rough streets of urban America, preaching that salvation was within reach of the city's downtrodden: paupers, immigrants, prostitutes, and blacks. The new city missions—which were run by men like Heth's admirer the Reverend Luther Crawford in New York—thus had a special role in dealing with the dislocating effects of modernization.[21] Even as the religious movements of the age of the Second Great Awakening drew on modern life and its new media as a source of energy, in a more conservative sense, they provided worldly and spiritual relief from all that was strange and bewildering in the modern world.

Because the new religious movements claimed that the divine presence dwelled within every human heart, they often called on the lowliest members of society to testify to God's power. Men may have been the leaders of most urban missions, but women and blacks were often the most zealous adherents. The historian Carroll Smith-Rosenberg has written that because "the immediate experience of the Holy Spirit, not the moral and orderly progress of the fathers, signified piety,"[22] the Second Great Awakening challenged paternal structures of religious authority and the gender arrangements that undergirded them. At least in isolated instances, the challenge extended to racial authority as well. In the lay ministry pulpits that were so central to the Second Great Awakening's expansion of Christianity's terrain, not just middle-class white women but blacks, former prostitutes, and other "untutored" folk were some of the most charismatic presences. While Heth was publicly singing hymns with ordained ministers in New York and Providence, the orator and former slave Sojourner Truth was preaching the gospel to thousands of whites at revivals in New York and Massachusetts, and other African American women such as Jarena Lee, Zilpha Elaw, Rebecca Cox Jackson, Julia Foote, and Sister Tilghman set out across the East with their holy messages.[23] Truth went on to become one of the best-known antislavery speakers in the country, but during her earlier religious phase, she was strikingly apolitical. This was consistent with the other women's public stances, as well. To gain a public identity at all was a difficult feat for any woman, and almost unimaginably risky for black women; to comment explicitly on their own oppression would only threaten their participation in the religious movements that gave them visibility.[24] In deference to the proprieties of race and gender, evangelical black women often appeared to revel in their "humble" status as vessels for God's word when they spoke in public.

Many of these itinerant African American female ministers became minor celebrities, and several of them narrated—or, in the few cases in which they were fully literate, wrote—cheaply printed memoirs to sell along the way. The best-selling of these was undoubtedly Olive Gilbert's 1850 rendering of Sojourner Truth's *Narrative*, which became required reading for abolitionists and sold well enough to finance a comfortable house for Truth.[25] In Gilbert's book, Truth was reported to have called herself a "self-made woman,"[26] but in arranging the production and promotion of her memoirs, as well as her tours, she depended heavily on the good offices of whites. Jarena Lee, by contrast, controlled her own finances by paying thirty-eight dollars of her own money to print a thousand copies of her memoirs, but who profited from the sales of the other black women's books?[27]

Joice Heth, too, had a "biography"—a cheaply printed sixteen-page pamphlet apparently produced in response to the religious controversy in Providence. This text (written by Lyman, as Barnum would later reveal)[28] highlights the entanglement of commerce and religion in the antebellum period as well as the vulnerability of black public figures to unscrupulous whites who controlled their appearances (Figure 7). Heth's biography, clearly a part of the promotional material of the tour, shares several other features with the popular writing about the lives of famous itinerant African American women religionists of the period. Like the memoirs of Lee, Elaw, Foote, and Truth, "The Life of Joice Heth, the Nurse of Gen. George Washington" advertised the forthcoming public appearances of its subject, who was presented as a humble vessel of spiritual truths. Rather than the grotesque curiosity promoted in the pages of New York papers, Heth was here a study in piety, humility, and morality. "The Life of Joice Heth" danced delicately around the controversy of her status as a slave, trying to fashion out of Heth's "life" a story that would be acceptable to detractors as well as advocates of slavery, by casting both her trials and her triumphs in a providential light. In this the text was more typical of life-writing about slaves than not. We are accustomed to think of the slave narrative as a vehicle of abolitionist protest, but this would have been a relatively new and uncommon function in 1835. Through the early nineteenth century, the burden of much biographical and autobiographical writing about slaves was to prove not the immorality of the institution of slavery but the black subject's potential for salvation, and the form common to most early slave narratives was that of the spiritual autobiography. Enslavement—for such writers as Olaudah Equiano and James Gronniosaw—was thus part of God's design: that which paradoxically tested the African in the earthly realm and provided his or her only point of contact with the Christian world.[29] As the poet Phillis Wheatley put it: "'Twas mercy brought me from my *Pagan* land, / Taught my benighted soul to understand / That there's a God, that there's a *Saviour* too."[30]

Such constructions (slavery as mercy) sometimes carried veiled meanings and muted protests—as recent scholars have pointed out[31]—and many of the narratives argued passionately against the worst of slavery's abuses. But in order for the works to be published, they had to avoid advocating a position as radical as the immediate end of American slavery and took, instead, what may be viewed as a "reformist" stance. Equiano sums this up best in his 1789 narrative: after relating some of the worst abuses he has witnessed, he challenges owners to treat "your slaves as men . . .

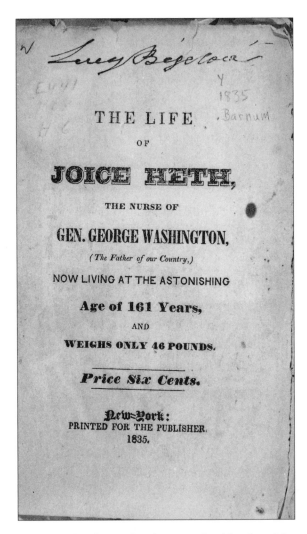

7. Pamphlet biography of Joice Heth sold at the exhibition. (© Collection of The New-York Historical Society.)

They would be faithful, honest, intelligent and vigorous; and peace, prosperity, and happiness would attend to you."[32] It is not clear whether "treating slaves as men" would involve freeing them.

Lyman's "Life of Joice Heth," true to form, does not let some of the horrors of slavery go unmentioned. After relating her birth in Madagascar in 1674, the author states that "at the age of fifteen, she was cruelly torn from the bosom of her parents and her native land by one of those inhuman beings, who, in those days, to enrich themselves, made merchandize of human flesh." This "protest," however, is more a rhetorical gesture than a political comment: the African slave trade had been legally abolished in all states since 1808 and was largely condemned as an inhumane practice even by slave owners. And fortunately for Heth, the text continues, she soon found herself in the service of "the Washington family, who were then living on an extensive domain, called the Chotank Plantations." These good people, who had no idea that a member of their household would one day become the Father of American freedoms and that another would become the oldest woman in recorded history, treated their slave with the utmost fellow-feeling. Unlike abolitionists' stories of cruel slave owners who raped their female slaves and then sold the offspring to the highest bidder, the Washingtons honored Joice's marriage to "a slave named Peter, belonging to Mrs. Atwood, a relative of the family of Washington, and living the next door neighbor," and kept her family of fifteen children intact. As with many spiritual autobiographies of slaves, her owners gave her religion, arranging for her baptism in the Potomac River in 1720; and "by her trusty and faithful discharge of such duties as were assigned her, she gained the full confidence of all the family, and was treated by them more as an hired servant than a slave." She had the run of the kitchen and the nursery, where, of course, she saw to the care of "little Georgy, as she now calls him." In fact, "she was the first person who put clothes on the unconscious infant, who was destined in after days to lead our heroic fathers on to glory, to victory, and to freedom."

How had she come into the services of her current exhibitors? Again the authors made sure not to impugn the morality of the Washingtons as Christians or as slaveholders, while still chronicling some of the pains of the slave. "At the age of fifty-four years," the narrative continues,

> she was formally sold and transferred, by a regular bill of sale, for the price of thirty-three pounds to Mrs. Atwood, who was the then owner of Peter, her husband. This was not done so much on account of the value of the services which she might render, as to accommodate her in the enjoyment of the constant company of her helpmate, (Peter,) who was

also at this time something in years, and a favorite domestic servant. By
this arrangement, they were permitted to be constantly together, both
employed in the lighter services in and about the house.

When Mrs. Atwood died, the old slave couple were once again kindly provided for. Despite the fact that "from the infirmities of old age, [they]
were unable to do much labor," they were taken in by "Mr. Boling . . . one
of the heirs of the estate" and were given what domestic work they could
manage. Mr. Boling treated them well until his death some years later
(followed shortly thereafter by the death of Peter), but the same could not
be said of his heirs. Over the generations, Joice "followed by legal succes-
sion, the branches of the family down to the present time," and often
found herself "very much neglected, laying for years in an outer building,
upon the naked floor." The terms of her sale to Lindsay and then to
Barnum are not discussed, but the authors do state that "in speaking of her
past condition, she expresses great thankfulness, that Providence should
so kindly provide the comforts of life, and make infinitely better her condition as she approaches towards the close of it." And perhaps in response to
questions about her exhibitors' possible coercion of her performances, the
author mentions that "she would not return to her former residence on
any account, and is highly pleased with the idea of her remaining as she is,
until death may finally close this mortal scene with her."

Although Heth was now portrayed as a pious, humble servant of the
Lord, her exhibitors never forgot that it was her status as an exceptional
creature that drew audiences. But they portrayed her preternatural old
age in religious terms as a "wonder," part of God's handiwork, rather than
as a medical aberration or a version of the human grotesque. The biography duly listed her diet ("a little weak tea and corn bread with rare cooked
eggs . . . coffee made very sweet," and as much "animal food" as her doctors would permit) and her fondness for tobacco, but these were merely
"her greatest temporal enjoyment." More important was her "great interest in conversing with pious persons, upon the subject of religion." This
devotion was not put on just for display, for "while alone . . . she will repeat
and sing hymns and psalms for hours together . . . that were commonly
learnt and sung a century and a half ago." Three certificates written by
aged white Kentuckians followed, each one attesting to Heth's great religi-

osity and to the authenticity of her story. All of these gentlemen had
known Heth since their youth, at which time she was already of great age
and blind; and all testified that the Washington story had not been fabricated or altered over the years. "She has ever been celebrated for her piety, and I believe no reward or threat could be offered which would in-
duce her to tell a falsehood," wrote one; another wrote that "she is very
religious and honest, and I believe the most implicit confidence may be
put in her word." (Two of these men were elsewhere identified as Mr.
Leland and Mr. Buckner, "the two eldest, most respectable and intelligent
inhabitants of Paris, Bourbon county, Kentucky." They also seem to have
traveled to Philadelphia with Heth and her previous exhibitor, Lindsay, in
order to offer their testimony.)[33]

Finally, Lyman stressed the Christian purposes of the exhibit and of the
pamphlet itself:

> In giving the foregoing brief sketch of the life and character of Joice
> Heth, the writer of this has but one single motive, and that is of charity
> towards the descendants of this living monument of antiquity.
>
> She has outlived all her descendants save five, and they are her great
> grand-children, who are now held in bondage by a highly respectable
> gentleman of Kentucky, who has generously offered to set them free on
> being paid two-thirds they cost him. This work, together with what may
> be collected from her exhibition, after deducting expenses, is expressly
> for that purpose, and will be immediately done whenever there can be
> realized the sum sufficient to do it. Two of them are said to be uncom-
> monly intelligent and active, quick to learn, and great favorites of their
> master. In consequence of his partiality towards them, they have been
> instructed to read, and have acquired by their assiduous application
> upon the Sabbath, a knowledge of the scriptures, of which they are very
> fond to learn. It is designed that they shall be instructed in the glorious
> truths of the gospel, so as to become fully qualified to teach their poor
> unfortunate race the true way to future happiness.
>
> If such should be the case, the writer of this little work would feel
> himself amply compensated for all his labor, by the happy reflection of
> having been instrumental, through the favor of the Lord, in opening a
> new channel through which might flow freely and effectually to those
> unfortunate beings, the glorious blessings derived from the knowledge
> of the gospel.[34]

In the view presented by this pamphlet, the exhibit degraded neither
Heth nor the spectators (as some would later claim it did); it was instead
an opportunity to aid in the spiritual development of the benighted African race, those "unfortunate beings" who lived in ignorance of the gospel—a common abolitionist appeal during this period. At the same time, it
did not take a radical abolitionist stance—the majority of Heth's owners
had been quite good to her and her family, and the most recent owner was
clearly trying to lift up his human chattel from a godless condition. Nor
was the intent of her current exhibitors in tension with the philanthropic
ideals of the good southern master. Newspapers in Providence and elsewhere in New England reprinted elements of this "biography" liberally,
and whenever Barnum and Lyman later came under attack for their exploitation of Heth or for purveying immoral entertainment, sympathetic
editors were induced to repeat the pamphlet's defense of Heth's piety and
her exhibitors' charity.

Heth's exhibit, however, was by no means transformed for all viewers
into a sacred event. Where her piety elevated her, her audiences' views of
race and the condition of her body continued to degrade her. The play of
the spirit and flesh was not unique for Heth. Although the Second Great
Awakening and the abolitionist movement provided African Americans
with their first real opportunities to play a part in public life, the response
from whites could be vicious when blacks appeared to overstep their
bounds. As one journalist wrote of Sojourner Truth's growing public stature, "she is a crazy, ignorant, repelling negress, and her guardians would
do a Christian act to restrict her entirely to private life."[35] Few of her com-
peers escaped similar, apparently gratuitous attacks on their mental capa-
bilities and supposedly "repelling" appearances, as writings by former
slaves frequently testify. Frederick Douglass describes in *My Bondage
and My Freedom* his dissatisfaction with George Foster, who arranged for
him to headline a subscription drive for the *Anti-Slavery Standard* and the
Liberator:

> Many came, no doubt, from curiosity to hear what a negro could say in
> his own cause. I was generally introduced as a *'chattel'*—a *'thing'*—a
> piece of southern *'property'*—the chairman assuring the audience that *it*
> could speak. Fugitive slaves, at that time, were not so plentiful as now;

and as a fugitive slave, I had the advantage of being a *"brand new fact"*—
the first one out . . . Some of my colored friends in New Bedford
thought very badly of my wisdom for thus exposing and degrading myself.[36]

This description makes Foster sound something like a sideshow barker,
and Douglass uses terms characteristic of freak show language to describe
his objectification: "curiosity," "novelty," "exposure." It is clear that in
some instances this perception of Douglass as a curiosity was a significant
draw for his public appearances. "We are so accustomed to mental stupid-
ity and moral dulness in the blacks that an exception surprises and startles
us," wrote one witness to a speech Douglass gave in Cincinnati.[37] He is
here viewed as a freakish exception to the rule of racial inferiority rather
than a representative of his race's potential—akin to a learned pig or dancing bear.

Douglas's was not the only African American public speaker to fight
through a web of images that associated public displays of blackness with
freakishness. Jarena Lee had to answer to charges that she was actually a
man in disguise,[38] and hostile audiences similarly questioned the sexual
identity of black women like the African American preacher Harriet
Livermore, the antislavery lecturer and poet Frances Ellen Watkins
Harper, and the French tragedian Rachel.[39] (Evidence of the ritual nature
of this charge is the fact that even Joice Heth was described as "exhibiting
himself" by one doubting editor in New York.)[40] This charge, which turns
outspoken African American women into bearded ladies, testifies to the
intense bodily scrutiny blacks faced on entering the public eye—a scrutiny
that would have been unseemly for whites to voice aloud in relation to a
"proper" white speaker. A legendary episode in the career of Sojourner
Truth provides perhaps the best-known incident of this sort. Asked to
speak at a women's rights convention in Indiana, Truth met the familiar
charge that she was actually a man got up in woman's clothing; a doctor
present then suggested that Truth bare her breast before the assembled
audience, and the audience voted in favor of the inspection. As a witness
recounted in a letter to William Lloyd Garrison:

Sojourner told them that her breasts had suckled many a white babe, to
the exclusion of her own offspring; that some of those white babies had

grown to man's estate; that, although they had sucked her colored breasts, they were, in her estimation, far more manly than they (her persecutors) appeared to be; and she quietly asked them, as she disrobed her bosom, if they, too, wished to suck! In vindication of her truthfulness, she told them that she would show her breast to the whole congregation; that it was not to her shame that she uncovered her breast before them, but to their shame.[41]

Like Lee and Douglass, Truth fought against being viewed as a grotesque curiosity and against the filter of freak show rhetoric and images that was distorting her message.

The degrading voyeurism to which blacks involved in morally serious work were regularly subjected makes explicable Leonard Cassuto's observation that the height of the freak show coincided with the height of the abolitionist movement;[42] to this conjunction we might add the Second Great Awakening. Both the political and the religious movement stressed the equality of all bodies in the eyes of God and used public displays to make the point; the freak show, in contrast, was there to argue the other side. A political lesson was inherent here. As Rosemarie Garland Thomson has written, the freak show helped define liberal individualism in the negative. If democracy required "the concept of an unmarked, normative, leveled body" as its presumptive subject, then the freak show's ritualistic display of aberrant, exotic, and anomalous bodies reinforced the idea that only certain classes of Americans were fit subjects for democracy.[43] Or, in slightly different terms, freak shows helped establish a sense of disembodiment in the white "norms" who visited them, a disembodiment that gave them access to the public sphere. Michael Warner argues that to secure a role in the public sphere of political debate was "to transcend the body" through "a logic of disincorporation and personal abstraction."[44] Audiences' perception of black speakers through the distorting lens of freak show grotesquerie demonstrates what Warner calls "the humiliation of positivity" that accompanied blackness, a positivity that made the body hypervisible when what was called for was the invisibility of "whiteness," of "normality."

When viewed outside of a religious frame, Joice Heth in Providence was clearly hypervisible, all body, and unfit for the public sphere. This could occasion either mockery or moral indignation. Counterbalancing the pamphlet biography's sanctimonious tones was an undercurrent of disgust in the Providence press. A reporter for the *Journal* began with a comical account of her pretensions to fame. "She says she was 'the first who put clothes on General Washington,' and also says she 'raised him.'—She now styles herself 'Lady Washington,' " he wrote. "Notwithstanding her immense age and mere skeleton form, her voice is strong and powerful, and her hearing of a whisper as acute as any person we have ever known. When any thing is whispered that she does not approve, she scolds like a very vixen."[45] In this comment, Heth was seen as both a freakish prodigy with hyper-developed senses and an over-proud negress. Two days later, the same paper ran a story entitled "A Good 'Un," which offered the following anecdote about her pride:

> Joice Heth, the "old one," not only retains her hearing perfectly, but also possesses the faculties of smell and taste to perfection. Yesterday, while many were in the Masonic Hall, where she is now exhibiting, someone had a bottle of cologne water with them, the flavor of which did not exactly suit her olfactory organ, which Joice immediately discovered, and cried out, "clear out with your *muskrat,* don't bring such stuff about me."
>
> Joice is also quite an epicure, and says she has lived long enough to know what is good and what is not. She asked for something to eat yesterday, and the nurse who attends her replied, "Yes, Joice, I will give you a fine piece of broiled mutton." "There, stop, stop," exclaimed Joice, "call up your dogs, for *mutton is de debil,* and fit for noting but de dogs—don't offer mutton to human persons." "Well," replied the nurse, "I know mutton is not very good, but it will do well enough for you." "For me," says Joice, "I'd tank you to understand dat I am *Lady Washington,* and want as good victuals as any body." This spirited reply convulsed the audience with laughter, and "lady Washington" was immediately supplied with a nice bit of chicken, and a good quantity of her favorite *Indian hoe cake,* baked in the ashes, which she says has been her principal food for the last 150 years.[46]

Heth is portrayed in these sketches as unworthy of her own status, even corrupted by it. Although she perceives that she is valued for her connection to the immortal Washington, she can only understand social elevation in terms of immediate bodily gratification: she believes she has the right to dismiss from her sensual range any scent, comment, or food not to her liking. In contrast to the biography's description of her practically ascetic pursuits of singing hymns to herself (broken only by the occasional smoking of a pipe), the *Journal* showed her skirting the edge of profanity in her speech, and she appears absurdly preoccupied with pleasures of the flesh and social advancement.

This portrayal gave off a whiff of class satire, directed downward and upward at the same time. The *Journal*, which catered to Providence's powerful middle class of merchants, professionals, and small-time entrepreneurs, typically flattered middle-class whites by portraying them as refined, polite, genteel citizens, and caricatured blacks, poor whites, and the old-money classes as "idlers." "When I compare together [the] different classes," editorialized a well-known preacher in the paper's pages, "I cannot think the difference between the rich and the poor, in regard to mere physical suffering, so great as is sometimes imagined. That some of the indigent among us die of scanty food is undoubtedly true; but vastly more in this community die from eating too much than from eating too little; vastly more from excess than starvation."[47] Heth's status as a grotesque, appetitive, status-hopping fraud gave her the worst features of both classes: the haughtiness and wastefulness of the rich and the vulgarity of the poor and nonwhite. As such, she was treated here as a real-life version of the immensely popular blackface stage character "Zip Coon," a free urban black dandy whose pretentions to upward mobility were the stuff of satire in countless stage performances throughout the decade.[48]

As Barnum well understood, the ambiguous coverage his "curiosity" received in Providence did not detract from the popularity of the exhibit, but added to it, for in it was the essential push and pull of repulsion and attraction that made Heth's display so compelling. Ministers and pious old ladies may have come to worship at her side, and some may have even thought they were contributing to an abolitionist cause; but children, in particular, seem to have taken delight in tormenting what they saw as a strange, freakish creature. The editor of *Harper's* recalled some thirty years later that "lively boy[s] would encourage Joice Heth, poking fun at her to her very face."[49] (This was one insult Heth did not take lightly: a newspaper editor reported that "if a child is within reach or even at the distance of any part of the bed, blind as she is, and has been for 80 years, she knows it and vociferously cries out—'away with you—clear out or I'll be after you.' ")[50] But the tension between the exhibit's supposedly lofty spiritual and political aims and the popular revelry surrounding her grotesque appearance was more than an isolated incident; to watch New Englanders reacting in conflicting ways to Heth is to watch them fumble with the meanings of race. At a time when whites were coming to see slavery as vaguely wrong but were uneasy with close contact with black bodies or the thought that blacks might possess anything like full humanity, Heth could function both as a sentimental victim and as an object of mockery. The opportunity to feel charitable toward blacks who were hidden from view and at the same time mock those who presumed to enter the public sphere was irresistible.

Future versions of the Heth story would also pick up on the tension between the sacred and profane, between Heth as a spiritual vessel and as a human grotesque. "For mutton is de debil" sounds practically polite compared with one version of the Heth of posterity: the beastly insubordinate slave who gorges herself on whiskey, tobacco, and vittles, swears a blue streak at her masters, and even threatens their physical well-being.[51] How can we explain these contradictions? As the Heth story moved on from town to town and, posthumously, from text to text, Barnum began to understand that it was not simply her freakishness, her religiosity, her nobility of purpose, her historical symbolism, her scientific interest, her acting, or even her impudence that made her valuable to him. Rather, her value lay in the multiplicity of these associations: Barnum himself could make others see in her whatever they most—or least—wanted to see. As he put it, the joke was that no matter what the association was, he always "pocketed the rhino." In that sense, it was not as important for Barnum to pass her off as any particular thing as it was to produce desire for her. Traveling through the North, this southern slave woman had become through a kind of alchemical transformation the ultimate northern artifact: a cultural commodity.

CULTURE
WARS

VENTURING FURTHER NORTH and west through New England, Barnum and Lyman found new challenges and new possibilities for the exhibit. At first the challenges were most clear. The harsh blue laws and the generally repressive feel of the cultural scene in Boston reminded Barnum of the "old Puritan fashion" of his Connecticut neighbors.[1] This was especially true in comparison with amusement-crazy New York. The Puritans' laws suppressing theatrical displays had only recently been relaxed in much of New England (Boston, for instance, opened its first theater in 1792, some sixty years after New York), and much of the old hostility toward public amusement remained. Anything that was not "noble," "refined," and "educative" was subject to the moral censure of the community's elite.[2] Added to this traditional Protestant distaste for theater was an upper-class resistance to raucous popular forms that catered to commoners.

Although recent scholars have characterized the "rich shared public culture" of 1830s America in contrast to the more fractious cultural hierarchy that developed in the second half of the century, we can see fault lines developing quite clearly in Bostonians' responses to the Heth exhibits and other popular entertainments.[3] These fault lines were not merely the result of aesthetic sensibilities, for Boston was a central stage for the contest between elite and working-class interests in the political realm, which always overlapped with the cultural. Small-scale riots had traditionally broken out after popular street performances through the 1820s and as such were generally tolerated; but as the riots (including one after T. D. Rice's performance of a blackface minstrel routine) grew in scale and began to be connected to issues of workers' rights, antiabolition, and other political issues, such tolerance eroded. The ruling class's response was to give teeth to the riot act, to professionalize the police force, and to scrutinize popular gatherings.[4]

The second quarter of the nineteenth century, as Isabelle Lehuu suggests, saw members of the conservative elite increasingly casting themselves as "managers of virtue," who policed popular tastes as a way of disciplining the working classes.[5] Much elite resistance to popular culture was directed against itinerant entertainers, who were commonly viewed as troublemakers and who often met with charges of vagrancy. Nevertheless, there was enough profit to be made in these entertainments that a lively contingent of rope-walkers, human curiosities, minstrel acts, and magicians could be found in Boston at any one time. Clashes with the cultural elite were practically inevitable. For instance, a traveling Jim Crow performer flogged a newspaper editor in the streets because the editor referred to him in print as a "vagabond"; on Joice Heth's arrival in Boston, James Salmon of the *Boston Gazette* wrote that she, too, was "a vagrant and not worth looking at."[6] The disgust registered in the elite journals and newspapers of Boston was often too deep for Barnum and his crew to combat openly or to fold into the carnivalesque fun of the exhibit, as they had in Providence. For example, Richard Hildreth, the editor of the *Atlas,* one of the leading voices of social conservatism in Boston, was not about to submit to Barnum and Lyman's attempts to gain free newspaper space:

> We have been annoyed the last week by a score of puffs dropped in our communication box—in poetry and prose—every one of which calls Joice Heth an interesting relic of antiquity, and declares that all the world are crowding to see her. One of them says that all visiters [sic] are "pleased with her appearance." If that be the case we should suppose that they might be very easily pleased. A more indecent mode of raising money than by the exhibition of an old woman—black or white—we can hardly imagine. We hope that the individuals interested in this exhibition will keep their scraps out of our communication box for the future—with much scrupulousness.[7]

Unlike the Providence ministers, whose disapproval of the exhibit hinged
on a specific interpretation of its political meaning (its implied involvement in the economy of slavery), this Whiggish editor dismissed the whole
enterprise as indecent.

Joseph Buckingham, the editor of another Whig paper, the *Courier,*
had for a time run advertisements for the exhibit, and so felt it a matter of
civic duty at least to attend it.[8] But once he did, the advertisements
stopped. His account of his visit makes clear the reason for this cessation:

> JOICE HETH. These are the words, which, printed in large capitals,
> and posted at every corner in the city, announce an exhibition at Con-
> cert Hall—an exhibition of a negro woman, said to be 161 years old, and
> said also to have been the nurse of Washington. The extraordinary spec-
> tacle of a living human being, supposed to have attained to double the
> ordinary life of the oldest of our species, tempted us to look in upon it.
> We do not profess much curiosity to see human deformity or human
> suffering in any of the shapes which it may please a superintending
> Providence to permit their existence, and we did not anticipate a plea-
> sure that could be great in degree or refined in character. But we were a
> little disappointed, notwithstanding. We had not anticipated a sight so
> melancholy and so disgusting. We will not attempt any description of it.
> Those who imagine they can contemplate with delight a breathing skel-
> eton, subjected to the same sort of discipline that is sometimes exer-
> cised in a menagerie to induce the inferior animals to play unnatural
> pranks for the amusement of barren spectators, will find food to their
> taste by visiting Joice Heth. But Humanity sickens at the exhibition. We
> can conceive no more exceptionable and reprehensible mode of taxing a
> community than this.[9]

Both editors offered a token protest against the conditions of Heth's exhibit, and Buckingham went as far as to compare her treatment to that of a
caged animal. But there is no suggestion in either piece—as there was in
Henry Cole's letter of protest to the *New York Sun*—that Heth herself was
worthy of better treatment, that she should have been comforted and
rested in her old age on account of her notable place in national memory.
Instead, the focus in both conservative Bostonian responses to the exhibit
is on the harm done to the community of spectators, whose senses and
sensibilities were "taxed" by the "disgusting" display of deformity.

Buckingham's penultimate sentence in the *Courier* piece expresses the enormity of the felt threat: it is "humanity"—not just those with social standing, taste, and morals—that "sickens at the exhibition."

Heth's race did not help. Four years before her arrival in Boston, the ruling coalition of clergymen, politicians, and other prominent citizens of Massachusetts had curtailed the celebration of Negro Election Day, a festival of African-derived dancing, cooking, and singing, over which an African American leader was elected to preside, even retaining some authority over the black community through the year. This ritual upheaval of social hierarchies came to be seen as a threat as the industrial revolution transformed New England's economy. As one early historian of Lynn put it, Negro Election Day had to go because of the deleterious effects on "the lower class of our own complexion"—a class whose rhythms of work and leisure were under increasing surveillance.[10] The arrival in town of Heth must have seemed to the Whig editors like a return of what so recently had been suppressed—a cultural form that stressed the wild fun of inverting social status. They were no doubt voicing their genuine distaste for the exhibit of a frail, perhaps sometimes bewildered, old woman before crowds of curiosity-seekers, but their responses were shaped by and spoke to larger social and cultural forces. In particular, the structure and scope of their disgust with the display of Heth's body are an index of genteel New Englanders' attitudes toward commercial culture, the lower orders, the public sphere, and the human body.

These Boston Whig papers catered primarily to moneyed gentlemen and would-be aristocrats, and their responses to the Heth exhibit typify the genteel idea that culture is the province of an upper crust of discerning gentlemen who act as moral guardians and gatekeepers of the public sphere.[11] This was part of the defense against Jacksonian democracy: the conservatives saw the propertied aristocracy as "natural" community leaders and the Jacksonians as a party of disaffected pretenders, devoid of taste, reason, and refinement. As Democrats won decisive elections at the national level and even won the mayoralty of Boston, the Whigs felt the ground slipping out from under them. And as the political field was expanding beyond the grasp of the elite, so was the cultural field, as reflected in the proliferation of irreverent commercial amusements—freak shows, minstrel acts, popular fiction, and irreverent papers—that aggressively

courted the working classes and often mocked the pretensions of the upper class to moral superiority.[12] In these conditions, the social elite exerted
on each other an enormous pressure for ideological consistency: according
to the editor of the *Atlas*, Richard Hildreth, to depart from the canons of
taste or politics was "to risk the consequences of those bulls of excommu-
nication which were fulminated from the pulpit and the press, and those
torrents of calumny, denunciation, and abuse, poured forth by a thousand
fluent tongues, against whomsoever deserted the ark of the covenant, and
allied himself to the uncircumcised Philistines."[13] Since Hildreth's and
Buckingham's responses to Heth were published in Whig papers with presumably Whig readers, they have the quality of internal policing: visit this
show and count yourself among the uncircumcised.

In writing about the "barren spectators" crowding to see the "disgusting" and "indecent" display, the Whig culture mavens read the exhibit as a
sign of the rabble crowding into the public sphere. But who actually visited Joice Heth? Barnum wrote that in Boston Heth was visited by several
eminent personages, including "an ex-member of Congress, his wife, two
children, and his aged mother . . . [The congressman] was one of the first
men in Boston, a gentleman highly esteemed."[14] Of course, Barnum was a
great liar, and it is probably best to take this testimony as a strategic account of his ongoing conquest of the North—first the all-powerful editors
of New York, then the ministers of Providence, now the proud old families
of New England—rather than as proof of his success with the high and
mighty of Boston. But as his comment suggests, the exhibit of Joice Heth
was never strictly a low-brow affair. Barnum's tenure with "Aunt Joice"
began not in a cheap oyster hall or tavern in New York, but in the elegant
dwelling house surrounded by the gardens at Niblo's. And in Boston, she
was exhibited in a small ballroom at the stately Concert Hall at the corner
of Court and Hanover Streets, where a refined Whig gentleman might be
presumed to feel at home. Furthermore, the admission price of 25 cents
would have discouraged many members of the working classes—both in
New York and in Boston—from shaking Heth's hand and asking her about
the swaddling and religious education of "dear little George." (Shoe-
makers, for instance, made about a dollar a day in the period 1830–1837,
and the popular museums that explicitly catered to working classes in the
1840s would charge a dime for admission.)[15]

Moving through the factory towns of Lynn and Lowell, Barnum understood that continued appeals to the upper classes would not fill his halls. He explicitly began to solicit the interest of female workers in the textile mills, who perhaps came to visit the show during their lunch hour or after work: newspapers advertised "tickets admitting eight ladies for $1.00," a discount of 50 percent.[16] Barnum's tacit admission of the social inequalities of the audiences he was soliciting is amplified by one of his few comments on the subject in his later writings. Discussing Heth's tour of factory towns in New England such as Providence, Lynn, and Lowell, Barnum wrote of the "cotton factories . . . in their glory" and the "great number of pretty girls, God bless them [who] are to be found there": "The girls in all manufacturing towns are fine creatures for exhibitions. Their sedentary lives, and their many privations, render anything in the shape of amusement a glory to them, and the satisfaction they receive upon all and every occasion, especially when they are escorted by their beaux, and what pretty girl is without them, renders their company as profitable to the exhibition, as it is pleasant to themselves."[17] Many of the Lowell textile workers had gone on strike a year earlier, calling themselves "daughters of freemen" and protesting wage cuts imposed by "Tory" employers who wished to make them "factory slaves." Despite these efforts, they still had no guarantee of a ten-hour day, and were required by their employers to live in dormitories and attend chapel.[18] Although Barnum's comment paints a rather rosy picture of these women's lives, he does fleetingly acknowledge their hardship and the dullness of their routines. Characteristically, however—and despite his Jacksonian sympathies—he sees in these privations an opportunity for profit rather than for solidarity.

Nevertheless, the newspaper records suggest that as Heth traveled through New England, her exhibit was increasingly interpreted—and often with disgust—as a symbol of cultural upheaval and disorder. The conservative gentlemen who denounced Heth's arrival in Boston saw themselves on the front line of the battle against the ascendancy of the "barren" masses, who would be exploited by vagabonds and humbugs like Heth and Barnum. The vagabonds seemed to be having the day, because the Heth exhibit, along with the exhibit of Afong Moy (the Chinese woman with "astonishingly little feet"), was a highlight of the fall season. Two decades later, a favored actor of the Shakespearean stage in Boston commented bitterly on the encroachments of such popular entertainments on the city's exalted field of culture. "Nothing has hurt my feelings so much," he wrote, "as to see crowds rushing, ready to break their necks, to witness a vile impostor, a gross humbug, while the best talent of the day, the most meritorious actor and actress that ever trod a stage, or embodied the sublime conceptions a Shakspeare, Byron, [or] Colman . . . have been puzzled to know whether it was best to blow out the lights and go home, or walk through their parts to the empty benches." Chief among these vile impostors and humbugs were the retinue and progeny of Barnum: "superannuated negro wenches, nurses of Noah and General Washington, stunted children, pasteboard mermaids, woolly horses, and other 'wonderful inventions.'"[19]

Stallybrass and White have written that the human body is often the site of struggles over cultural propriety and social hierarchy. Transgressions against dominant culture and attempts to control those transgressions "obsessively return to somatic symbols, for these are ultimate elements of social classification itself."[20] As a powerful but deeply ambiguous somatic symbol, Heth herself continued to draw considerable interest from certain quarters of the New England press, particularly among the more populist, typically Democratic papers. In addition to the grotesque fascination it had elicited in the New York press, her body here served as the site for indirect attacks on the elite culture that would repress or disavow it. For instance, Charles Greene, perhaps the leading Jacksonian journalist in Boston, enthusiastically endorsed Heth's performance, as it was part of the upsurge of entertainments that challenged the stranglehold of the elite on New England culture.[21] In replying to James Salmon, the *Gazette* editor who had commented that Heth was nothing but a vagabond, Greene found a new opportunity to personalize his politics. Salmon had written that the vagabond Heth was "not worth looking at," but Greene gleefully reported (or perhaps invented) Heth's zippy response: "I'm as handsome as *you* are any day, old daddy Salmon, and can *sing* twice as well."[22] If the upper classes wanted to dismiss popular revelry over the grotesque body, the response of those below was to turn the tables and remind the elite—in strikingly nondeferential terms—of their discomfort with their own bodies.

A crucial element of social classification that Heth's body represented, of course, was race. Boston, like Providence, was an early center for abolitionist activity, especially since William Lloyd Garrison's founding of the *Liberator* in 1831. Neither the Whig nor the Democratic party (nor their journalistic outlets), though, favored the propositions broached by "radicals" such as Garrison and George Thompson, the British abolitionist who had just toured the States. All summer long in 1835, Boston's Democratic mayor, Theodore Lyman, found the populace in "a very heated, and irritable state" over the activities of abolitionists. Their mood began to boil over when it was reported that at Andover, Massachusetts, while Heth was in Boston, Thompson gave an alarming address in which he declared "that the slave-holders ought to have their throats cut." Without a fully professionalized police force, Lyman was unable to control the streets, and on October 21 an angry mob seeking Thompson broke up a meeting of the Anti-Slavery Society in Boston. They did not find Thompson, but they did find Garrison, and settled on dragging him through the streets of Boston at the end of a rope.[23]

David Grimsted notes that on the same day several other mobs took antiabolition action in Utica, New York, and Montpelier, Vermont, and speculates that this was part of a coordinated—if disavowed—attempt on the part of northern Jacksonian Democrats to convince the South that they were serious about protecting slave-owning interests. Although neither Whigs nor Democrats had a stake in upsetting the fragile peace between North and South, it was the Whigs and their propertied constituents who were more concerned to protect the urban social order that was threatened by the mobs.[24] Certainly the Democrats were the more stridently antiabolitionist of the parties and more eager to provide justification for the long-term, if not permanent, continuance of slavery. Barnum, a Democrat through his mid-career whose position on slavery never seemed quite self-consistent, expressed a common Democratic position on the slavery issue in 1845 when he wrote, "I am no apologist for slavery, and I abhor its existence as much as any man; but the rabid fanaticism of some abolitionists is more reprehensible than slavery itself, and only serves to strengthen instead of weaken the fetters of the enslaved."[25] These words are the very language of the mob, as Grimsted presents it. Participants in antiabolition mobs generally characterized themselves as protectors of social order and abolitionists as rabid fanatics—Barnum seems to be echoing the hue and cry for Thompson and Garrison that swept the streets of Boston as his performing slave was working the crowds at Concert Hall.

It is remarkable, given the surrounding atmosphere, that the exhibit of
Heth in Boston neither provoked a riot nor was subject to the inquiries of
abolitionists, as it had been in Providence. Barnum's shrewdness, once
again, no doubt helped him escape the heat; despite the petty journalistic
mudslinging that the exhibit touched off, it seems to have functioned as a
safe space for interpretive play with issues that were so frightening outside
the Concert Hall itself. The theme of racial identity, so divisive and dangerous in the ordinary social world, was here an occasion for half-con-
scious improvisation. Coverage of the exhibit touched upon but never
quite conformed to the central political interpretations of race that were
hardening in the Jacksonian period. As Alexander Saxton has argued, the
majority of Democrats were no more racist than the majority of Whigs;
they simply gave a more shrill voice to their racism, portraying blacks as
animalistic and biologically inferior to whites. As opposed to this "hard"
Democratic racism, Whigs adhered to a "soft" racism, in which blacks
were not viewed as vicious beasts whose animal passions had to be held in
check by force, but were instead the moral and intellectual equivalent of
children, who needed to be shielded from the complexities of civilization.
Whig intellectuals in New England, according to Reginald Horsman, generally rejected scientific accounts that suggested whites and blacks were
different species, favoring biblical accounts of a common origin. According to Saxton, Democrats generally imagined race to be an absolute deter-
minant of savagery or civilization, whereas Whigs considered the difference between lower-class whites and blacks to be no greater than the
difference between upper-class whites and lower-class whites. For Democrats, race was the most important category determining the social hierarchy; for Whigs, race was simply "one difference among many."[26]

Perhaps because they were not fully conscious that they were writing
about "race" when they wrote about Heth, the Boston editors found themselves floating free of this structure of racial thinking. Instead, their improvisations on the theme of Heth's identity sometimes resulted from idio-
syncratically held positions, sometimes from competitive positioning
among the papers, and sometimes from their sense of Heth's uniqueness,
her uneasy fit in the categories of racial and social hierarchy.[27] Still, the
broad outlines of the journalistic response to Heth in Boston mark it as a
cultural skirmish in a wider cultural war over race and class, even if neither
side seemed quite aware of the relation between the battle and its larger

context. One hybrid mixture of "hard" and "soft" racist views that converged on the exhibit of Heth was that of W. Warland Clapp, another Whig editor. During the Heth display, Clapp wrote in an unrelated column that slaves would rise in murderous, beastly fury if encouraged by "fanatics" like Thompson and Garrison. Departing from the standard Whig line that blacks were childlike creatures in need of protection, Clapp viewed them instead as a force of nature more powerful than "a high pressure steam engine of ten thousand horse power." But upon visiting Joice Heth, Clapp was impressed by her natural docility and amiability. It is "altogether astonishing," he wrote, "to witness so much playfulness in the second childhood of any individual."[28] His astonishment makes sense given his apocalyptic view of black fury; he saw Heth not as an exemplum of her race but as a "marvel," something that escaped the usual categories of biological and social classification. And the Whiggish *Courier* editor Joseph Buckingham, cited above as objecting so strenuously to the display, adopted the ordinarily Democratic language of black animalism (she was like "an inferior animal"). He used this image, however, not to pillory blacks but to defend Heth from "barren spectators," a position much more in line with his paternalistic Whig outlook.

Whatever their ideological viewpoints, those most interested in promoting Heth's display took pains to show that she was not suffering in her current state. Back in New York, the editor of the *Sunday Morning News* read of the *Courier*'s attack on the exhibit, in which the editor "seems to consider it cruel to impose upon her the trouble of answering questions to gratify the curiosity of visitors." Referring back to and embellishing the pamphlet biography of Heth, the *Morning News* replied with the familiar argument that her exhibitors were truly her "protectors," that she had formerly lived "in a state of destitution and misery truly wretched: her house a mere shed, not capable of sheltering her from the storm—her bed but a truss of straw, and her food of the meanest kind, and sometimes barely sufficient to satisfy the cravings of hunger." Living in this condition, "helpless and value-less," she was taken into the care of

> humane persons, with her own and her owner's consent. Since then she
> has experienced the kindest care . . . she has a good bed to lie upon, the
> most palatable and wholesome food—her pipe and whiskey in reason-
> able quantity; and she expresses freely her gratitude for all the good

things she enjoys, and is herself perfectly content with her condition . . .
If the Courier had become acquainted with the true history of this
woman, he would have entertained different views of the subject.[29]

Heth was not a "breathing skeleton" reduced to the condition of an "inferior animal" playing tricks; instead, she was fully human, capable of making choices, "freely" expressing gratitude, and understanding her condition "perfectly."

Both the *Courier* and the *Morning News* were posing as her defenders,
one protesting her exploitation (or, more exactly, protesting the solicita-
tion of public interest in her exploitation) and one calling for her continued protection by "humane" owners and an adoring public. But this defense, earnest as it might have been, shows Heth caught on the horns of a
rhetorical dilemma. On the one hand, her would-be liberator, who saw her
exhibit as coercion and torture, found Heth herself "disgusting" and beyond "any description"—she was a subhuman wretch ("a breathing skeleton") whose own humanity seemed to have been completely erased, if indeed it ever existed. On the other hand, the man who took seriously such
things as her "happiness," her "will," and her "consent" argued that she
couldn't have been less than happy being subject to the whims of her exhibitors. What neither writer considered was that onlookers were not in a
position to gauge Heth's will or, rather, that Heth was not in a position in
which she could express it to them or even perhaps to herself. A fundamental condition of slavery in the United States was that the enslaved
could not testify against any white person and could not act in self-defense
when whites were the aggressors. Saidiya Hartman has written that these
injunctions amounted to the slave's submission "not to the will of his master only but to that of all other white persons," and allowed "the slave to be
used in any capacity that pleased the master or whomever."[30] Because she
was a slave, therefore, Heth's "consent" could *only* be a matter of seem-
ing; whether she "wanted" to perform for her master was a question that
could never truthfully be answered because, as slaves knew too well, to say
"no" was impermissible.

It might be argued that those looking in on her performance believed
that Heth was no longer a slave, that she had been freed from her bondage
and therefore could have expressed her desire not to perform if she had

wanted to. In this sense, she would be no less "free" than nonblack human curiosities, such as Afong Moy or the Virginia dwarfs, who were also performing across the North under the supervision of their exhibitors. But several factors make this argument collapse. First, acculturated as she was to slavery, Heth could hardly have been expected suddenly to speak her mind before large crowds of whites, when she knew full well that her exhibitor stood to lose (and would probably punish her) if she even attempted petty acts of insubordination in public. (Indeed, Barnum gleefully bragged in later accounts of his ingenious methods of keeping Heth in line.) Second, "freaks" of all races during this period were often under a system of control by their exhibitors so absolute as to approach slavery, and they were certainly not free to protest the conditions of their labor in public. And finally, the idea of "consent" itself, as David Gerber has argued, is meaningless unless "one has a significant range of meaningful choices."[31] As an infirm, paralyzed, blind, ill woman nearing the end of her life, Heth may well have taken some measure of comfort in her soft bed, her food, her pipe, her whiskey, and even the attention paid to her. But did she have a choice (much less a meaningful one)? Without one, she could not have given her consent.

And yet Heth continued to delight many of her onlookers, not only in ways that seemed to express her own delight, but often in ways that seemed playful, irreverent, slightly subversive. Erastus Brooks, editor of the *Essex Gazette*, entertained his small-town readers in Haverhill with an account of his visit to Heth in Boston. Finding her "the greatest wonder in New England if not in America," Brooks wrote that she "is remarkable not only for her great age but for a strength of mind, a fervent piety and withal a cheerful spirit that we have never seen equaled by those fifty and even eighty years younger than herself—could you hear her voice without having seen the 'wreck of matter,' you would have taken her to be a woman of deep piety and sound judgment." Despite this piety, she was not above making sport of members of the audience:

When a gentleman asked her what she intended to do with her money, "Use it," was her brief and yankee answer. When another person repeated the question, she answered that she "intended to buy a *wedding dress.*" "Whom do you intend to marry?"—"Yourself sir," she replied, "if

I can find *no one else.*" In answer to one of her *jeu-d'esprits* a gentleman told her that "she was *too old for him!*" "And so are a great many others *too old for me,*" continued this widowed mother of fifteen children, and half a dozen generations.[32]

The *Essex Gazette,* it should be pointed out, was in the midst of a power struggle that touched directly on issues of race and slavery. In the context of this struggle, the apparent *"jeux d'esprit"* of a black woman's joking about how she might use her money to attract a white suitor takes on more serious undertones. Brooks, a businessman who had inherited control of the paper, was eager to give up the editorial reins, and had in the previous year turned the *Gazette* over to an ambitious young editor and poet named John Greenleaf Whittier. Whittier had written a forceful abolitionist tract called *Justice and Expediency,* and his passionate abolitionist verses would later make him, in Frederick Douglass's estimation, "the slave's poet"; he would go on, after the Civil War, to become a nationally recognized icon of the Union, whose birthday was celebrated in northern public schools.[33] When Brooks hired him, however, he was a largely unknown young man of twenty-seven, and Brooks could hardly have expected that while editing the paper, he would make a widely publicized appearance with George Thompson in which the two would be pelted with eggs, stones, mud, and vegetables. Whittier's description of his political activities in the pages of the *Essex Gazette* helped convince Brooks that Whittier was the wrong man for the job, and so by early 1835, Brooks himself was back in charge. The damage Whittier had done to the paper's reputation was lasting, however, and the *Gazette* continued to come under fire for propagating abolitionist hysteria. Brooks saw fit to make a response: "We defy you to show a single line of denunciation in the Gazette since it has been under our control against Slave holders or the opponents of abolition, either of the North *or* South. We publicly declared long since, that irreparable injury had been done, by all parties from unchristian discussion and denunciation, and by the abuse of assumed power and the dealing out of harsh epithets."[34]

Accordingly, when on his trip to the big city Brooks looked in on the life of a slave (or a former slave—he didn't elaborate what he thought her status was), he drew far less startling conclusions than the "slave's poet" would have. His conclusion that Joice Heth was "cheerful in spirit" and "always seemingly happy" accords with the *Morning News* reporter's view that the exhibit was not coerced, but fully consensual. Even if we grant that the reported dialogue had really taken place, some details of Brooks's account might make us wonder about his conclusion. First, Brooks took the banter about the wedding dress to be part of Heth's delightful playfulness. But what could she have been thinking when a visitor asked her what she would do with the money made from her display, knowing as she did that Barnum and Lyman were pocketing all of it? Her *jeux d'esprit* in this light seem rather more mordant than playful. Brooks also reported what he took to be Heth's happy submissiveness to God: "She has the zeal of a martyr and owns no dependence but on her Redeemer, as she says with great emphasis. God willing she could wish to die now, but still awaits the summons of death with pleasure, and a willingness to submit to Providence. 'God's will be done' is her fervent oft-repeated prayer." The "great emphasis" she placed on having no dependence on anyone but God can be interpreted first—as Brooks apparently took it—as a sign that Heth was not dependent on any human and was happy with her condition. But when we consider that Heth *was* dependent on Barnum, and knew it, the comment takes on two additional, and perhaps not contradictory, meanings. Her words could have been ventriloquized, part of the "routine" that Barnum drilled into her in order to fabricate a consistent life history. But the "great emphasis" with which she pronounced her independence from human control might have been intended in a different spirit. As Eugene Genovese has written, Christianity provided the seeds of resistance for the slave, "for it placed a master above his own master and thereby dissolved the moral and ideological ground on which the very principle of absolute human lordship must rest."[35] Heth's comment may have been her little reminder, if not to Barnum or her white audience then perhaps to some other person, that her spirit, unlike her body, could be possessed by no mere human.

For whose benefit, if not her own or Barnum's, did she place this "great emphasis"? There was, from this point of the exhibit until the end, one other black woman present at all times, and it is interesting to speculate on what sort of relationship Heth might have had with her. In Boston, wrote Barnum, he had hired for the care of his aging property an "attendant, a

faithful coloured woman."[36] The presence of the nurse of the nurse of
Washington was noted in subsequent advertisements for the exhibit; she
was "in continual attendance," and in addition to caring for Heth herself,
gave "every attention to the ladies who visit this relic of bygone ages."[37] A
free black woman who nonetheless could not support herself or her family
without catering to the needs of whites, she might have taken solace in
Heth's words of spiritual fulfillment and their implication of a final release
from submission to the will of others.

Some observers stressed Heth's consent in her exhibit, and others characterized her performance as coerced; Barnum and Lyman (Lyman especially), meanwhile, were shaping a plan that would cast the exhibit not as
an expression of either consent or coercion, but as a simulacrum of human
agency. The origin of this plan, according to Barnum, was a meeting with
Johannes Nepomuk Maelzel in Boston. As Barnum began the display of
Joice Heth in the smaller of the two exhibition rooms at Concert Hall,
Maelzel, the former "court mechanic" of the Austrian throne, occupied
the larger one, exhibiting his astonishing mechanical contraptions, including automata, musical toys, and dioramas.[38] One of his chief attractions
was the Panoramic Spectacle of the Conflagration of Moscow, in which,
every evening at 8:45, a miniature Napoleonic army would invade a minutely rendered diorama of the Russian capital, to the accompaniment of
military music; the scene would turn to night, and a small flame would appear on the horizon and grow until it enveloped the city; the Imperial
Army would retreat, alarms and church bells would sound; and, finally, a
mine would explode beneath the Palace of the Kremlin, leaving it a heap
of smoking ruins.[39]

Even more famous than this startling contraption, though, was an entertainer who since 1769 had fascinated, outraged, and bewildered crowds
across Europe and the United States. This was the automaton chess
player. Exhibited first by Baron von Kempeln in the court of the Empress
Maria Theresa, this apparently machine-driven dummy had defeated
Benjamin Franklin and many of the elite chess players of Europe in a series of widely publicized matches in Paris, stumped the great mathemati-
cian Johann Jacob Ebert, and inspired a short story by E. T. A.
Hoffmann.[40] The von Kempeln family sold the chess player to the enterprising Maelzel in 1805, and the new proprietor saw an opportunity not

just to position himself among the nobility and eminent personages of Europe, but to make money. After successful tours of Europe, he began in the late 1820s to exhibit the chess-playing contraption to a newly industrializing American Republic, which was developing a healthy appetite for amusements that played on the idea of the "intelligent machine."[41] Was this automaton, in the words of Edgar Allan Poe, "a *pure machine*, unconnected with human agency in its movements"? Or, as Poe sought to prove, was the explanation "that its movements are regulated by *mind*—by some person who sees the board of the antagonist"?[42]

Maelzel was perhaps the most successful cultural entrepreneur the world had known before Barnum, but he was in 1835 near the end of his career. He had not presented a major new attraction to the public since 1818 (and none new to America since 1827), and his famous chess player—swathed as always in Turkish robes and apparently animated by nothing but the numerous gears inside the table over which it "pondered" its moves—was now generally assumed to be a hoax. The question of how the hoax could be detected still had the power to attract a steady stream of visitors, but not the throngs it once had. According to Barnum, when he and his new sensation arrived in Boston, "the crowd of visitors to see Aunt Joice was so great, that our room could not accommodate them, and Mr. Maelzel was induced to close his exhibition, and give us his large room." If Barnum is to be believed, Maelzel recognized in the younger man the next bearer of the flame of modern amusements. "When your old woman dies," he said to Barnum, in heavily accented English, "you come to me, and I will make your fortune. I will let you have my 'carousal,' my automaton trumpet-player, and many curious things which will make plenty of money."[43]

In fact, the old woman did die within four months, but by then Maelzel had already fled to Cuba, in the wake of the widely publicized revelation that his automaton was operated by none other than William Schlumberger, a diminutive chess genius who was hidden cleverly behind a series of sliding panels among the machine's gears. In Cuba both Maelzel and Schlumberger died of the yellow fever. But forging on from Boston, Heth would soon have a new role to play, in which she, like Schlumberger, would perform as an intelligent machine.

LOVE, AUTOMATA,
AND INDIA RUBBER

BY LATE SEPTEMBER, "the dark daughter of Madagascar," "the venerable nigger," "the vagrant," "this rare piece of antiquity, the solitary relic of a former age," the "skeleton" "who has not flesh enough remaining to make a grease spot, or entice a Jersey mosquitoe," "the living mummy," the "wonderful," "extraordinary," "disgusting," "fastidious," "lively," "curious" Joice Heth had been displayed before the public for nine months.[1] During the previous eight weeks she had barely had a day free of travel or exhibition, and many days had included both. Through mid-October, she and her retinue—Barnum, Lyman, and her private nurse—moved on to the Mechanics' Hall of Lowell, to Willard's Building in Hingham, back to Concert Hall in Boston for another week, to Stowell's Rail Road House in Worcester for two days, to Union Hall in Hartford for three days, to Springfield for three more, and back to New York's Niblo's Garden to fulfill a second engagement. Newspaper advertisements hinted at Heth's declining health ("This is the LAST OPPORTUNITY which can ever be afforded to the citizens of New England, of seeing this wonderful Woman," "she will be 162, if she lives till February," "death won't always forget her"),[2] but still she was exhibited six days a week, from nine A.M. to one P.M., from three to six, and from seven to nine.

At Niblo's, Heth's second visit coincided with the ninth annual fair of the American Institute, a major tourist attraction—drawing tens of thousands of visitors by 1835—that showcased new products (everything from artificial legs to ornamented window blinds) and celebrated the entrepreneurial spirit of New York (Figure 8). As rapid industrialization and its related dislocations led to increasing labor strife in the city—between 1831 and 1835 New York laborers had formed over fifty unions and waged nearly forty strikes—the fair was the employers' forum for projecting an image of the workplace as a place of innovation and social harmony.[3] Members of the American Institute included many early capitalists, masters who had large numbers of journeymen and apprentices in their employ and were no longer directly involved in the production of the goods from which they profited; nevertheless, they cast themselves, in the rhetoric of the day, as "mechanics"—a term that harked back to the days of the industrious artisan and implied no such division of labor. As such, the lines of social distinction that institute members drew were not between employer and employee but between "mechanic" and "aristocrat." In the 1835 fair at Niblo's, a controversy arose over the fact that the "ladies and gentlemen" paying admission to the spectacle were ushered in through the front door and treated with a great deal of solicitude, while the "mechanics" who were displaying their wares (or the wares of those who worked for them) were forced to enter through the rear and on several occasions were treated rudely.[4] This gave the members of the institute a splendid opportunity to claim victim status, to make themselves out as the rough and disrespected laborers from whose ranks most had long since risen. Such disputes notwithstanding, Niblo's was thronged with visitors, many of whom wandered across the garden to visit Joice Heth in her room. Her exhibit was more crowded than ever, and to allow a smooth flow into and out of the exhibit, Barnum had to open a separate exit from Heth's apartment and prod Heth into cutting her hymns and stories short.[5]

The display of Heth and the display of the fruits of industry at the fair were not as dissimilar as they may seem, since the wondrous new inventions and innovations showcased at the fair made enterprise itself seem like a novelty act. If the 161-year-old woman was an example of wonder commodified, the astonishing contraptions presented by the American Institute were commodities imbued with wonder. Perhaps the most wondrous commodity on display—and one that would shortly become linked with the puzzle of Joice Heth's identity—was India rubber. A natural

8. B. J. Harrison, *Fair of the American Institute at Niblo's Garden*, watercolor drawing, c. 1845. Heth was exhibited in a private room at the October 1835 fair, also held at Niblo's.

waterproofing agent derived from the sap of trees in the Brazilian Amazon region, caoutchouc (as the natives and many Europeans called it) had been the object of European and American commercial speculation since the eighteenth century; waterproof India rubber boots enjoyed a notable vogue in the early 1830s.[6] But such ventures inevitably foundered on the fact that India rubber grew brittle and often cracked in the winter, and melted into a putrid jelly in the summer. Still, the stuff seemed to have limitless possibilities for a wide variety of industrial enterprises in the North, where factories began to churn out waterproof clothing, caps, shoes, life preservers, wagon covers, and other items, all of which held up only in moderate weather. One newspaper suggested that with a few refinements, India rubber would become "one of the most important elements for manufacturing that has been discovered since the introduction of the great staple commodity of the South."[7] In short, it was to be the North's answer to cotton, and would release northern industry from reliance on the raw materials of the South.

In this context, the researches of Charles Goodyear—descendant of one of the first families of New Haven and the son of the inventor of pearl buttons—were met with widespread public interest. Goodyear's prize-winning display at the American Institute's fair at Niblo's Garden in 1835 demonstrated that India rubber could be made pliable enough to fashion beautiful copper-plated and lithographic engravings, as well as a "map of the world, which is exceedingly fine . . . [and] has only to be *blown up,* and a man has a globe, which he may afterwards fold up and put in his pocket."[8] Even more promising than these decorative uses for the "mechanics" at the fair was Goodyear's continuing investigation into the stabilization of India rubber, which only a few years later would culminate in his invention of vulcanization. This process, which used heat and sulfur to bond the tree sap more solidly, would soon make India rubber nearly as ubiquitous as plastic would become over a century later.

This ubiquity is reflected in the surprising frequency of the image of India rubber in literature of the mid-nineteenth century. It is not surprising that a writer as alert to popular sensations as Edgar Allan Poe has his American narrator noiselessly stalking "the man of the crowd" all over London while wearing "caoutchouc over-shoes," which permit him to "move about in perfect silence." But caoutchouc seemed also the vehicle of escaping the city to learn the lessons of nature: Francis Parkman wore an "india rubber cloak" on his exploration of the American West, and Walt Whitman wrote that on his "perpetual journey" of self-discovery, he would be wearing "good shoes, . . . a staff cut from the woods," and, of course, "a rain-proof coat." The stuff had political and metaphysical implications as well. Henry David Thoreau, arguing in "Resistance to Civil Government" that "that government is best which governs least," used caoutchouc to illustrate his point: "Trade and commerce, if they were not made of India-rubber, would never manage to bounce over the obstacles which legislators are continually putting in their way." Even his Concord neighbor Ralph Waldo Emerson used a popular brand of vulcanized clothing in a somber metaphor: "The dearest events are summer-rain, and we the Para coats that shed every drop."[9]

More important for Goodyear than this cultural success, India rubber's commercial success would eventually make him the Connecticut Yankee second in money and fame perhaps only to Barnum. In fact, it seems likely that Lyman and Barnum stopped in on Goodyear's display at the fair, for when in the next month Lyman traveled with Heth to Goodyear's hometown of New Haven, he—like so many other Americans—had India rubber very much on his mind.

The trip to New Haven would be without Barnum, who was finding himself enamored, from a business point of view, of an Italian-born "professor of equilibrium and plate dancing" named Signor Antonio.[10] Barnum encountered Antonio at the Albany Museum, where Heth was entertaining visitors from October 28 through November 3. This eclectic institution, housing works of fine art, a cabinet of curiosities, and, in the evenings, lecturers, musicians, human *lusus naturae,* and other performers, was fairly representative of the early nineteenth-century American museum. As scholars have shown, museums were not then the high-brow "segregated temples of the fine arts" they would become later in the century; rather, they were "repositories of information, collections of strange or doubtful data."[11] In a typical museum, one could find a piece of wood from Noah's ark, wax figures of notable personages, stuffed animals, dinosaur bones, a "monstrous tapeworm" extracted from a human intestine, and mummies alongside masterworks of art; in addition, singing dwarfs, ventriloquists, magicians, operators of dioramas and other contraptions, and lecturers on phrenology or craniology all found space to entertain and instruct their audiences. With their mixture of the educative and the sensationalistic served up at affordable prices, such museums catered to as wide a range of social classes and tastes as any cultural institution in early nineteenth-century America.[12]

Signor Antonio's act at the Albany Museum, Barnum later wrote, "was as surprising as it was novel," for "the balancing and spinning of crockery was nearly or quite new in this country—to me it was entirely so."[13] An advertisement at the Albany Museum gives a good sense of the performer's abilities: Antonio's "splendid feats of Equilibrium" included "balancing of

pipes, forks, swords, plates and bowls, causing the latter to whirl around
with inconceivable rapidity," as well as such mysterious maneuvers as "the
Highland Tiger Ball" and the "Chinese Defense, a feat never attempted
by any other performer in this country." Hearing that Signor Antonio had
no engagements scheduled beyond that week, Barnum quickly arranged
an interview with him, at which it was agreed that Antonio would work for
Barnum for the following year. He would change his name to Signor
Vivalla ("I did not think 'Antonio' sufficiently 'foreign'"), tour the country
with Barnum, and agree to bathe regularly ("an operation to which he had
apparently been a stranger for several years"). Being a freeborn man, Signor Vivalla, unlike Joice Heth, was in a position to negotiate a wage, and
Barnum agreed to pay him twelve dollars a week. As the cost of living in
New York was just above a dollar a week, this was a considerable sum.[14]

With Vivalla in tow, the company left Albany for New York City and
stayed in Barnum's old lodgings on Frankfort Street. Here Heth had her
first real rest since August, while Barnum visited his wife Charity and their
two-year-old daughter, Caroline, at their boarding house in the city. (Ever
reluctant to discuss his emotional life, Barnum makes no other mention of
his family in all his writings about the tour.) During this time, Barnum
meditated on what course to pursue with his two protégés. It appears that
the impresario noticed a curious phenomenon in regard to Heth: that
while she had usually been exhibited in rather genteel establishments, it
was the more populist newspapers and journals that had followed her career most closely. Or perhaps the city's increasing regulation of novelty
acts in summer gardens like Niblo's had extended to the Heth exhibit,
forcing Barnum and Heth—like so many acts now deemed scurrilous or licentious—to find a new home on a commercial stage.[15] Whatever his ra-
tionale, Barnum decided to display both of his performers in the Bowery,
the center of working-class cultural activity in the city, rather than in another staid pleasure garden like Niblo's.

The Bowery—what one historian has called "New York's plebeian bou-
levard, the workingmen's counterpart to fashionable Broadway"—featured dozens of theaters, exhibition houses, taverns, dance halls, gambling
houses, and brothels, all catering to a boisterous, often indecorous audience.[16] Among the most disreputable of all, as George Foster wrote, was
the Franklin Theatre. Here, among other attractions, seminude "model

artists" were on display "for the benefit of half a hundred impotent and di-
lapidated old lechers and twice as many precociously prurient boys."[17] Although Foster is describing activities at the Franklin a decade after
Barnum's display of Vivalla, it suggests that the Franklin was a good many
rungs down the ladder from Niblo's, which was, as Barnum had written,
"the only place of amusement where the shining lights of righteousness
will be seen." At the Franklin, Signor Vivalla played to a packed house,
with Barnum himself appearing onstage to help arrange the crockery, to
hand "the professor" a musket for a trick in which Vivalla hopped around
stage on one ten-foot-high stilt while firing at a target. Forgetting (or wishing to forget) his earlier escapades with Colonel Lindsay and the defecat-
ing "learned goat," Barnum wrote that this was "my first appearance on
any stage." Signor Vivalla remained at the Franklin for a week, pulling in
fifty dollars a night for Barnum and receiving a reception "such as only a
Chatham or a Bowery audience could give."[18] (Apparently this did not include sparking a riot or being showered with vegetables or obscenities,
which were common responses to Bowery productions.)[19]

Heth was set up in a saloon at the corner of Division Street and the
Bowery, with Levi Lyman in charge of daily operations. The record of
Heth's residence in the Bowery is thin, what with Barnum devoting most
of his attention to feats of plate spinning, and with the "indolent" if clever
Lyman running the show. Still, it is safe to surmise that the antiauthority
element of Heth's performance (the mock refinements of "Lady Washington") would have played well there. Bowery audiences, largely made up of
craft workers, small employers, day laborers, journeymen, and apprentices
from neighborhood butcheries, furniture shops, and shipyards, favored
carnivalesque entertainments that poked fun at two targets: blacks and the
rich. The most popular of these entertainments were the blackface acts
that had leapt to national prominence three years earlier with T. D.
"Daddy" Rice's electrifying performance of "Jim Crow" in the Bowery. In
fact, Rice had followed roughly the same path as Heth, starting out on
stage in Louisville and moving eastward through Cincinnati and Pittsburgh to New York. And like Heth's, his act of impersonation was open to
improvisation and audience involvement.[20] Primed for the inverted minstrel world of "brack" presidents, dandies, and "larned skolars," Bowery
audiences would certainly have welcomed a chance to greet the black

woman so intimately caught up in the greatness of George Washington. Or, if they were unbelievers, they might happily go to jeer.

One interesting exchange remains on record from the Bowery exhibit. Throughout her tour of the Northeast, Heth had been open to scattered charges of inauthenticity, but most of the doubters wasted little time or ink writing about her. Starting in Boston, Barnum and Lyman tried to pre-empt public expressions of skepticism by offering visitors a refund "if they are not satisfied that her age is, as claimed, 161 years."[21] But James Gordon Bennett—the notorious editor of the *New York Herald* who made a career of exposing frauds, rogues, sexual misconduct, and the like—would not be satisfied by such an offer. We have earlier seen that, according to Levi Lyman's later account published in the *Herald,* Bennett was the one major New York editor whom Barnum and Lyman hadn't paid off, and that Bennett had been prevented from training his skeptical, inde-pendent eye on Heth during her first visit to New York by the fire that burned down the *Herald's* office. Now back up and running in October, Bennett's hugely popular rag (it was, like other cheap papers, literally made out of old rags) catered largely to working-class New Yorkers, the same group that formed the core audience for minstrel shows and other rowdy entertainments in the Bowery. Exhibiting his usual brashness, Bennett offered a tantalizing suggestion about the Nurse of Washington: "Joice Heth, now exhibiting himself [*sic*], is doubtless a gross imposition." (Somewhat cryptically, he added, "Ask Mary Washington, at the corner of John and Cliff street.")[22] A response came the next day in a letter to the editor:

> Mr. Bennett, I observed in yr. paper of Monday the suggestion that the exhibition of Joice Heth is a hoax. I believe that is the general impres-sion of all before seeing her, but none afterwards. When she was at Niblo's a couple of months since I visited her, firmly believing the exhi-bition an imposition, but before I left the room I confess I was perfectly convinced of the truth of all said concerning her. In the first place her appearance exhibits the most remarkable marks of age. The documents which accompany her, including a bill of sale from the father of George Washington, certainly establish her age beyond question, and that they are real originals, appears positive from the fact that they have been published in the Kentucky and Virginia papers and I believe never ques-

tioned. I believe no person can behold her without perfect satisfaction. She is at all events a most interesting curiosity, generally talking, laughing or singing—and her exhibitors (to whom I am not known) are certainly very fair, for they advertise to refund the money to any visitor who may leave her either incredulous or dissatisfied.[23]

Whether or not this letter came from Barnum, Lyman, or someone else, it marked the first stage in a new dispute over Heth, which focused not on her propriety or fitness for exhibition but on the authenticity of her story. Although Bennett's doubts about the very grounds for exhibiting her would seem to have posed a potential problem for Barnum and Lyman, they succeeded in converting this question into yet another opportunity for whipping up public interest. In New Haven, the question of Heth's authenticity moved in a spectacular new direction, as she was said not only not to be the 161-year-old nurse of George Washington, but not to be a human being at all—in fact, not even a living creature—but a Maelzel-like mechanical contraption. In a related matter, she was also said to have fallen in love. Needless to say, in a town absorbed with the researches of Charles Goodyear, all of this hinged on the question of India rubber.

In early December, Barnum and Signor Vivalla were on tour in Washington, D.C., and Philadelphia, where Vivalla was engaged in an international trial of skill with an American circus juggler named J. B. Roberts. Meanwhile, Lyman was left with Heth, and he set up shop at Hamilton Hall in New Haven. There Heth stayed for what appeared to be a relatively uneventful week,[24] until a certain story took hold, apparently first as a joke. It all began with a newspaper editor in Newport, New Hampshire, who wrote:

> We not only believe she is as old, but a great deal older than those who are with her pretend. We have a notion that she was born in Egypt some 3000 years ago, that she is not, in fact, a living person, but a mummy— and that she is made to talk, scold, sing, &c. by the aid of a galvanic battery concealed about her person.[25]

This article seems to have caught the eye and fired the imagination of one of Heth's visitors in New Haven. The next day, the *New Haven Daily Her-*

ald reported receiving a mysterious communication about Heth's identity from "The Lady in Temple Street" (or someone pretending to be a lady from Temple Street), which it refused to print. New York's *Sunday Morning News,* however, did not pass up the opportunity.

> A female correspondent, of the New Haven Herald, has lately made a grand and important discovery which she has propounded to the editor of that paper in a communication which he, having the fear of a prosecution for libel before his eyes, most ungallantly declines to publish. We have no hesitation in characterizing it as the most brilliant discovery ever made in this country, not excepting the lunatical observation which at the time created such a sensation.[26] The correspondant [*sic*] of the Herald has ascertained that Joice Heth is not a real bona fide woman, made up of the usual bones, muscles, blood vessels and nerves appertaining to the sex, that the withered, emaciated dried up object whom we have all considered a venerable relict [*sic*] of antiquity—a living mummy—a connecting link between the present and the past—is nothing more nor less than a composition of caoutchouc, made up by some of those cunning fellows who deal in gum elastick overshoes and waterproof boots . . . What a commentary upon the gullibility of mankind. It is worse than all the perpetual motions, leather whales and manufactured mermaids and sea serpents that ever were exhibited.
>
> Some of our readers may perhaps think that we are too credulous with respect to this discovery, that we give it our belief without sufficient proof; but the fact is it bears probability too strongly written in its face for us to entertain for a moment a doubt of its truth. When we consider the inventive genius of our countrymen, and the great improvements which have been made in the manufacture of india rubber articles, and above all when we consider how many fashionable forms, which on a sunshiny day can be seen perambulating the streets of our city, are made up by the art of the milliner,—who can deny the possibility, nay, the extreme probability of the truth of the discovery which the correspondent of the Herald has announced?[27]

On the face of it, this article looks like extended journalistic play, a bit of filler on a slow news day—especially in light of an earlier, lengthy *Sunday Morning News* article in praise of Heth. As the paper's later coverage of the Heth autopsy would indicate, however, this New York editor appears to have believed the story of the "Lady in Temple Street," who was almost certainly none other than Levi Lyman.[28]

The *Sunday Morning News* editor was no doubt rather foolish—by turns too credulous and too skeptical—but the story of Heth's being an automaton was actually more elaborate (if not much more plausible) than his rendering of it might suggest. Several key elements were left out of the article. If Heth were an automaton, what would account for her improvised comments, her responses to questions, or even the lifelike feel of her body? Filling in some of these gaps is Barnum's own account of the imaginary mechanism from his 1854 autobiography. In this text, numerous details about the humbug are either misremembered or fabricated—for instance, Barnum claims that the episode occurred in Boston, immediately after his meeting with Maelzel, and that it was his brainchild; in fact, it occurred in New Haven, when, as Barnum acknowledges, he had "left Lyman to exhibit Joice." (The automaton story was an especially good joke to carry out in New Haven, appealing as it did to civic pride about "the great improvements which have been made in the manufacture of india rubber.") Nevertheless, this is still the most thorough account extant of the fabrication of the "automaton" story:

> When the audiences began to decrease in numbers, a short communication appeared in one of the newspapers, signed "A Visitor," in which the writer claimed to have made an important discovery. He stated that Joice Heth, as at present exhibited, was a humbug, whereas, if the simple truth was told in regard to the exhibition, it was really vastly curious and interesting. "The fact is," said the communication, "Joice Heth is not a human being. What purports to be a remarkably old woman is simply a curiously-constructed automaton, made up of whalebone, India-rubber, and numberless springs ingeniously put together, and made to move at the slightest touch, according to the will of the operator. The exhibitor is a ventriloquist, and all the conversations apparently held with the ancient lady are purely imaginary, so far as she is concerned, for the answers and incidents purporting to be given and related by her are merely the ventriloquial voice of the exhibitor."

Maelzel's ingenious mechanism somewhat prepared the way for this announcement, and hundreds who had not visited Joice Heth were now anxious to see the curious automaton; while many who had seen her were equally desirous of a second look, in order to determine whether or not they had been deceived. The consequence was, our audiences again largely increased.[29]

How effective was the hoax? As Barnum would have it, an elderly lady in attendance, the mother of a respected Boston congressman, "was closely scrutinizing Aunt Joice, under the immediate direction of my helpmate, Lyman." When the old white woman took Heth's wrist in her hand to check for a pulse, she called out, "There, it is alive after all!" Lyman asked for her reasons, to which she replied that "its pulse beats as regularly as mine does." His response was, "Oh, that is the most simple portion of the machinery . . . We make that operate on the principle of a pendulum to a clock." The woman then began proclaiming loudly that "the thing is not alive at all," at which point her son, greatly embarrassed, stepped in to draw her away from the exhibit. Clearly this incident never happened in quite the way Barnum told it, but no doubt such stories of audience gullibility were widespread and added to the sense of surreal fun surrounding the exhibit. Even one's sense of touch could be beguiled.

One of the more curious developments in the six-month run of the exhibit, this new twist enlisted Heth—perhaps without her knowing it—into the history of the automaton. These self-moving mechanisms, powered by springs, reservoirs of water or steam, or pendulums acting on pulleys, levers, wires, gears, and valves, were among the first complex machines created by humans.[30] Several key themes course through the history of their exhibit, which dates back to at least the medieval period in Europe. Lorraine Daston and Katharine Park have shown that in the earliest exhibits, generally at courts, automata were fashionable among nobility because they "embodied a form of symbolic power—over nature, over others, and over oneself." In addition, "automata functioned as ideal servants: beings . . . over whom their owners could have . . . perfect control." In the Renaissance and early modern periods, however, the focus on such exhibits as often stressed their perfect resemblance to living forms, rather than their mimicry of the social order. The point of the automaton was still to demonstrate power—but rather than the power of their sovereign, at whose will they would dance or walk or swim, exhibits highlighted the power of their creators, who were imitating the creative power of God to animate raw matter.

With mechanical singing birds, toy soldiers, moving pictures, fortune tellers, organ and harpsichord players, artists, and scribes forming a crucial part of the canon of late sixteenth- and early seventeenth-century *Wunderkammern* (cabinets of curiosity) across Europe, the increasingly sophisticated contraptions began to raise questions about the boundaries of human power over nature. Would it be possible to create an automaton so refined in its movements that it was indistinguishable from a living being? In the first half of the seventeenth century, this question resonated with—and perhaps even influenced—the profound philosophical reevaluation of man's place in the universe that gave birth to the modern skeptical method. René Descartes—Daston and Park's study suggests—formulated and brought to a pitch of philosophical intensity a kind of questioning that was already in wide popular circulation concerning automata. Although Descartes believed that only differences in complexity and scale separated what he called "the machines made by artisans and the various bodies which nature alone constructs," he did not believe that humans would ever be able to match God's intricacy and variety. Nevertheless, his vision of the collapsing boundary between art and nature led him to use the automaton to articulate the central crisis in his *Meditations.* In that text, his desire to arrive at a bedrock certainty about what it was possible to know swirls around the question of whether the people passing by his window are really men or "hats and cloaks which may cover automata."[31]

Over the following centuries, Descartes's question—clearly abstracted from the realm of early modern amusements—would itself be put back into popular circulation. Although serious Enlightenment thinkers scoffed at the idea that the artificial and the natural were indistinguishable, exhibitors of automata continued to erode the distinction. Moving beyond the usual attempts to conceal the principle behind the artifice, they labored to mystify even the basic distinction between the real and the fake. A staple of late eighteenth- and early nineteenth-century chicanery, according to Hillel Schwartz, was "false automata"—a genre of contraptions that "allowed magicians a wider ambit of responses to audience demands than did mechanical automata, but [which] were presented so that the mystery seemed to lie entirely within the clockwork." The surprise in these exhibits always came when the contraption or figurine exhibited some sign of "free will": an insult, an attempt to escape from the master, an irrational or spontaneous gesture.[32] Descartes had written that language and flexible behavior adapted to circumstances were what could finally distinguish humans from machines,[33] and indeed, it was those qualities that, to the discerning eye and ear, gave away the "false" part of the false automaton: Maelzel's chess player pausing before retracting his hand and "reconsidering" his move; a human ventriloquist responding to audience questions through a wax bust with spring-operated lips. Levi Lyman's orchestration of the Heth-as-automaton hoax appears, then, as an endgame in this cycle of human impersonating machine impersonating human. For here, in Heth's unwitting performance as the machine imitating the woman imitating the nurse of George Washington, the circuit of natural and artificial becomes a feedback loop, with the point of the original impersonation lost. There is a sort of agentless performance going on, which—though done by a human—mimics and reverses the structure of a machine that does not know it is performing. Cartesian skepticism, as passed off in the automaton market, now appears as something shopworn, exhausted, at the end of the line.

But how did Heth move so quickly—in the imagination of Lyman and the public who read about her and possibly examined her in this new light—from being a human curiosity to an artificial one? Once again, this conjunction repeats the logic of the early modern automata of the *Wunderkammern* and its offshoot, the early nineteenth-century American museum, in which wonders of nature were exhibited side by side with wonders of art, with the point often being that it was difficult to tell which was imitating which. Like Descartes, Francis Bacon was drawn to *Wunderkammern* and other displays of curiosities for evidence of the collapsing distinction between art and nature, but Bacon's emphasis was on natural rather than artificial oddities: monstrous births, human horns, and nature's fabulous forms were evidence of "nature at play," seemingly imitating the fecund imagination of the artist. Indeed, according to Daston and Park, human monsters through the seventeenth century were often viewed as "works of art, awakening wonder in onlookers by their rarity and oddity, as well as by the ingenuity of their maker."[34] In the wake of Lyman and Barnum's meeting with Maelzel in Boston, Lyman appears to have made a connection between the monstrous and the artificial that harks back to the early modern period: if Heth drew customers when she was advertised as a wonder of the natural world, it would require only a subtle shift to draw them again by advertising her as a wonder of the artificial world.

Unlike the typical false automaton, however, in this exhibit the human being who actually animated the fake machine apparently did not know that she was performing. (In contrast, William Schlumberger, hidden among the gears of the automaton chess player, had to know that his moves were regarded as those of a machine.) The performance clearly would work best in this way: a Heth who was told to be a machine could only have gummed up the process with bogus herky-jerky motions, a robotic voice, or some other giveaway. In this way, her performance had the same unwilled status as that of William Pinchbeck's "Pig of Knowledge," which was exhibited in Newburyport in 1798. Advertisements for this creature claimed that it "reads print or writing, spells, tells the time of day, both the hours and minutes, by any persons watch in the company, the date of the year, the day of the month, distinguishes colours, how many persons are present." The performance was so impressive, Pinchbeck claimed, that audiences suspected the pig was in actuality an automaton; he both combated and furthered this speculation by advertising it as "a real living animal."[35] The audience's suspicion of the mechanism behind the pig's actions can highlight the sheer irrelevance of Heth's will in her performance as a "fake fake"—it was a performance that went on *through* her body without her intending it.

In this way, the episode was a rich fantasia on themes of human agency and power that had run through the exhibits of automata both real and fake since the medieval period. First, insofar as the automaton was a figure that both moved itself and was animated by the will of another person, it played on the connections between the body and the mind that went to the very core of definitions of humanity itself. If human behavior was to be distinguished from either animal behavior or the action of a machine, it would be necessary to posit a distinctly human quality—intentionality, rather than automatic, mechanistic behavior—behind those actions. For this reason, figures of apes had long been popular as automata, since they appeared similar to human beings but behaved as a "beast machine," as

they were called in the medieval period.[36] The figure of the ape, then, doubled the automaton's blurring of the human and the inhuman by introduc-
ing a set of associations with a creature whose intentional status was likewise blurry.

A second issue raised by automata concerned the extension of the human will over matter, a quality that attracted many automaton makers into
industrial innovation. For instance, Jacques de Vaucanson, the famed inventor of the automaton duck and flute player, went on to develop an ap-
paratus for the automatic weaving of brocades; Friedrich von Knauss, who
invented an automaton writer, later invented the typewriter. Many makers
of automata also developed ingenious prosthetic devices such as mechanical hands, literally to extend human agency beyond the realm of the
body.[37] This conception of automaton-as-prosthesis raised questions of
power and submission to human will that had been asked of automata
since the medieval period—automata were, according to Michel Foucault,
the very image of "docile bodies" on which models of power could be elaborated.[38] It was a similar association, one suspects, that led to the creation
of many automaton "negroes" in the antebellum period, including a
singing black toy that was on display in Charles Willson Peale's museum in
New York at around the time Heth was in New Haven.[39] Black people and
apes were fitting forms for automata since they both posed—in different
degrees—questions for white audiences about bodies that resembled
dominant conceptions of the "human" but that may or may not have
lacked fully human powers of intentionality or rational agency. Black automata, additionally, repeated at the level of amusement slavery's system
of bodily domination. One of the common justifications for slavery, after
all, was that blacks were not capable of rational thought, that their actions
were guided more by animal instinct and emotion than by intelligent calculation. In their natural state, the argument went, they were like beasts;
but in a perfect state of slavery, they could become, if guided by a master's
rational will, something like machines or prosthetic devices. ("They are la-
bor-saving machines themselves, every one of 'em!" a wicked master as-
serts in *Uncle Tom's Cabin*.)[40] The "false automaton" story grafted onto the
body of a black woman, then, amplified the usual play between free will
and submission, between mechanical performance of labor and possession
of human agency that accompanied most such exhibits, and linked those

issues—in perhaps a preconscious way—with questions of race and slavery.

The editor of the *Daily Herald* of New Haven, as we have seen, chose not to run the story about Heth's being an automaton, but once the story was in circulation, he began to develop in print a related fantasy about Heth, one that was based not on her automatism or lack of human agency but on its opposite: the intense power of her will, even her deviant sexuality. In interpreting the following, it is worth bearing in mind that New Haven had recently been the site of an intense battle over race and sex. As skilled white workers felt threatened by the introduction of factory production and by competition with free blacks for jobs, the news of the abolitionist Arthur Tappan's plans to finance the practical education of a group of African American men in New Haven met with enormous resistance. Calling Tappan an "amalgamationist" (a proponent of miscegenation) for his beliefs that intermarriage should be legalized, a garbage-throwing mob surrounded his house, then moved on to burn down the residences of local blacks. An unofficial "posse" then began raiding black-run brothels and arresting white customers, thus symbolically containing the threat to white racial purity posed by any drift toward amalgamation within their own ranks.[41] It is in this context that Joice Heth, no longer a mechanical contraption, was said to have fallen in love with a white man.

Silas Mix was a twenty-eight-year-old lawyer from one of the most prominent families in New Haven. A graduate of Yale University, he had joined the law firm of the Hon. Nathan Smith, who had a booming New Haven practice. Judged by the Yale alumni association to have "as fair promise for the future as any lawyer of his age in the State," Mix soon involved himself in state politics, an effort that culminated in his election as representative for New Haven in the Connecticut General Assembly in 1832, and his appointment as executive secretary of the governor the following year. But signs of mental distress soon became visible. His arguments in court grew more and more tangled, and he involved himself and his clients in disputes that wandered far from the original issues of the trial. As he grew increasingly moody and irritable, his once-flourishing business began to fall off, and his "loping, cadaverous" figure was often seen wandering the streets of New Haven, seeking out potential lawsuits.[42]

Eighteen months before Joice Heth came to town, the *New Haven Daily Herald* began to report on Silas Mix's odd behavior. What particularly caught the paper's attention was an incident in which Mix threatened to sue the city if he was not paid a ten-dollar retainer for his services in a case involving the exemption of certain buildings from taxation. The problem was that the city claimed it had actually fired him from the case, and that he had been making a nuisance of himself ever since. When the *Daily Herald* began to pick up the story and to mock Mix's actions, the editor received from a sheriff's deputy a lengthy communication in Mix's elegant hand, beautifully done up in foolscap and ornamented with pink ribbons. This epistle contained not only a lengthy explanation of Mix's actions but a demand that the paper publish his version of events and pay him six thousand dollars for damage to his reputation, with an implied threat of a suit for a larger sum if payment was not received promptly. This threat, of course, brought nothing but further editorial scorn, and Mix was pursuing his libel action when Joice Heth visited New Haven in December of 1835.[43]

Just after it refused to print the full text of Mix's accusatory letter, the *Daily Herald* also refused to print the letter from the "Lady in Temple Street" who claimed that Heth was an automaton. In the paper's explanation of this refusal, the two cases became strangely intertwined:

> The "*Lady in Temple Street*" who insists upon it that *Joice Heth* is made of India rubber, and is nothing but a fiction, a "real mockery," must excuse us for not giving her speculations on the subject to the public. We begin to find it will not do for us to assume the responsibilities of our anonymous correspondents. If we were to declare the venerable personage alluded to a non-entity, who knows how soon she and our *protege* would send us another visitation of red tape and foolscap, to the tune of some 20,000 dollars. Silas, they say, is a great friend to antiquity, and astonishingly gallant to the sex. There are strange affinities in these days.—Joice and he might reconcile the discrepancies of age by their natural sympathies.[44]

It was a common trope in the mid-nineteenth century to compare the mental faculties of the insane to those of children and nonwhites, particularly those descended from Africa.[45] The suggested union of Heth and Mix was therefore both a "strange affinity" and a "natural sympathy"—strange for its kinky mixture of ages and races, natural for its suggestion that an insane white man was a suitable match for a black woman. In playing with this trope, the *Daily Herald,* beacon of New Haven social conservatism, revised the initial proposition of the Lady in Temple Street that Heth was so "different" a creature as not to be a human "made up of the usual bones, muscles, blood vessels and nerves appertaining to [her] sex." Rather than having a fake body and producing only an illusion of will, in this new fantasy, she had a body that was all too real, and a will that was unrestrained by any principle of decorum or civilized restraint. Grotesque and grotesquely sexual, she was outside the circle of respectable society; she was thus an appropriate match for a downwardly mobile white man who had violated the genteel rules of decorum. In the context of the antiamalgamation riots in New Haven, the *Herald's* story was typically Whig. Déclassé whites and blacks were figures of equal fun; amalgamation was not so much a real threat to society as an illustration of the need for social hierarchy.

A full-fledged improvisation was under way. The Lady in Temple Street shot back the next week:

Messrs. EDITORS:—

   I observed in the "little daily," some days since, in answer to my communication which you did not feel inclined to publish, that you are in favor of amalgamation, and that you think that Silas and Joice would make good help-meets. We ladies think there could not be a better match;— for Silas, by entering into matrimony, would stand a chance to have plenty of "little ones" coming on to help him out of his troubles,—and we ladies in temple street will give Silas our hearty well wishes for success, if he should take your hint and enter into matrimony with Joice. I, for one, think that every young gentleman ought to enter on the marriage list; it adds to their respectability—and only think how all the young men would follow suit, if Silas should set the example! We should have but few old maids in this goodly city to "pine away and die" for the want of a good husband.

   A Lady in Temple Street[46]

Assuming that this was Lyman writing, one can only speculate on a new type of publicity being manufactured for Heth, in which a titillating set of associations, however joking, would lend a new, sexualized charge to visitors' scrutiny of her body. The idea of amalgamation with a white man, however, was not entirely out of keeping with Heth's earlier stage history; one could argue that the idea of her suckling and dressing the infant Washington always gave off a spark of interracial sex, and that the reported affair with Mix simply displaced visitors' libidinal interest in her story, affixing it to a less prominent object than the Father of the Nation.

Whatever the case may be, the *Herald* did not let up on the story, continuing to link Heth with Mix long after the lawyer's "intended" had left town. When Heth died two months later, the newspaper ran the first two verses of an execrable elegy supposedly written by the unbalanced young lawyer:

> Joice Heth is dead, that good old slave,
> We ne'er shall see her more;
> She served General Washington
> Forty long years or more.
>
> And now she's left that wooden box
> That she was carried in;—
> I hope she's where she's better off
> Than in this world of sin.[47]

The editor offered his sympathies for Mix's distress, and expressed his hope that "the bereaved partner won't go mad." This hope notwithstanding, Mix's deteriorating mental health forced him to close his practice a few years later, and in 1850 he was confined to the Retreat for the Insane in Hartford, where he died in 1882. He was never married.[48]

SPECTACLE

DESPITE HER REPORTED AMOROUS ACTIVITIES, Joice Heth took a turn for the worse in New Haven, and when her exhibit at Hamilton Hall had run its course on January 27, 1836, all future engagements were canceled. She had been "ailing from a cold," newspapers reported, and "medical aid was procured to prolong, if possible, her already protracted existence." Lyman took her to the house of Barnum's brother Philo in Bethel, where, with the aid of her private nurse, he hoped she would recover. But these efforts failed, and on February 19, she passed on to the "land of pleasure" about which she had so fervently sung.[1] Barnum, back in his New York boarding house after his Washington tour with Vivalla, was greeted by a horse-drawn sleigh, whose driver handed him a note from Philo informing him "that Aunt Joice was no more." Her body, however, still lingered—in fact, it was in the very sleigh outside Barnum's door. Barnum later wrote that he "at once determined to have it returned to Bethel and interred in our village burial-ground." But for the present, he lodged it in a small room of his boarding house, for which he had the only key, and meditated on what else he might do.[2] And in the end he decided that the show must go on.

The questions surrounding Joice Heth's identity—both her claims to extraordinary old age and her status as the former nurse of George Washington—were only intensified for the popular press when she died. If she was as old as advertised, how had she managed this extraordinary feat, and what finally brought on her death? And if she wasn't, how could her story be disproved? In order to probe these riddles, several newspapers in New York immediately began clamoring for an autopsy, which was carried out six days after her death and which provided the most successful, sensational, and even spectacular event in Heth's career on the stages of the North. In a way this is not surprising. Many human anomalies had attracted the attention of anatomists upon their death since at least the end of the fifteenth century, and writings about these postmortem investigations were disseminated widely in both learned journals and popular broadsides in the late seventeenth and eighteenth centuries.[3]

In another light, though, one senses something radically new taking place upon the death of Joice Heth, something that could not have occurred in the days before cultural entrepreneurs became true capitalists. The penny press, aided by enterprising showmen like Barnum, helped create in nineteenth-century America a template for what Guy Debord has called the "society of spectacle," a set of social arrangements in which citizens are linked to one another through the act of cultural consumption. In the realm of entertainment, audience members came to train their eyes on the object before them rather than on the social relations they held to the object (and to one another); as such, "the spectacle is the opposite of dialogue," and "spectators are linked only by a one-way relationship to the very center that maintains their isolation from one another."[4] Gone were visitors' and readers' interactions with Heth and with one another; in their place came a horrifying and fascinating "event," which would consume the press for weeks, even months.

New types of entertainment, born of new social relations, themselves engendered new social relations. The creation of mass media in Jacksonian America was linked inextricably with the creation of mass politics, in that both fostered a sense of uniform citizenship and belonging for white males regardless of social class. But as Alexander Saxton's study of the penny press has demonstrated, this sense of inclusion had its boundaries: the nativism and racism of both hard-core Jacksonians and their newspapers of choice helped reinforce the idea that participation in a democratic culture was one of the spoils of race.[5] The violent spectacle of Joice Heth at the table—created and perpetuated by Barnum and the new commercial press—was a spectacle of inclusion and exclusion, masculinity and femininity, whiteness and blackness, social life and social death.

Science, too, played a key role in both the spectacle and the national discussion of race. Although scientific inquiries into racial difference had been ongoing since antiquity, it was only in the 1830s that the scientific community came to a position that James Brewer Stewart has called "racial modernity": a consensus that the existence of superior and inferior races was a "uniform, biologically determined, self-evident, naturalized [and] immutable" truth.[6] Heth's itinerant exhibit had occasionally caught the attention of scientists, but their interpretations of her body had never gained ascendancy over religious, ethical, or historical interpretations. In addition, the questions that scientists asked were rather scattershot and never yielded conclusive answers about much of anything. With her death, though, science quickly became the court of last appeal, promising once and for all to "fix" her identity and, symbolically, to organize some of the competing meanings surrounding Heth's exhibit. The new focus on fixing her identity (who or what is she?) rather than interpreting her story (what does she mean to us?) takes on an implicitly deterministic overtone when viewed within the context of scientific attempts to essentialize race in the antebellum period. The Heth autopsy—like other spectacular displays of race created by the emerging mass media—dramatized some of the new meanings of racial identity and provided an opportunity for whites to debate them (in a displaced register) as they gazed upon or read about her corpse. To look at the spectacle of the death of Aunt Joice is to perceive a white, urban, northern audience being shaped by—and in turn giving shape to—the interlocking issues of racial identity and modernization in the antebellum period. As felt in the ordinary lives of white spectators and readers, these issues were the source of enormous anxiety; the achievement of Barnum, Lyman, and the editors of the penny press was to turn them—for considerable gain—into fun.

While the body of Joice Heth was hidden in Barnum's boarding house (he does not tell how it was stored or whether he resided with it), rumors of an impending autopsy were reported enthusiastically in the New York press. The idea of an autopsy had been discussed since at least the preceding fall: one newspaper reported in September that "some physicians have given it as their opinion, that, if after death, she were to be eviscerated, her body would not turn to putrefaction."[7] To this clamor, the *Sun* provided the lone half-hearted note of dissent:

> We were somewhat surprised that a public dissection of this kind should have been proposed, and were half inclined to question the propriety of the scientific curiosity which prompted it. We felt as though the person of poor old Joice Heth, should have been sacred from exposure and mutilation, not so much on account of her extreme old age, and the public curiosity which she had already gratified for the gain of others, as for the high honor with which she was endowed in being the nurse of the immortal Washington.[8]

This same paper had earlier printed Henry Cole's objection to the exhibit, which argued, on similar grounds, that "SHE who nursed the 'father of our country,' the man to whom we owe our present happy and prosperous condition" should not be "exhibited as 'our rarer monsters are.'" Consistent with Cole's objection to Heth's exhibit in life, the *Sun* professed to view her autopsy not as an indignity for Heth herself, but as a mercenary assault on the memory of Washington. In this sense, the newspaper looked like—or posed as—a defender of mythic history and premodern notions of "honor" against the unsparing, modern clinical eye of the anatomists, whose medical gaze could not distinguish between patriotic relics and human meat. But this protest was disingenuous, for two days earlier, the same paper had led the call for such an autopsy to be performed:

> We can only say that an opportunity for illustrating the effects of such extreme old age upon the human system is not likely to occur again very soon, and that the investigation, conducted by a competent hand, would doubtless form an instructive and valuable record in anatomical science. The old woman's soul, we trust, is quite comfortable in heaven, where, perhaps, distinctions of color are of less consequence than they are here; and if the surgeons, by dissecting her body, can trace the causes of her having been so long getting thither, it might be useful to those who are in more haste. But, independently of this consideration, the examination of the anatomy of very aged persons, affords one of the most curious and instructive studies in the science.[9]

The "half inclination" to defend the memory of "the immortal Washington" was therefore not simply a nod toward a popular icon, but an indirect acknowledgment that competing values were at stake: national memory and "honor" were competing with the needs of science to make use of rare materials for an important study. It was, as will become clear, Heth's race that tipped the balance in favor of science.

The *Sun*'s status as the first successful commercial paper in the United States should make us question whether the disinterested pursuit of scientific knowledge was its top priority. The paper's endorsement of the dissection of a human curiosity—particularly a black woman—was not itself an anomaly, but rather a tried and true route to the creation of spectacle, a sensational fix to boost readership. A precedent had been set as early as 1815 with the death of Sartje Baartman (a.k.a. the "Hottentot Venus"), a native South African woman of the San tribe whose presumed steatopygia—an excess of fatty tissue that gave her abnormally prominent buttocks and distended labia—had made her an object of intense popular and scientific interest as she had been exhibited across Europe. In London, where she was led across a stage wearing a costume that resembled her skin as closely as possible, hers was one of the most successful shows of the early nineteenth century, perhaps because, for an extra charge, viewers were allowed to poke or prod her buttocks. Moving on to Paris, she was exhibited in an animal show and came under the close scrutiny of zoologists and physiologists who forced her to submit to nude examination. When she died, the prominent French zoologist Georges Cuvier dissected her and presented to the scientific community a written report and her actual, excised genitals in a jar, and he apparently sent her skin back to England, where it was stuffed and put on display.[10] Baartman's story was covered widely in the United States press; in fact, in a transcontinental spin-off exhibit, her nephew was later exhibited in Philadelphia.[11] As planned, then, Heth's autopsy was an early but not unprecedented instance of the imperious gaze of anatomists joining forces with commercial interests, making scrutiny of the racialized female body a crossroads of science and popular culture.

One apparent distinction between the cases of Baartman and Heth is that the anatomical study of Baartman had an explicitly racialist goal (Cuvier wanted to demonstrate that the Hottentots were biologically closer to animals than to Europeans), while the proposed autopsy of Heth was justified by a seemingly race-neutral inquiry into "the effects of extreme old age on the human system." As we have seen, however, the discussion of Heth's age was invariably connected with issues of biological difference between the races. The relative adaptability of different races to different climates—and hence their different aging processes in different climates—was not only a question debated by mid-nineteenth-century biologists, but had been an important part of the national discussion of race since Thomas Jefferson's famous refutation of the naturalist Count de Buffon's claims that the typical European's physical constitution was ill suited to the climate of the New World.[12] It would have been clear to many readers—and certainly to editors—that to probe the causes behind Heth's longevity would be to probe the nature of racial difference itself.

Such a project put the event on the leading edge of a wave that was about to sweep across the scientific community and popular culture alike. Jefferson claimed that, despite his "suspicion . . . that blacks, whether originally a distinct race, or made distinct by time and circumstances, are inferior to the whites in the endowments both of body and mind," racial differences had not yet "been viewed by us as subjects of natural history."[13] Toward this end, the scrutiny of racial "types" that began with human curiosities like Baartman and Heth would become more thoroughgoing in the researches of the American School of anatomy, which dominated the field in the 1850s. Led by Samuel George Morton and Louis Agassiz, the American School sought to prove the African race's physiological uniqueness and mental inferiority through such means as measuring the cranial capacity and other physical features of large numbers of racially typed specimens. As with the story of Sartje Baartman in Europe, this type of racial science in the States overlapped with the concerns of the emerging mass culture, which provided lessons in racial anatomy by other means.

The *Sun's* mention of the "distinctions of color" that would supposedly evaporate as Heth departed the mortal world is therefore disingenuous, considering that her death afforded a clear opportunity to heighten or at least underline those distinctions. One truth that the autopsy might disclose, according to a rival paper, was that blacks lived longer than whites if cared for properly.[14] Scientific scrutiny of Heth's body, many editors hoped, would help establish this fact, which would be congenial to proslavery interests. But the editors knew, too, that the autopsy itself—and not just its findings—would likely be seen by readers as an object lesson in the meanings of racial "distinctions." If their wishes for an autopsy came true, Heth would be facing one of the greatest humiliations imaginable to nineteenth-century Americans, whether black or white—a posthumous assault on her bodily integrity. Ann Douglas has written that the corpse was imagined in the antebellum period as a spiritual object, a body that had found heavenly repose after a life of competition and struggle.[15] But it is necessary to restrict this meaning to "respectable" white corpses, for those of blacks, the poor, and criminals usually met a fate different from that of the whites who ended up in tranquil cemeteries. Extending the stigma these bodies bore in life, they continued to be subjected to indignities in death—chief among them the anatomist's knife. A consideration of Heth's dissection must therefore begin with an examination of its place in the world of antebellum pathological anatomy, where, once again, race, scientific knowledge, and spectacle converged.

An essential part of the modernization of medical practice in the nineteenth century was the new emphasis on autopsies in medical training. Michel Foucault has written of the autopsy's position as a foundational practice in the creation of modern consciousness. The pathological anatomist's dispassionate, clinical view of disease and death recast the human body as an inherently knowable system, an object that could be perceived according to a set of rational rules.[16] Beginning in the late eighteenth century in the United States as well as in Europe, the medical community's desire to set forth these rules led to an unprecedented demand for corpses. This need, however, clashed with residual premodern beliefs about the sanctity of the corpse—particularly the idea that disturbing the body could prevent its resurrection.[17] Perhaps because of this clash of views, the legal status of dissections was murky. Until Massachusetts passed the first anatomy act in 1834, dissection was illegal in every state in the Union (although the law was rarely enforced), and New York did not pass a similar act until 1854.[18] Several states did allow executed criminals to be dissected, but this was not enough to provide a steady stream of study material for medical students. In order to meet demand, medical faculty had to resort to covert measures, the most common of which was grave robbing. This practice was in most states a misdemeanor offense, but generally went unpunished in the courts, since it was clear by the late eighteenth century that the furtherance of medical knowledge depended in large part on such illicit traffic.

If the law did not provide adequate protection for the hallowed corpse, however, laypeople would: there was hardly a medical school in the first half of the nineteenth century that escaped riots against its faculty for their desecration of grave sites. The racial politics of this mob rule were consistent with those of the great doctors' riot of New York in 1788. One later writer described the events that led to the disturbances: "Usually the students had contented themselves with ripping open the graves of strangers and negroes, about whom there was little feeling; but this winter they dug up respectable people, even young women, of whom they made an indecent exposure."[19] These riots and others like them in the early national period helped antebellum doctors and anatomists understand that their reputations and even their security depended on producing an illusion of social distinctions among corpses that reproduced those among living bodies. Paupers, criminals, and blacks continued to be most prone to be cut open, and slaves provided the best material of all for morbid anatomy. Not only were their surviving kin powerless to raise trouble about the commodification of their corpses (in 1788, members of the African American community in New York sent a petition to the city's Common Council urging protection of grave sites in the Negro burial ground, apparently to no avail),[20] but their bodies had been commodities to begin with.[21] In the eyes of some anatomists, therefore, a plantation was like a mine for laboratory materials. A scene from William Wells Brown's 1853 novel *Clotel* makes this clear. Carlton, a free-thinking northerner visiting a plantation in Louisiana, comes across a curious "wanted" ad in the *Natchez Free Trader*. A Dr. Stillman is offering to pay cash for the acquisition of *"fifty . . . sick Negroes,* considered *incurable"* by their owners. This Stillman is associated with a local college, whose prospectus advertises its peculiar regional advantages to men of science: "No place in the United States offers as great opportunities for the acquisition of anatomical knowledge. Subjects being obtained from among the coloured population in sufficient numbers *for every purpose,* and proper dissections carried on *without offending any individuals in the community!"*[22] Respectable white corpses, these "individuals" no doubt maintained, should remain the property of the living, but should never be transformed into commodities.

The differential treatment of black and white corpses extended one of the dominant social meanings of "race" into the world of the dead. As recent scholars have shown, the maintenance of racial distinction hinged on conceptions of property rights: whites were the only racial group in the United States that had an inalienable right to own property, including most importantly a Lockean property in the self. Blacks were at the other extreme, since they not only possessed no such right, but could become someone else's property, and could be bought and sold as commodities.[23] The social inequality of corpses thus reveals a collective fantasy about the metaphysics of racial demarcation: that whites would own themselves in perpetuity, even after death.

As Barnum and the penny press's editors saw, the cluster of social meanings adhering to Heth's dead body actually increased the considerable value it had held in life. Its connection to Washington continued to make it a curiosity, nearly a holy relic, in its own right. It was also prized material for scientists because of its rarity (the remains of medical curiosities usually generated top dollar in the market for corpses)[24] and because of its significance in the loaded debates about race, biology, and region. In addition, popular interest in racial science transmuted Heth's scientific value into commercial value. And finally, her blackness exempted those responsible for her autopsy from the clamor against human dissection and turned them into actors in a spectacle of white domination. Perhaps lending support to this last, unspoken social meaning is the fact that the final punishment meted out for the highly publicized slave uprising in Southampton, Virginia, four years earlier was the dissection of the rebel leader Nat Turner. After he was executed, reports cite, his body "was delivered to the doctors," who, in addition to performing an autopsy on his corpse, "skinned it and made grease of the flesh." A final by-product of the dissection, one report states, was "a money purse made of his hide."[25]

Soon after Heth died, Barnum contacted Dr. David L. Rogers, a respected New York surgeon, professor of surgery at the New York College of Physicians and Surgeons, inventor of a tool for excising inflamed tonsils, collector of medical curiosities (his medical cabinet included a shelf of diseased and deformed stomachs in jars), and future surgical chair of Geneva College.[26] Rogers had been to visit Heth some months earlier, and had expressed his skepticism about her age to several friends. Not only did Heth's pulse "almost invariably beat at the rate of 75, instead of considerably more than 100, which would most probably have been their rapidity at the extreme age which she assumed," but she had *"none* of the concomitants" of great age: deafness, a feeble voice, senility, or grave impairment of bodily function.[27] (Her blindness, he concluded, was the result of an illness that she may have developed early in life. He apparently did not comment on her paralysis.) Speaking to Barnum, Rogers had "expressed a desire to institute a postmortem examination if she should die in the country," and Barnum had "agreed that he should have the opportunity, if unfortunately it should occur while she was under my protection."[28] (In another rendering of the story, Barnum is more forthright and more callous: "I shed tears upon her humble grave—not of sorrow for her decease—but of regret on account of my having lost a valuable and profitable curiosity.")[29]

Accordingly, the autopsy was arranged for February 25, in the amphitheater of the City Saloon on Broadway (next door to the American Museum, which Barnum would later purchase and use to exhibit hundreds of human and natural curiosities). Word spread quickly of this last opportunity to see and evaluate Heth's body. As with her living performances, this posthumous one was not free to the public; in fact, the price of admission went up to the astonishing level of 50 cents, the equivalent of a good seat at the opera. Nevertheless, close to 1,500 people turned out. In the audience were medical students, editors, clergymen, and other interested citizens. (It is not clear whether he was in attendance, but the great diarist, socialite, and former mayor of New York, Philip Hone, noted the event in his diary.)[30] Presumably few if any women were present, since the viewing of dissections was thought to be a threat to their moral character.[31] The take for Barnum and Lyman was approximately $700.

Rogers's willingness to participate in such a spectacle may seem surprising by today's standards, but Barnum's ruse was potentially as beneficial to the medical community as it was to the emerging culture industry of editors and showmen. In order to convince laypeople of the importance of anatomy in the advancement of science, anatomists took every opportunity to display their knowledge in public. In the 1760s the first anatomical theater was constructed in Philadelphia, mainly as a place of instruction for the students of William Shippen, Jr. But this space was also used to perform a postmortem examination of conjoined twins for a ticket-paying audience. Dr. Rogers himself had participated in several high-profile anatomical examinations before Heth's. In 1830 he had dissected the body of the notorious pirate Charles Gibbs, and later turned over a "Fac-simile of the Penis" of Gibbs to the Grand Anatomical Museum of New York. And five years later he set out to perform a dramatic "galvanic experiment" on the body of the late Manuel Fernandez (an associate of Gibbs). Hoping to demonstrate the existence of "animal electricity"—the supposed "vital spark" that animated all living beings—he subjected the body to a series of precisely located electrical shocks. He did manage to make the dead man's cheek, lips, little finger, and toe twitch, but a reporter for the *New York Sun* reported that it was a rather disappointing show.[32]

At noon, when all the visitors were in place, Heth's body—or so it seemed—was placed in a mahogany coffin and taken to a makeshift operating table set up in the amphitheater. Barnum, Lyman, and Rogers advanced to the table, accompanied by the famous reporter Richard Adams Locke, who had been granted an exclusive for his paper. Since Heth had reportedly been dead for six days, Rogers would probably have injected the corpse with a mixture of oxymuriate of mercury, rectified spirits of wine, turpentine varnish, and vermilion in order to preserve the tissue and remove odor.[33] Standing before the emaciated body, Rogers stated that he would be looking primarily for "ossification (or conversion into bone) of certain parts of the body which, in subjects of ordinary longevity, were cartilaginous." For instance, he had found that the heart of a woman he had examined in Italy, who had died at age 115, had been "almost entirely ossified," as had "all the mass of cartilage about the sternum and the other bones of the chest." He then turned to the corpse on the table.[34]

Before we turn to Heth's actual dismemberment, it is worth considering the position articulated by Saidiya Hartman, who writes challengingly of the dangers of re-producing spectacular scenes of the black body's historical humiliation. She is writing of scenes of whipping, rape, mutilation, and suicide during slavery, but her questions are relevant to the scene of dissection before us:

> What interests me are the ways we are called upon to participate in such scenes. Are we witnesses who confirm the truth of what happened in the

face of the world-destroying capacities of pain, the distortions of torture, the sheer unrepresentability of terror, and the repression of the dominant accounts? Or are we voyeurs fascinated with and repelled by exhibitions of terror and sufferance? What does the exposure of the violated body yield? Proof of black sentience or the inhumanity of the "peculiar institution"?[35]

Hartman's suggestion is that such scenes can too easily amount to either pornography or a self-serving "empathy" for the victims, an empathy that is so facile as to block an understanding of the real differences between observer and victim. Her solution is to avoid the spectacular altogether and to focus instead on the terror inherent in those routine aspects of slavery that are not physically brutalizing. In writing about "the terror of the quotidian" manifested in slaves' coerced songs and dances rather than about spectacular scenes of rape, beating, and torture, she avoids exploiting the allure of displays of suffering; instead she examines "the diffusion of terror and the violence perpetrated under the rubric of pleasure, paternalism, and property." Heth's "live" exhibit would have been a good subject for Hartman's study; her autopsy would have been out of bounds.

Why, then, should we view Heth under the knife? Perhaps focusing on her dismemberment will add to an overflowing stock of images of black subjection in the service of dominant white culture, images that desensitize whites to actual African American suffering. Or maybe, in calling up spectacular scenes of racial humiliation from a more distant past, we will become lost in narcissistic self-congratulation for our own empathic response to Heth's posthumous humiliation and our own superiority to the viewers who took pleasure in it. Perhaps this will simply become a new source of pleasure.

My view is that while these dangers are real, to pass over the climax of spectacular abuse and degradation in this story would obscure a central ethical question. That is, it would risk leaving the impression that the Heth exhibit was not only a species of what Hartman calls "the terror of the quotidian" but was an actual improvement of the lot of an old slave woman. The "terror" of the exhibit is, in places, hard to find. Although Heth was compelled to work for Barnum—if not necessarily against her will, then certainly in disregard of it—it can be (and often was) argued that for all her enforced travels and exhibitions, she remained surprisingly lively, taking evident joy in aspects of her exhibit: the attentions paid her by thousands of strangers, the company of ministers and local luminaries, the approval and delight of onlookers who encouraged her to sing, joke, tell stories. She was ill and dying, but do we have proof that this is not how she wanted to spend her final months? If she were free, can we know absolutely that she would not have wanted what she was getting?

The story of her death and dissection makes this reasoning untenable. What Heth's sensational autopsy reveals, and what cannot be expressed without describing it, is the way that pleasure and aggression can be bound up with each other, especially when it comes to playing with race. Song and dance, the autopsy tells us, can seduce us into violence. Just as lynching became a form of entertainment (well into the twentieth century, souvenirs and postcards were often sold at the scene),[36] so entertainment can be a form of lynching. Hartman suggests that historical distance can inure us to the horror of a scene of abuse, but I think it can just as easily help us make sense of that horror. Singular as the autopsy was, it was composed of thoroughly conventional elements; these elements, no longer being conventional, dislocate us, force us into an estrangement from the event and might make us more aware of watching ourselves looking, or even create the uncanny sense that the event is looking back at us. In responding to the story with its amusing twists and turns, its demented lawyers and automaton lovers, its outrageous promotions and titillating exposures, we may find ourselves re-creating the sense of allure that accounted for the exhibit's success. In turning to the story's grisly end, however, we are forced to confront the deep entanglements of pleasure and aggression that were only faintly legible in the tour of Joice Heth, which now seems simply the prelude to her dismemberment.

Stretching the skin of her abdomen tight with his fingers and gripping his knife like a pen, Rogers cut into Heth's midsection along the direction of the muscular fibers. Upon examination of the internal organs, he pronounced each "to have a perfectly natural and healthy appearance." In particular, he noted that the liver was "of a proper size, and free from disease." Next he carved through her chest—presumably with a small handsaw[37]—and he examined the heart and surrounding bones most thoroughly. Here he recalled for his audience the case of the 115-year-old Italian woman whose heart he had found nearly turned to stone. In Heth's case, though, the coronary artery was not at all ossified, nor were any of the valves. At the arch of the aorta he did find "the slightest degree of ossification," but nothing beyond what might be expected for a woman of ordinary longevity. Further up were several adhesions on the left side of the lungs, "which he thought had probably been of long continuance, and also many tubercles in the lobe, which he presumed to have been the cause of death." (This finding of tuberculosis would explain the many descriptions of Heth's worsening "cold.")

Forcing the sutures of the head open "was no . . . easy matter," according to one eyewitness; "in fact, a good deal of violence was necessary." No other audience response to this struggle to sunder the skull and examine the brains is recorded, but the drama seems to have been worth the 50 cents. After all, what was being sought was not simply the cause of death, the verification of something in the bones, the body, the organs. Instead, as Rogers carved apart Heth's body looking for proof of his medical hypothesis, the audience was looking for something more abstract, the answer to a series of questions and relief from a certain anxious confusion. Was her story true? Was she whom she claimed to be? If not, how had so many been fooled? Was someone behind her, coaching her, drilling her, forcing her to speak? If she was not exactly an automaton, as the "Lady in Temple Street" had suggested in New Haven, was she some sort of human puppet? Or was the story Heth's own? Had she pulled one over on the newspapermen, the doctors—even her own exhibitors? Had she outwitted the audience members themselves? To open her head was a fitting final gesture in the solution of the mystery.

The sutures of the head were "quite distinct," it turned out, and the brain itself appeared "healthy"; on these evidences and "numerous others in the whole pathological anatomy of the body," Dr. Rogers concluded that "Joice Heth could not have been more than *seventy-five*, or, at the utmost *eighty* years of age!"[38] One might expect this finding to have ended the controversy and resulted in the exposure of Barnum and Lyman as great humbugs. (Barnum's name had first been published in connection with Joice Heth just before the autopsy took place, as "the gentleman who had charge of her for some time past.")[39] Such an exposure was the goal of the *New York Sun*, whose star reporter Richard Adams Locke had hovered over the corpse on the dissecting table, recording his findings in clinical detail for publication in his paper the next morning. Instead, Locke's report set off a frenzy of denials, counterclaims, and disputations that would consume the popular press for weeks. In these, Heth's dissection triggered questions of identity, authenticity, and medical authority; her story in turn became, for a moment, the center of the swirling culture industry that was taking shape around her.

II
RESURRECTION

AUTHENTICITY AND COMMODITY

DESPITE THE PROMOTERS' PROMISES of certainty, the autopsy of Joice Heth merely unleashed a proliferating set of rival claims about its findings, many made in earnest belief, many fabricated, and many in speculation. Doubtless numerous claims have been lost to posterity, but an almost bewildering number have survived through the agency of antebellum New York's lively and combative cast of newspapers. During this period, newspapers were establishing for themselves a central authority in the lives of a great many readers—especially those in cities, and even more especially in New York. A crucial aspect of this authority was their ability to expose the inauthentic, but in their rush to do so, they often fell prey to the very inauthenticity they sought to expose; as David Henkin has written, the newspaper's authority during this period was "paradoxically and disturbingly crucial to the recognition and exposure of the fault lines in the ground upon which it stood."[1]

As dozens of papers announced their sole possession of the "truth," the story they were investigating increasingly came unstuck from any tangible referent. This, in Jean Baudrillard's view, is one of the central effects of capitalism on culture: to produce a free-floating system of signs—imitations, copies, counterfeits—that come to constitute their own economy.[2] The papers' mixture of skeptical, credulous, aggressive, and hostile responses to the corpse, to the event, and to one another frames the conversion of Joice Heth from an object of curiosity to a purely textual commodity; that conversion, in turn, marked an opportunity for the press to try out some of its new roles, and for Lyman and Barnum to prey on the instability of those roles. What seemed stable beneath the shifting surfaces of the press coverage, though, was a common bond that all the participants— save the figure on the table—shared: their whiteness and their maleness. It is the push and pull between these silently cohesive social factors and the voluble discord surrounding the grounds of knowledge, authority, and identity that make this episode appear as a distorting mirror of the public sphere and the capitalist culture of antebellum America.

In 1830 there were sixty-five daily newspapers in the United States, supported largely by political parties, government contracts, and wealthy individual subscribers; in the early national period, according to Alexander Saxton, the press "belonged to and served the upper-class coalition" that ruled the country.[3] But in 1833 an outbreak of cholera that wreaked havoc on the New York publishing industry prompted the unemployed twenty-three-year-old journeyman printer Benjamin Day to look for a novel way to do business. Given his modest background and political views (like many other printers, Day was active in the radical Workingmen's movement), he decided to start a paper that would be affordable for common workers and would appeal to their interests. As opposed to the six-penny papers that published the bulk of daily journalism, Day's new paper, the *Sun*, charged only a penny. Day's politics were strongly pro-Jackson, but he chose to separate himself from Democratic Party editorial control and seek revenues solely from subscriptions, street sales, and advertising. The result was the first successful commercial paper in U.S. history. Day's success gave rise to several other "penny" papers in New York, most notably James Gordon Bennett's *Herald,* which began operation early in 1835. These papers were united by their freedom from patronage, their brash, innovative style of reporting, their self-confident antielitism, their exposure of hoaxes and swindles, and—paradoxically—their boisterous infighting. Occasionally these squabbles turned ugly, and the early history of the penny press is filled with trials for libel, including a case in which Day sued Bennett in January 1836.[4]

The papers were also united by their racism and opposition to abolition. In the *Sun*'s first year, Day did allow that his second-in-command George

Wisner occasionally snuck in "his damned little Abolitionist articles," but Day soon fired Wisner for this; in his place he installed Richard Adams Locke, who was soon to become the most prominent journalist of his day (and who, as we know, would have the exclusive position beside Dr. Rogers at Joice Heth's autopsy). From 1835 on, the *Sun's* line on slavery was consistently antiabolitionist—notwithstanding Bennett's sneering claim in 1837 that his rival's sheet circulated "principally among the Negroes of this city."[5] There is no difficulty in divining the *Herald's* editorial view of race and slavery. In a January 1836 editorial titled "The Abolition Question," Bennett wrote: "The blacks of the South are held in servitude by humane, kind, and careful masters—the blacks of the North are slaves to pilfering, idleness, intemperance, and vice . . . As to freedom, there is just as much in one case as the other." Abolitionists, he argued, not only were stirring up trouble but were traitors to their race: they were quick to point out the slightest injustice done to blacks but felt "not a particle of sympathy towards . . . the thousands upon thousands of the mechanics of the north, 'bone of our bone, flesh of our flesh,' toiling night and day for their bread."[6]

In contrast to their overt racism, Day and Bennett conceived of their papers (or at least hoped that they would be conceived by others) as instruments of egalitarianism and authority for all white males. Bennett wrote in 1835, "Formerly no man could read unless he had $10 to spare for a paper. Now with a cent in his left pocket, and a quid of tobacco in his cheek, he can purchase more intelligence, truth, and wit, than is contained in such papers as the dull Courier & Enquirer, or the stupid Times for three months"; Day made many similar claims. Nevertheless, the nature of the class politics of these penny papers has been the subject of debate. Did the papers, as Bennett suggested, enable upward mobility for workers? Or did they represent a new business interest that had no real stake in promoting working-class consciousness? Some historians of journalism take the editors at their word; Saxton, however, points out that as the papers became successful and their own production processes came to mirror those of capitalist society at large, they began to obscure, rather than assert, the class interests of their readers.[7] In addition, the editors did not want to alienate their advertisers by urging workers to assert their own rights. As a result, during the frequent labor strikes of the period they were more likely to urge restraint on all sides rather than working-class militancy.

Although the papers rarely encouraged their readers to take political action to further the interests of the working class, they did speak to them in what Michael Denning has called a "mechanic accent." Giving New York's workers a brash new voice to help them make sense of their experiences, the *Sun* and the *Herald* served as both agents of and defenses against modernization, which Jonathan Crary defines as

> a process by which capitalism uproots and makes mobile that which is grounded, clears away or obliterates that which impedes circulation, and makes exchangeable that which is singular. This applies as much to bodies, signs, images, languages, kinship relations, religious practices, and nationalities as it does to commodities, wealth, and labor power. Modernization becomes a ceaseless and self-perpetuating creation of new needs, new consumption, and new production.[8]

The papers' forthright commercialism cleared away the obstacles of respectability that impeded the circulation of scandal, spectacle, rumor, and a certain kind of play with social identity. At the same time, through their early use of steam (and later telegraph) and their increasingly hierarchical divisions of labor, they were on the advance guard of capitalist technology that was uprooting the artisanal system of labor. And yet they were in the awkward position of catering primarily to readers who were in danger of being dispossessed by the very developments the papers represented. The comb makers, hatters, printers, blacksmiths, cabinet makers, medicine manufacturers, ship builders, and various petty entrepreneurs who made up the mechanic class were in the 1830s in danger of finding their skills rendered obsolete by emerging technologies and their labor commodified by a new breed of capitalists. As a way to sidestep that contradiction and maintain their hold on both the tobacco-chewing workers and their bosses who advertised in the papers, the penny press peddled stories that gave workers a symbolic sense of their own mastery. Giving readers mysteries to solve offered a form of play with problems of legibility and identity that were so vexing in the social world. To solve these puzzles was one form of symbolic mastery; appealing to white readers' racial superiority was another.[9]

Richard Adams Locke was a Cambridge-educated Englishman and a lineal descendant of the philosopher John Locke. Six months before Heth died, he had produced what Edgar Allan Poe called—with barbed praise—"the greatest HIT in the way of SENSATION—of merely popular sensation—ever made by any similar fiction either in America or in Europe": the great moon hoax. According to a series of articles Locke wrote in the summer of 1835, it had been his great fortune to visit the world's leading astronomer, Sir John Herschel, who was then conducting lunar researches with his massive telescope on the southern tip of South Africa. To the astonishment of the reading public, the moon turned out to be populated by other-worldly buffalo, leaping goats with beards, long-legged birds, and spherical creatures that rolled across a moonscape containing volcanoes and vast forests. Most extraordinary of all was a race of flying men, who seemed to be a cross between bats, orangutans, and humans: their "long, semi-transparent wings" prompted "Herschel" to denominate them *"vespertilio-homo,* or man bat." If one read between the lines, however, other features more resembled stereotypical attributes of the African race: their hair was "closely curled, but apparently not woolly," and their faces and bodies were—in the standard racist description—similar to those of the "orang-utan." As if this were not subliminal cue enough, Locke concluded with a subtle reference to their childishness and oversexualized nature: "They are doubtless innocent and happy creatures, notwithstanding some of their amusements would but ill comport with our terrestrial notions of decorum."[10] The "greatest HIT" of American popular culture before the Joice Heth autopsy was thus another riddle involving race and the probing eye of science.

After the "Moon Story" appeared in the *Sun,* many other papers picked it up, with some—initially including Bennett's *Herald*—taking it quite seriously. When Bennett discovered that he had been duped, however, he offered a stinging rebuttal in print and was forever after on the alert to root out his rival's bogus reporting; over the next few years, he charged that Locke's humbuggery was behind virtually every piece of news that the *Sun* uncovered before the *Herald* did. In the aftermath of the Joice Heth story, he turned his all-devouring skepticism once again on his old antagonists Locke and Day. (He was unaware that his own skepticism would shortly be turned against himself.) Locke's dispatch to the *Sun* concluded that Dr. Rogers had proved "that [Heth's] pretensions to the extraordinary longevity of 161 years, all her stories about suckling General Washington, and about her fondness for 'young master George,' have been taught her, in regular lessons, for the benefit of her exhibitors."[11] Dozens of newspapers across the country took this finding as authoritative and reprinted it, but not the *Herald.* Although Locke's report would seem to have confirmed Bennett's long-standing disbelief in Heth's authenticity, Bennett found different grounds on which to discredit his rival after Lyman visited him in his office the following day. In reprinting the *Sun's* "long rigmarole account of the dissection of Joice Heth"—along with sniping editorial commentary in brackets—Bennett announced that the *Sun* had been duped. Remarkably, it was the central premise of the autopsy, and not any particular findings about Heth, that was the problem:

> *Joice Heth is not dead.* On Wednesday last, as we learn from the best authority, she was living at Hebron, in Connecticut, where she then was. The subject on which Doctor Rogers and the Medical Faculty of Barclay street have been exercising their knife and their ingenuity, is the remains of a respectable old negress called AUNT NELLY, who has lived many years in a small house by herself, in Harlaem, belonging to Mr. Clarke. She is, as Dr. Rogers sagely discovers, and Doctor Locke his colleage [*sic*] accurately records, only eighty years of age. Aunt Nelly before death, complained of old age and infirmity. She was otherwise in good spirits. The recent winter, however, has been very severe, and so she gave up the ghost a few days ago.[12]

Bennett's explanation for this humbug dates back to the controversy over the "Moon Story." Bennett believed that Dr. Rogers—a close friend of Locke's—had had a hand in this earlier hoax. Since Locke and Rogers were known to be teaming up again in investigating the Heth story, the autopsy in City Saloon provided a golden opportunity for those taken in by the moon hoax to exact revenge upon those who had hoaxed them. Accordingly, Bennett reported, a New York doctor who had been publicly fooled by the moon hoax had decided to turn the tables on his tormentors by "contriving to pass off" the body of Aunt Nelly for that of Aunt Joice. Wearing his callousness like a badge, Bennett concluded that "Aunt Nelly, neglected, unknown, unpitied when alive, became an object of deep science and deeper investigation when she died. She was as old and ugly as Joice herself, and in that respect answered the thing exactly."

Bennett consistently portrayed the *Herald* as a bedrock of solidarity among white readers struggling to find a stable identity for themselves, and as a zone of authenticity among the confusions of city life. The effect of this new entry in the Joice Heth debate, though, was only to loosen what had previously seemed stable, to throw open new questions that deferred resolution. In the debate that followed, the murky status of Heth's corpse became a hinge for questions of identity and authenticity. The *Herald* claimed that the body not only was not what it had been passed off as (the nurse of Washington), but was not even what it appeared to be in the present (the corpse of the woman who had claimed to be the nurse of Washington). In contrast, the *Sun*—even while demonstrating the inauthenticity of Heth's persona—stuck to the idea that the body was, always had been, and would continue to be a uniquely valuable item well beyond death. In fact, as the paper reported three days after the autopsy: "We have heard it hinted that . . . the exhibitors of this old negress . . . mean to have the body embalmed dry like a mummy, and send it to England with an old male negro who is to rejoice in the name of Joice's husband, and to swear he is 180 years old, with proper certificates, letters of Gen. Washington &c. to corroborate his story."[13] Despite having published two articles protesting Heth's exhibit (once during her life and once in death), the *Sun* here celebrated the possibility of continuing the posthumous performance indefinitely. Heth had been a valuable commodity in life, and there was no reason for her exhibitors (or, one could argue, the *Sun* itself) to stop reaping benefits from her simply because of her demise.

This suggestion marks the distance traveled from the realm of carnivalesque road show to that of mass-media spectacle. In life, Heth had been a performer who straddled the line between affirming social distinctions of race and trespassing them; now in death she was thoroughly objectified, turned into mere matter, a corpse on a table, even a performing mummy. Instead of reading about the status inversions involved when audience members shook hands with Heth, heard her stories and songs, indulged her pretenses to be "Lady Washington," or imagined her in love, readers of the *Sun* were being asked not to respond to Heth, but simply to buy papers and the claims they made. Inasmuch as the freak show in the modern period became part of the culture of spectation-as-consumption, Susan Stewart has written, it resolved itself in a "horrifying closure" in which "it does not matter whether the freak is alive or dead."[14] Heth was to be viewed, not spoken to; she was an object to be comprehended or fantasized about, not a living part of the carnivalesque upheavals of a social system; and, arguably, she served these needs better in death than in life.

The play with social identity that this story represents mirrors but also distorts the flux in social relations experienced by readers of the penny press. The ubiquitous exposés of swindlers, hoaxers, and other fraudulent social actors in the penny press and other early mass circulation journals reveals the anxieties of readers about the dizzying relations of the social world. In cities suddenly crowded with strangers—would-be social climbers, potentially unscrupulous confidence men on the make—how could one know for certain another's "real" social identity? In the eyes of many whites, however, blacks represented one satisfyingly stable group. Their opportunities for mobility were radically restricted—by society, certainly, and also presumably by their limited mental capacities—and they therefore seemed socially legible.[15]

But in the case of Heth's autopsy it was the black woman whose social (and even material) identity was in flux, while scientists and journalists tried to pin her down. Barnum and Lyman furiously fanned the flames of uncertainty. "The gentleman who has been exhibiting Joice Heth, called upon us on Saturday," Bennett reported, after he had published his Aunt Nelly theory, "and stated positively that he sent Joice Heth to his brother, at Hebron, in Connecticut several weeks since, that she is yet there, and was alive and well at the last accounts. He got several copies of the Herald, exposing the hoax, to send to her."[16] According to the *Evening Star,* another Jacksonian paper in New York, the *Herald*'s Aunt Nelly story was bogus: "It is attempted to make it appear that Joice Heth, lately examined by a number of physicians and students, was not the Joice Heth lately exhibited here as a very aged person. We know the fact that it is the same; and that the person who had charge of her carried her to Connecticut, where she has been decently interred and a monument is about to be erected over her grave." Despite exposing the *Sun*'s rival, however, the *Evening Star* contested Locke's report on different grounds, claiming that Rogers's findings were "nonsense" because "no *post-mortem* examination on a subject over seventy can indicate the age or near it." [17]

Attacked on several fronts, the *Sun* shot back the next day, charging that the various exposés of the *Sun*'s being duped were themselves the result of hoaxes:

> The exhibitors of Joice Heth, not content with making $10,000 or $12,000, by their humbug representation of her age when alive, and by exhibiting her body at 50 cts. a head after she was dead, have been amusing themselves with hoaxing some stupid editors with the story that the body dissected the other day at the City Saloon, was not that of Joice Heth, but of some other old negress, with which they had hoaxed the doctors. One of these editors, if the despicable and unprincipled scribbler to whom we allude can be so termed, believed this story of the non-identity of the body, and proclaimed it in his loathsome little sheet, not knowing that the persons who had deceived him came directly from his office to ours, and boasted of their new exploit! These persons also put an advertisement in the Transcript telling the same ridiculous story, for the purpose, as they said, of "setting the newspapers fighting;" but we, of course, knew its falsehood, for we had seen the body, living and dead, long nails or rather "claws," as the Star calls them, and all.—The Star, however, of last evening, has sense of propriety enough to oppose this second attempted imposition, and, we doubt not it will in a few days acknowledge the first. With the agents in this infamous imposture, we have hitherto dealt very mercifully, but, if they proceed further, we will make this city rather uncomfortable for them.[18]

The agents, Barnum and Lyman, need not have proceeded further, since the newspapers were already doing their bidding. Bennett, the "despicable and unprincipled scribbler" (of whom Day elsewhere wrote that his "only chance of dying an upright man will be that of hanging perpendicularly upon a rope"),[19] stuck to the story of "the non-identity of the body"—even reprinting several certificates written by residents of Harlem backing up the "Aunt Nelly" claim. He retorted that the *Sun*'s editors were not to be trusted, since they had recently been indicted of a misdemeanor in stealing correspondence intended for a rival paper.[20]

Further, Bennett claimed that Barnum and Lyman had admitted to *him* long since that Heth was alive and well and living in Connecticut. It is possible that Bennett made this up to support a faltering story, but it seems fairly safe to conclude—given his barrage of attacks against the *Sun*'s deliberate falsifications in the past, and given the shape of subsequent events—that Barnum and Lyman were playing both sides of the argument and had convinced him of the Aunt Nelly story. It is not clear exactly what the two showmen hoped to gain by this. Perhaps they were setting the stage for some triumphant reunion tour with a new actress in Heth's place; perhaps they had some obscure financial stake in embarrassing Bennett; perhaps this was simply the first stage in their revenge for Bennett's failure to accept their original claim about Heth's longevity and connection to Washington. More likely, it was simply a random note played in an improvisation session, part of the free-floating system of signs that might later be organized in some unforeseen way—as they eventually were—for profit.

The improvisation on Heth's inauthenticity and the possibilities of knowledge and authority continued. Even without Barnum and Lyman's admission, Bennett argued that Locke's report of the autopsy was so riddled with error (such as "the ridiculous assertion that the pulse of every old person returns to the rapidity of youth") that it made the *Sun*'s exposé "ridiculous." To these men who were "fit for the penitentiary," Bennett offered a wager of $350 (or "half [Locke's] *post-mortem* proceeds") that the corpse would be proved "by an impartial judge" not to be Heth's.

Making matters even more complicated, a writer in the *Transcript* (a short-lived third penny paper in New York) challenged Rogers and Locke from a position of apparently equal scientific authority. One might have expected this paper to offer an unusually insightful analysis of the autopsy, since it was the only paper in New York to offer a regular column called "Coroner's Inquest." And indeed, the *Transcript*'s article on Heth was written by "a respectable surgeon residing in the upper part of the city, who was present at, and assisted in, the post mortem examination of the body," and who signed his name simply "TRUTH." In it, he did not dispute that it was Heth who was dissected, but instead sought to demolish Rogers's forensic logic. The writer expressed his doubts about "the *whole* account given of Joice Heth by the proprietors, but to doubt that she had attained an age far, very far, beyond the usual, and even the unusual duration of human life, would be to fly in the face of the most tangible indications of longevity." The problem was Rogers's lack of scientific objectivity:

> The article in question was evidently written for the mere purpose of advocating the *a priori* opinion of the Surgeon, "highly eminent in his

profession of Anatomical knowledge and skill," who conducted the examination. That gentleman made up his mind that Joice Heth was not a very old woman; and like all theorists, found proofs "as plenty as blackberries," and "strong as holy writ," in support of his preconception.— This opinion he was heard to express within an hour before the inspection of the body. It is unfortunate that the writer of the article in the Sun has said so much—he should not have told that Dr. Rogers had determined that her age was not at the utmost over eighty—it would have sounded much better if it had been a spontaneous discovery, and to have let it burst upon us as a new light, in meridian effulgence—something in the manner of the "Moon Story."

TRUTH then attacked Rogers's interpretation of evidence: the pulse rate of extraordinarily old persons did not necessarily continue to increase with age, as Rogers had claimed; Rogers generalized about extreme longevity without sufficient evidence; he failed to do a dissection of the eye; he did not consider Heth's extraordinary emaciation; and he misinterpreted the lack of ossification in Heth's vessels and internal organs. Since this last finding was the lynchpin of Rogers's and Locke's argument, TRUTH took considerable care to dismantle it. He agreed with the premise that the cartilage, internal organs, and vessels of people over the age of fifty tended to ossify. But how was it, he wondered, that there was so *little* ossification in the body of Heth? After all, the "wise-acre editor" seemed "willing to allow" that she was eighty, so "it follows that the vessels which carried the stream of life through the physical system of Old Joice Heth, had resisted the usual process of ossification for at least thirty years beyond the common period for that disposition to take place; and if for thirty years, why may it not for a hundred years?" The signs of absence of aging in Heth could be taken not as evidence of youth but as an indication of an unnatural aging process—in other words, there was some extraordinary principle at work in her that kept her body from breaking down. Finally, TRUTH played the race card:

Another important physiological fact should be stated, which is, that blacks have a much greater tenacity for life than whites, and were it not that, like the domestic horse, they are broken down by servitude, they would live to much greater ages than the Circassian race—and in the case before us, had it not been for the affection of the lungs (one lobe of which was tuberculated with serous effusion in the left cavity of the chest,) together with what must have been fatigue to her, traveling and being subjected to the annoyance and importunity of her visitors, it is not improbable that the vital spark might have continued to flicker considerably longer.[21]

Predictably, Locke responded the next day, denying that the man calling himself TRUTH had had any role in the postmortem examination. Since no other source mentions the presence of a second surgeon at the operating table, it is probably safe to assume that the *Sun* was correct. So what would be TRUTH's motive for writing? Because Barnum never took credit for this aspect of the hoax, one can only assume that TRUTH was in actuality none other than Levi Lyman. Lyman's unusual gift (one for which Barnum is generally given sole credit) was to insert plausible claims into the machinery of the popular press and gum up their ability to claim authority over anything. He undoubtedly knew—here as in so many other cases—that the claims would be quickly dismantled; his point, however, was not to establish truth but to defer its final hegemony, to keep the process of questioning and arguing going as long as possible. Although the *Sun* rushed in to defend itself against this charlatan (who was not even really a charlatan, but a fake charlatan), Lyman's tactic served the paper well, allowing Locke yet another opportunity to assert his authority in the face of the inauthentic. The potential gains for Lyman and Barnum were once again rather unclear and seem to have been taken as an article of faith. (Indeed, five years later, Barnum would convert Lyman's deliberate mystifications into personal gain, while Lyman himself would drop out of the entertainment game altogether.)

To return to the matter at hand: Locke was not content simply to dismiss the claims of "TRUTH" on the grounds that he was not present at the autopsy. Instead, he rearticulated Dr. Rogers's findings and argued that TRUTH's revisionist interpretation of the autopsy constituted "begging, or rather superciliously assuming the whole question, in opposition to negative anatomical proof." Just as predictably, another reply from TRUTH followed in the *Transcript* charging that the *Sun* refused to take up any of the particulars of his argument, and asserting again that Rogers had asked him to assist in the autopsy. Meanwhile the *Herald* was still pushing the Aunt Nelly theory, and the *Morning News* (which a month

earlier had the distinction of being the only paper to swallow the story of
Heth's being an automaton) declared that nothing could be certain. And
so it probably seemed to readers, since the autopsy now had at least three
distinct outcomes: Heth was a fraud; Heth was alive; Heth was the real
thing. Even Silas Mix, whom the *New Haven Daily Herald* saw fit to bring
back into the picture, was offered as an authority. Heth could not have
been so old as claimed, for the editor knew that "our Silas . . . could not be
betrothed to any thing over a centenarian."[22]

The multiplicity of responses to the autopsy obscures the fact that a
fundamental reduction in the scope of interpretation was taking place. In
1836 (as at the turn of the twenty-first century), even as capitalist mass
media appeared to offer a vast proliferation of voices and choices, it also
tended to collapse those voices into each other.[23] In this early version of
that paradoxical process of expansion and narrowing, competition among
the papers produced an extraordinary range of viewpoints, but an almost
numbing sameness characterized them as a group. This sameness resulted
from the shared desire of each editor to distinguish his product from his
competitors' by offering an authoritative "explanation" for the strange turn
of events in the Heth affair. The papers were a source of confusion that
billed themselves as the end of confusion, the collective voice of instability
that promised mastery.

The particular image of this mastery was an unadorned corpse of a black
woman at the mercy of scientists and editors, each picking apart the body
to enhance his cultural prestige or simply to keep up with the competition.
For the most part, the penny papers showed a somewhat surprising degree of restraint in not dwelling on the titillating aspects of this scenario,
but perhaps this was only because these aspects were so obvious that there
was no need to comment on them in order to create a prurient effect. The
voyeurism implicit in the scenario was intensified by the surrounding debates over the propriety of dissection itself. During a period in which sheltering women from public scrutiny was a major ideological preoccupation,
public indignation over grave-robbing anatomists was particularly sharp
when white women's bodies were at stake—the "violation" of the grave
site becoming doubled as a metaphoric rape if a "proper" female was to be
cut open. One important reason that black corpses were subjected to dis-

section more often than white corpses, then, was to protect whites—particularly white women—from the possibility of posthumous indecent exposure and violation.[24] The corollary to this defense of dead white female bodies was a heightening of white males' sense of sexual thrill at the prospect of autopsies of other women. This thrill was further provoked by the leering masculinity of the penny press. (This quality would be amplified over the next few years in spectacles involving young, beautiful, murdered women.)[25] One of Bennett's post-postmortem taunts at Dr. Rogers, for instance, was to hint that he had performed the autopsy out of a necrophiliac desire for Heth—after all, while she was alive he had "examined her more thoroughly than can be expressed in a newspaper, but medical men can easily imagine it."[26] The implication was that he had enjoyed this examination, and wanted to have one last go at her body.

It was not only in the Joice Heth case that the penny press's play with images of white mastery over black corpses verged toward necro-pornography. Shortly before reporting the Joice Heth autopsy, several New York papers ran an article billed as a doctor's reminiscence of his days in medical school. In this grisly story, a group of medical students play a prank on a colleague by putting a black female corpse (presumably being readied for dissection) under his sheets, which he discovers after he disrobes and stumbles into bed after a night of drinking. After stowing the corpse under his bed for the night, he gets back at his buddies by slicing off "some fine large steaks from the buttocks of black Sue," giving them to his landlady to fry up the next morning, and watching his friends eat them. After he tells his friends what he has done, they dose up with medicine to vomit their meal.[27]

The story of "The Negro Steaks"—clearly a fiction but presented as fact—indulged in and denied necrophiliac and cannibalistic urges in a particularly anxious and noxious way. Stories of cannibalism were enormously popular reading during the antebellum period, and, like the story of Black Sue, they usually involved an interracial encounter. The standard picture, though, was one of whites watching in dismay as members of "savage" races devoured the flesh of humans. Africans, after all, were widely assumed to be the most cannibalistic of races, and this was a sign of their savagery, their moral inferiority to whites. As one advocate of slavery put it, "the horrid and heart-appalling practice of *cannibalism* has, in *all* ages, attached more to the African race than to any other people of the earth."[28] But of course "The Negro Steaks" reversed the usual scenario, with the member of the "savage" race herself becoming a meal for white men. One of the most common nineteenth-century interpretations of cannibalism was that it represented savages' mode of revenge on their enemies, and here, too, the medical student was revenging himself on his buddies. But for what cause? Quite simply, for his forced sexual contact with the corpse, whose blackness and deadness were equally grotesque features.

A main point of the story, it seems to me, is to call up readers' worst fears about the fate of the human body at the hands of anatomists, and then to deflect those fears by limiting their realization to the body of a "negro." In the popular press, anatomists were perceived doubly, on the one hand as exemplary modern men, experts who could probe the meanings of the body in accordance with the new science, but on the other as akin to savages or perverts, humans who did not respect the sanctity of the human body. The clinical detachment that was so essential to the modern conception of medicine (and that was one of the presumed markers of the civilized modern mind over both "savages" and premoderns) could also be seen as itself a type of savagery. The joke of this story was to exaggerate that savagery by a couple of degrees: not only would the anatomists carve up a corpse, but they might sleep with it, eat it. But the resolution hints at the way in which black corpses became the vehicle by which the competing views of anatomists' work were reconciled. Modern science could comport with civilized behavior if it practiced its savagery on savages. Rather than an outrage, anatomists' behavior would become a comfort, or at least a joke.

In a similar way, the editors of the penny press felt licensed to practice their rhetorical savagery on Heth, imagining her body probed, sliced up, embalmed, and after all this, still fit for a dirty joke or two. Whites who mobbed abolitionists on the grounds of their promoting miscegenation responded in much the same way—negating their own prurient interest in interracial sex with violence. That the mobs were defending against their own sexual interest in blacks is suggested by numerous factors, including the frequency of attacks on black-run brothels, the extraordinary popularity of sexually suggestive blackface minstrel plays, and, most strongly, the inevitable imputation of "amalgamationism" to abolitionists who favored nothing of the sort.[29] The penny press's savagery was a linguistic version of mobbing, or a deflection of mob sensibilities into a commercial terrain. In these stories, they indulged readers' sexual interest in black women and practiced rhetorical violence to protect them from that interest. A few months after the postmortem examination, Bennett used the autopsy of Heth as an index of his own aggression; he wrote of some rivals who had been abusing his name, "Let the drivellers around me bark as much as they please . . . I will kill the loafers and get fifty cents a piece for their skins."[30] The mixture of aggression and voyeurism of both "The Negro Steaks" and the Joice Heth story proved irresistible. It was this mixture that prompted journalists and readers to linger over Heth's gruesome finale for months—even, at the prompting of Barnum, for years.

EXPOSURE AND
MASTERY

GIVEN THE IRRESOLUTION of the Heth story to this point, readers of the penny press in the spring and summer of 1836 must have expected that more twists would be forthcoming. But, perhaps sensing oversaturation in the papers and impatience on the part of the editors, the exhibitors left off for the time being and pursued other interests. For one thing, Barnum's promised tour of Europe with Heth's remains never came about, as he still had a profitable living performer, Signor Vivalla, on his hands. Over the next few months, Vivalla continued to spin crockery for Barnum in theaters and circuses, at Peale's Museum in New York, and in taverns, concert halls, and other venues in New England and the mid-Atlantic. When the tour began to lose steam and profits evaporated, Barnum contracted with the successful Connecticut circus manager Aaron Turner to have Vivalla join his show. Barnum was by this point paying Vivalla eighty dollars per month; Turner agreed to pay Barnum this figure plus 20 percent of the profits of the circus, with Barnum acting as ticket seller, secretary, and treasurer. Leaving his wife and daughter in Bethel, Barnum once again took to the road. In the fall and summer of 1836, Barnum, Vivalla, Turner, and the gang of horses, ponies, riders, musical bands, clowns, and magicians made their way across New England, New York, New Jersey, Pennsylvania, Delaware, Maryland, the District of Columbia, Maryland, and Virginia.[1]

It is not clear what Lyman did with himself in the summer of 1836, but one day in September, while Barnum and his crew were somewhere in Virginia, Lyman ran into James Gordon Bennett—the man he had duped so thoroughly with the Aunt Nelly story seven months earlier—on a New York street. Bennett's usual method of settling disputes of professional honor was either the lawsuit or the street fight; in fact, he had already tangled three times that year with rival editor James Watson Webb alone, losing the fights badly.[2] And now, in Barnum's account, Bennett proceeded to "blow [Lyman] sky high"—perhaps a prelude to a physical challenge—for having made a fool of him. Lyman calmed him down, explaining that it had all been in good fun, and promising to grant him the biggest prize in the Heth sweepstakes yet—an exclusive interview in which he would tell the "real" story of how the hoax had been concocted.[3]

On September 8, the *Herald* ran the first of a series of five front-page installments of "The Joice Heth Hoax," based on Lyman's dictation to Bennett.[4] The paper had only recently begun the innovative practice of running news, instead of advertisements or public notices, on the front page, so this story counts as one of the first front-page news stories in U.S. history. In addition, by the third installment of the series, Bennett had arranged to have the promotional woodcut of Heth—dressed in a lacy bonnet and displaying her talon-like fingernails—accompany the text (Figure 9). This was one of the first illustrations of any kind accompanying a news story in an American newspaper, and apparently the first of a human figure.[5] Taken together, the placement, graphics, and marketing of "The Joice Heth Hoax" reveal some of the ways in which the commodification of news was transforming print culture. Since revenues for publishing newspapers had in the past come largely from political parties, with advertisers and subscriptions making up whatever deficit remained, there had been no need to make a profit or even to market the papers particularly aggressively. But now, with the pressures of the marketplace dominating the perspective of editors like Bennett, the need to be noticed above the din of competing papers led to innovations in format, style, and promotion. With ubiquitous newsboys crying their wares in the street, with large-font boldface print announcing the unraveling of a celebrated hoax, and with Joice Heth herself staring out at passersby, the newspaper, in essence, became an advertisement for itself.[6]

The Joice Heath Hoax.---No. 4.

Aunt Joice and her exhibitors were now on their
way to New York. As she was bundled up in the
Rail Road Cars, people gazed, wondered, looked and
some laughed. Her exhibitors were the gravest men
in the world—seldom smiled—seldom discomposed
their features.

9. Front page of the *New York Herald,* September 24,
1836. (© Collection of The New-York Historical Society.)

In attempting to expose fraudulent practices, the penny press editors found a way to push their product while playfully addressing their readers' anxieties about the deceptions latent in capitalist culture—a theme the commercial press was in a unique position to address. The Heth exposé (which was really a mock exposé) offered numerous variations on this theme of counterfeiture, providing an array of deceptions for readers to work through, always promising a final resolution, but always holding out. This collaboration—or contest—between Lyman and Bennett would help develop Barnum's signature style, which Neil Harris has called the "operational aesthetic"—an urban form that "structured problems of experiencing the exotic and unfamiliar by reducing that experience to a simple evaluation."[7]

From the first installment, the *Herald*'s "Joice Heth Hoax" cast the self-making northern confidence man or swindler as an emblem of Yankee ingenuity, rather than of threatening inauthenticity. This story was in fact yet another of Lyman's hoaxes, mixing known elements of the Heth exhibit and dissection with utter fabrications that tended to aggrandize himself and Barnum. To start with, rather than admitting that Barnum had procured the rights to exhibit Heth from her earlier exhibitor R. W. Lindsay, the first installment records a more dramatic account of Heth's discovery. A few years back, it begins, "a gentleman from New England," presumably Barnum, is traveling through Kentucky with a Virginian friend until they reach Paris, in Bourbon County. Stopping at the plantation of William Bolen, an acquaintance of the Virginian, they learn "by mere accident that Mr. Bolen had an old negro woman who had been blind in her bed for 30 years, and was a great natural curiosity." Despite the fact that the woman is only sixty-five years old, the New Englander finds her to be "a most singular and *outré* being—almost a mummy alive—and more curious than any thing [he] had ever seen," and he proposes to exhibit her across the country "as a negro woman of extraordinary age." After giving Mr. Bolen "an interest in the speculation," the two arrange to have "Aunt Joice" carried off her bed ("on which she had groaned, and cursed, and swore, and drank whiskey . . . for 30 years") and taken to Louisville, some sixty miles from Paris. They hire a room, stick up handbills, and advertise in the papers the exhibit of a 110-year-old negro woman. But they meet with only moderate success, since, as the Yankee concludes, "The old slave of Bill Bolen creates no attention—who the devil cares for her—'Joice Heth be damned,' the people will say." Instantly, he dreams up the idea that her age can be raised and the story of her "having lived in the family of the sainted Washington" appended.

The Yankee is now thoroughly in control of the exhibit (the Virginian is never mentioned again), but he has several men in his employ helping him with the details and logistics of the exhibit. Their first task is to teach Joice how to pull the story off, how to get her to learn the intimate history of the Washington family and her role in it, how to respond to audience questions—how to be, in short, an actress or impostor as well as a natural curiosity. In this, they have some initial trouble. When she is quizzed too hard about the details of her story, she curses the exhibitors and threatens to tell her "massa" that they have been abusing her. Appealing to her pride, the New Englander asks her if she is not capable of remembering what she has learned. She replies: "I remember every word old massa Bolen told me fifty years ago," and she continues her studies without incident. But another problem lies in the fact that she appears too vigorous to have reached the biblical old age imputed to her: "She had a wild, huge, and unregulated appetite, and would eat as much, and more than any ordinary person in good health. As her exhibitor was a great friend of temperance in eating and drinking he wisely concluded to put her under a good and well devised regimen. She was therefore fed for weeks on eggs and whiskey, till she was brought down to mere muscle and bone."

The story Lyman was feeding Bennett to this point stresses precisely those elements that Lyman and Barnum had been careful to deny in their earlier representations of Heth's act. Not only was the exhibit a profit-making "speculation" for the Yankee exhibitor and the slave-owning southerner rather than an antislavery benefit, but rather than improving her condition from the harsh neglect of slavery, here the exhibitor had taken a vibrant if infirm old woman groaning and cursing from her bed, subjected her to a regime of coerced performances, and taken steps intended to worsen her health. Moving on through Cincinnati toward Pittsburgh, the Yankee exhibitor scrutinizes his property and thinks how he can "improve" it further. The main problem, he thinks, is her teeth: a 161-year-old woman could hardly be expected to have even the "three or four old stumps" that yet remain in Aunt Joice's head. Thinking to trick her into consenting to their removal, he first asks her how she would like to have a dentist give her a new set of teeth. She is delighted with the idea until the exhibitor informs her that the dentist will have to pull out the old ones first. At this, she rips off a stream of "awful imprecations" and insists on retaining her natural teeth. Wheedling and coaxing her, the company involved in the exhibition finally get her drunk on "good whiskey," at which point she gives "a reluctant consent to have the old teeth pulled out, only to get a new set." A few nights later, when Aunt Joice has forgotten her drunken consent, the exhibitor grabs hold of one of her teeth and rips it out, earning him a string of curses and threats. He nonetheless manages to wrench out the remaining teeth, and placates her with whiskey and eggs.

In the three subsequent installments of "The Joice Heth Hoax"—each filling several columns in the minute print of the *Herald,* making it by far the longest story of the year—the company moves through Pittsburgh, Greenburgh (Pa.), and Philadelphia, gradually adding bogus documents, religious hymns, and more intricate stories to the fabric of the exhibit. The pattern of Heth's crotchety resistance and whiskey-drenched compliance continues, but despite some close scrapes (most notably the realization that a forged 1727 bill of sale from the family of Washington refers to Heth's being sold in the "State of Virginia" when Virginia was in fact still a colony), the party manages to convince editors, doctors, priests, philosophers, patriots, and even Revolutionary War veterans of the authenticity of Heth's claims.

A coup de grâce is the diddling of Nicholas Biddle, director of the Second National Bank of the United States and the most hated public figure among Jacksonian Democrats. Under Biddle's direction, the Bank contained all the deposits of the federal government, and its profits went not to taxpayers but to stockholders. The Bank, Jackson alleged, was therefore the embodiment of a massive conspiracy among the old-money elite to concentrate all the nation's wealth in their hands; furthermore, it intruded on the political process to arrange the election of officials who would protect its interests. He devoted much of his first term in office to killing this "hydra-headed" monster, and by 1835, when Joice Heth came to Philadelphia, Biddle had been defeated and was a figure of fun for the Jacksonian press.[8] In the *Herald*'s exposé of the Heth tour even the 'Monster' himself, Nicholas Biddle, had been seen peering into the old withered features of the nurse of Washington, and satisfying himself whether she was in favor of the Bank, or against it. Mr. Biddle is a gentleman every inch. He is the most polished man in this country—he is equally acute and sagacious. He accordingly could never be so ill-bred as to doubt for one moment the solemn assertion of a lady of such character and pretensions—such documents and advocates as Joice was now surrounded with.[9]

Biddle's gentility—his polish and his trust of breeding and character—are of course no match for the wily Jacksonian confidence man and his agents. The exhibit in Philadelphia became, for a moment, a test of self-making against the established, moneyed order.

Jacksonian Democrats' hatred of the Bank has sometimes been taken as an indication of their opposition to capitalism, but historians now tend to view it as part of a desire to expand the capitalist field by attacking consolidated wealth and creating opportunities for the mechanics.[10] In line with this interpretation, Yankee's conquest of Biddle leads to his own capitalist enterprise. Before mounting an all-out assault on the city of New York, the exhibitor decides to look for a business partner, someone to whom he can "sell a few shares of Joice" and finds "a purchaser in a very clever little fellow down in Front street." The Yankee asks this Lyman figure if he knows the Bible and if he can "pray pretty slickly." On getting affirmative answers, he says:

> "Well, I guess you'll do.—I'll sell you a share of the smartest old nigger woman you ever did see—how much on her will you take? Capital spec she is."
>
> "Why," says the other, "I would like to take the four quarters of such an article, if she was but white and comely—but a nigger I can't say I can stomach, as yet. I've only belonged to the Abolition Society for three weeks."

The Barnum figure, the Yankee, is essentially treating Heth as a certain amount of capital, which can be divided into shares. The Lyman figure hears only the part of the offer that suggests he "take" a "nigger woman," and his mind immediately leaps to "the Abolition Society," which presumably promotes interracial sex. The joke is that he assumes that he's being offered a black prostitute, a proposition that was coming to seem increasingly dangerous to white males in New York. Brothels featuring black and interracial women for hire and catering largely to white men were quite popular through the early 1830s in New York, particularly in the Five Points neighborhood. But as Timothy Gilfoyle has shown, just as the popular outcry against abolitionists began to feature charges of "amalgamation," authorities were cracking down on these institutions and their promotion of "racial pollution."[11] The mixture of race, sex, and money here is thus more than a casual joke—it is a reminder of the volatile mixture of fascination with black sexuality and simultaneous resistance to the designs of abolitionism that was so familiar to working-class white readers. This common expression of working-class resentment of abolitionist activity cast in sexual terms was one to which the *Herald* itself frequently gave voice, as in this 1835 article: "STRANGE TASTE:—At the recent meeting of the Female Anti-Slavery Society in Boston, a number of colored wenches were present. This is the strangest taste of all—that white women would be willing to equalize in this way. They must have had a few black beaux to whom they were engaged to be married."[12]

Just as in the Lyman figure's joke, to court abolition is to court interracial sex, which is enough to scotch any deal. The figure of Joice Heth is thus made an instrument for upward mobility and white male participation in the capitalist system, and at the same time an object of derision, a body whose grotesque sexuality can't be "stomached" for fear of contamination. The elements in tension in the joke are the desire to change one's economic and social status (the exhibitor tells the would-be speculator that "Joice would make [us] money like smoke in New York") and the sense that there are some social lines that simply shouldn't be crossed. Money is the lure, but race trumps all. What is happening, in one of the first long-running features in the first mass medium, is a virtual fantasia on the powerful Jacksonian themes of social mobility balanced by racial essence, but done in such a compressed and indirect manner as hardly to raise an eyebrow.

The story makes an appeal to readers' regional pride as well. Northern city dwellers are consistently portrayed as more sophisticated and shrewd than the gullible southerners and small-town citizens who are fooled by a hoax that is only half developed. And the portrait of Joice Heth's northern master is of an even more shrewd exploiter of the slave's body than the southern "Massa Bolen"—it is the Yankee who is the true exemplar of the master race, for he can compel black bodies to work to the point of death and beyond. This is because he understands that labor is not the only basis of value, that the northern economies of "speculation" and entertainment provide novel opportunities to invest in the raw materials, even the waste, of the South. Joice Heth becomes, in his hands, not just a commodity but an example of capitalist alchemy: value produced out of nothing—an ingenious counterfeit bill. In this way, "The Joice Heth Hoax" in the *Herald* served as a half-joking version of that paper's many serialized exposés of notorious frauds, swindlers, and "stock-jobbers." Karen Halttunen comments that "the proliferation of moveable wealth, especially negotiable paper, in the early nineteenth century, and the growing confusion and anonymity of urban living, had made possible for the first time a wide variety of swindles, frauds, forgeries, counterfeiting activities, and other confidence games."[13] The dream of making something of nothing, like winning the lottery, must have appealed enormously to penny press readers.

The serialized "Joice Heth Hoax" was cut off abruptly after four main installments and a few added teasers—well before the spectacular autopsy—when Bennett apparently realized that Lyman was pulling his leg again. (Barnum had of course not "discovered" Heth on a Kentucky plantation, nor had he invented her story; as he later admitted, she was exhibited first by R. W. Lindsay.) But in casting the Barnum figure as a cultural hero for the same sorts of manipulations of value and confidence that the penny press elsewhere denounced so thoroughly in its exposés of swindlers and forgers, the *Herald* voiced its ambivalent relation to capitalist culture. As the first purely commercial journalistic enterprise, the penny press was itself an important part of the capitalist expansion whose excesses it exposed. In keeping with this ambivalence, the penny press portrayed Barnum as that liminal figure who was symbolic of both the dangers and the possibilities of capitalist culture: the confidence man.[14] But in the same story that aggrandized Barnum for his deceptions, Heth herself was made to seem a blank slate whom the white man animated with his schemes. Her role in the deception was displaced entirely onto the will of this strange northern "master"—and if she offered any resistance at all, it was for all intents and purposes snuffed out by pouring whiskey down her throat.

By a pure coincidence, however, the *Herald*'s "Joice Heth Hoax" may well have played a minor role in one now-famous North Carolina slave's resistance to her oppression. In her 1860 memoir, *Incidents in the Life of a Slave Girl*, Harriet Jacobs describes a confidence game she played with her master with her own freedom at stake. In order to escape her master's unwanted sexual advances and plot her eventual escape from slavery, she holes up in a crawl space above her grandmother's house. By lying low for seven years, she tries to give her master the impression that she has already escaped so that he will not be on the lookout when she does flee. To this end, she decides to write him a letter describing her life in New York and to have a free friend of hers deliver the letter to a "trustworthy seafaring person" who will carry it north and mail it back to North Carolina with a New York postmark. To help her authenticate the letter, her friend gives her a page of a New York newspaper, which will provide her with street names. As Jacobs writes, "It was a piece of the New York Herald; and, for once, the paper that systematically abuses the colored people was made to render them a service."[15] The year was 1837 and the paper was presumably a few months old, having been used to line a commercial hatbox brought south by a peddler. It is quite likely, therefore, that the paper she read as a means to deceive her master contained some news about the Heth hoax, and it is possible that it had Joice Heth's picture on the front page.

After the *Herald*'s bogus exposé cut off, relatively little was heard about Joice Heth for another six years. Newspapers made joking asides about the affair in thinly related contexts (an article about great families, for instance, jokingly mentions the dissection of Heth as an attempt to understand how "the preservation of the breeds of men and horses improve[s] the race and beautif[ies] creation"),[16] but the "truth" behind the hoax was never revealed. Meanwhile, Barnum continued on with Turner's circus through October, then struck out on his own with Vivalla, "a negro singer and dancer named James Sandford," several other musicians, horses, wagons, and a tent. In Raleigh, North Carolina, Barnum reports that Sandford "abruptly left me," which suggests that his performance may have been coerced in the fashion of Heth's, or at least that he was not remunerated with the same generosity that performers like Vivalla had been. Barnum found himself without his star attraction, but, resourceful as ever, he wrote: "Being determined not to disappoint the audience, *I blacked myself thoroughly,* and sung the songs advertised . . . It was decidedly a 'hard push,' but the audience supposed the singer was Sandford, and, to my surprise, my singing was applauded, and in two of the songs I was encored!"[17] After finding a replacement for Sandford, the group passed through the Carolinas, Georgia, Alabama, and Kentucky, where the new "negro singer" drowned in the river at Frankfort. Barnum gives no indication in any of his autobiographical writings of the circumstances under which this drowning took place, but given what else he does disclose about his dealings with African American employees and subordinates, we might suspect that the replacement singer, like Sandford, was trying to make a getaway.

Similarly unfortunate was a young black man who found himself calling Barnum "massa" during the winter of 1837–38 in Vicksburg. According to a biographical sketch of Barnum written by "a very loving friend" of the showman (whom Barnum's most thorough biographer concludes to have been Barnum himself) and published in the *New York Atlas* in 1845, the Yankee Barnum purchased a steamboat to help him up river, as well as a slave to act as his valet. (This was well after all northern states had abolished slavery.) When he suspected the "nigger" of stealing from him, Barnum "gave him fifty lashes, and took him to New Orleans, where he was sold at auction." At the end of his journey, he sold the steamboat, taking as payment "cash, sugar, molasses, and a negro woman and child. He shipped his sweets to New York [and] sold his negroes in St. Louis."[18] Two years after his abolitionist pose in Providence, Barnum was participating fully—and apparently without hesitation or discomfort at his role—in the economic and disciplinary regimes of slavery: whipping a resistant slave, buying and selling women and children as commodities.

Barnum himself made an escape from the increasingly weak limelight of the roadshow shortly thereafter. "Thoroughly disgusted with the life of an itinerant showman," he headed back to New York in June of 1838 looking for work in a "respectable, permanent business." In the aftermath of the great financial Panic of 1837, this was hardly a propitious time for speculative ventures; after advertising that he had $2,500 to invest in a new speculation, Barnum reported receiving scores of propositions from quacks, frauds, and even an admitted counterfeiter. He eventually entered into partnership with a German manufacturer of cologne water, bear's grease, blacking, and waterproof paste. Sadly, this man, despite a slew of worthy recommendations, proved to be "a scamp," and in 1840 he ran off with the $2,500, leaving Barnum with only the recipes for his rather dubious products. Fortunately Barnum had a few profitable concerns running on the side. One of these was managing the performances of John Diamond, "who was really a genius in the dancing line . . . [and] justly celebrated as the best negro-dancer and representative of Ethiopian 'breakdowns' in the land." ("Negro-dancer" here does not imply that Diamond was black; he was, rather, an early blackface minstrel. As fellow showman Thomas Low Nichols hyperbolically put it, "There was not an audience in America that would not have resented, in a very energetic fashion, the insult of being asked to look at the dancing of a real negro.")[19] Seeing few options for success in New York, Barnum reluctantly returned to what he knew best, and with Diamond, a singer/storyteller, and a fiddler, he made his way back down to New Orleans. There, however, Diamond danced off into the distance, having extorted a great deal of money from Barnum. Some other players in his retinue, meanwhile, were trying to pull their own stunt in St. Louis, advertising that *they* were exhibiting the real Master Diamond. Catching wind of this, Barnum threatened to sue; the troupe then managed to dig up R. W. Lindsay—Joice Heth's original exhibitor—and convince *him* to sue Barnum on trumped-up charges that he had failed to pay him for "a pipe of brandy" owed him in the Heth transaction. After spending the night in jail, Barnum countersued his tormentors, returned to New York, and "re-resolved that I would never again be an itinerant showman."[20]

Although he always remained connected with the show line, what he did over the next five decades was to craft an unprecedented public persona for himself that exceeded anything he could possibly create in a simple "act." Through a mixture of writing and self-advertising (often indistinguishable from each other) and the management of increasingly bold cultural productions, he would become, in the words of one obituary writer, "the most widely known American that ever lived," and in Barnum's own account, a veritable one-man tourist attraction.[21] In launching that celebrity, though, he looked not to the future but to the past. Bluford Adams notes, "in view of Barnum's lackluster career in the five years since Heth's death, it isn't surprising that he would return to her as a basis for a public persona."[22]

Heth's return came, unsurprisingly, in the unruly world of the commercial newspaper. In 1841 Barnum got a job writing articles for a new Democratic paper, the *New York Atlas*. In April of that year, he began publishing in the *Atlas* the first in a series of autobiographical writings—a project to which he would return about once a decade for the next half century. What is curious about this first attempt at autobiography is that it not only is the template for the later, book-length works, but also reads like a mockery of them. In essence, Barnum mystified his own autobiography before he wrote it, creating a counterfeit before there was an original. This was altogether fitting in the career of a man who thrived on the inauthentic, and in a culture in which legitimate currency often looked more fishy than bogus bills. (See Figure 10.)

In this work, "Adventures of an Adventurer, Being Some Passages in the Life of Barnaby Diddleum," Barnum trumpeted his own rise (lightly fictionalized: read *Barn*aby Diddle*um*) in an aggressive, vernacular voice that was the hallmark of the Jacksonian Yankee, a shrewd aspiring merchant who uses his wiles to achieve upward mobility.[23] After a quick, picaresque survey of his early years, he retells the story of the *Herald*'s "Joice Heth Hoax" from a particularly egomaniacal perspective. "Crown me with fame—erect a monument to my memory—decree me a roman triumph—I deserve all—I stand alone—I have no equal, no rival—I am the king of Humbugs—the king among princes," begins the first chapter on his involvement with Heth.[24]

The story stays fairly close to the lines of the Lyman/Bennett version of "The Joice Heth Hoax," but, starting with the discovery of Heth in Kentucky, it exaggerates both Heth's worthlessness as a slave and the Barnum figure's ingenuity, and speaks even more clearly to readers' taste for violence and their sense of racial solidarity. The plantation scene, in particular, subtly expresses one of the most common features of working-class white racism of the antebellum period—an assertion of black laziness that

10. P. T. Barnum at age thirty-four in 1844, after he wrote the first of his reminiscences of the Joice Heth episode.

was in implicit contrast to white workers' diligence. As the story begins, Barnaby Diddleum (presumably pronounced "Diddle 'Em") visits the plantation of a friend in Paris, Bourbon County, Kentucky. When Diddleum asks him about "the lions of the place," his friend replies:

"There are none . . . unless you will rank as a curiosity old aunt Joyce" [*sic*].

"And who the devil's old aunt Joyce?" I asked.

"Oh a remarkably old negro woman that I am cursed with; she is about as old as Methuselah I believe—she has been bed ridden for twelve years, during which time she has had a capital appetite, and seems no more inclined to join the black spirits of her departed brethren, than she did twelve years ago. She bears a charmed life, I fancy, and lives on for the sole purpose of picking my pockets by remaining, while I live, on the pension list."

I felt a great curiosity to see the woman who was thus swindling my friend by her disgusting pertinacity to cling to life at his expense, and accordingly went with him over to his plantation where at length I was introduced, without much form or ceremony, into the apartment of the venerable Joyce. She was very comfortably lodged, and seemed to me to be exceedingly happy. She was exempt from all work—the horror of a negro. She enjoyed the elysium of her race—idleness, to its fullest extent, and she was evidently determined to hold on to the good things of this life as long as possible; nor did she feel the smallest desire to forsake the bed-ridden comforts of the flesh for the uncertainties of an after life. I was struck with this at once—but I was struck more with her extraordinary appearance of age. She looked like a galvanized mummy. It was enough to make a man's hair turn grey to count her years. I thought this woman a great curiosity, and that she might be turned to some account by being exhibited.[25]

The emphasis on Heth's idleness, her "natural" abhorrence of work, and the financial burden she posed for her master fits perfectly with Orlando Patterson's discussion of the "parasitism" of slavery, in which "the slaveholder camouflaged his dependence, his parasitism, by various ideological strategies. Paradoxically, he defined the slave as a dependent. This is consistent with the distinctly human technique of camouflaging a relation by defining it as the opposite of what it really is."[26] The particular version of parasitism here has the slave enjoying an unreasonable leisure while "picking the pocket" of the master—a complaint that today sounds ludicrous but that was frequently voiced in the antebellum period. The characterization of labor as "the horror of a negro" was a common complaint that masters and other white observers lodged against black slaves—who, of course, had ample reason to be horrified by the conditions of their labor and to resist their masters' attempts to subject them to an ascetic regime of work.[27]

But in the context of a self-made white man puffing his own rise in New York, this representation of a slave's parasitism on her master takes on an additional meaning. What, after all, could the reference to Heth's "remaining . . . on the pension list" have to do with the condition of an aged slave? This seems, in the light of the *Atlas*'s base readership who were aspiring to upward mobility, to have far more to do with the race and class politics of the urban North than with those of the planter South. The portrait of the indolent Heth was the polar opposite of what was likely expected of readers of "The Adventures of an Adventurer" in the workplace. George Lipsitz and David Roediger note that urban working whites during this period were increasingly subjected to new regimes of industrial discipline in the workplace—regimes that punished them for failing to adhere to strict standards of punctuality, productivity, and sobriety. Through popular amusements, most notably blackface minstrelsy, they constructed an image of blacks as all that they had left behind, "a representation of the natural self at odds with the normative self of industrial culture."[28] Jim Crow's liability to dance at the drop of a hat, Zip Coon's abhorrence of manual labor, and Heth's enjoyment of "the elysium of her race" were all a part of this ideological construction of black laziness, a construction that bespoke both disgust and longing on the part of white readers and minstrel-goers.

This opening gambit in "Adventures" thus does several things at once. Besides expressing a familiar northern artisanal or working-class apology for the practices of southern slavery (the *Herald*, remember, had characterized freed blacks as "slaves to pilfering, idleness, intemperance, and vice," whereas southern slaves were "held in servitude by humane, kind, and careful masters"), it gave its readers an implicitly flattering self-image by portraying the black race as all that they themselves were not. And finally, it provided the grounds for lashing out at the objects of their scorn. Saidiya Hartman has observed that accounts of "slave idleness [and] intemperate consumption . . . justified coercive labor measures and the constriction of liberties."[29] These justifications filtered into the popular northern consciousness; for here, although the kindly master has spared harsh punishments to the aging slave who is eating and drinking him into poverty, Heth's "disgusting pertinacity to cling to life at his expense" clearly licenses readers' desires to see her subjected to harsh discipline. As the story unfolded, they got their wish. After Diddleum realizes that Heth "might be turned to some account by being exhibited," he puts a proposition to her master:

> "You want to get rid of aunt Joyce?" said I.
> "I do."
> "I'll do it. What will you give me?"
> "Oh!" he said laughingly, "she must die a natural death."
> "To be sure," said I, "and be as well or better taken care of than now. I have a crochet in my head by which I may probably make something out of her. At all events, I'll take her off your hands if you give me something handsome."

Although the master's assumption that the Yankee is offering an invitation to murder his slave is proved false, it appears warranted by the protagonist's aggressive phrasing of the question. Indeed, this scene initiates Diddleum's will to exert power over his future touring companion, a will that only grows stronger throughout the serialized story. The Kentuckian master readily assents to Diddleum's plan, agreeing to pay him half of what Aunt Joice would cost him if she were to languish another year on his plantation, and unambiguously making her "the property of Barnaby Diddleum." It is clear that Heth's new master will allow none of the indulgences of the old one—as soon as she is sold, she is "raised from her lethargy, and commanded, at my sovereign will and pleasure, to arise and commence her travels." As in "The Joice Heth Hoax," her teeth are pulled out, she is fed a scanty diet, and she is once again portrayed as resistant to this new regime:

> I did not exhibit her immediately, for the old girl was rather cantakerous [sic]. She had led an easy life of it. She had enjoyed a sinecure situation with her old master, and she by no means relished the idea of having her old bones trotted about the country, as she foresaw they would be from one extremity to the other without much rest or ceremony. So leaving the old girl to rip out oaths by the volley, an accomplishment that she

was remarkably proficient in, I began for a short time to look about me for amusement . . .

I soon got Joyce into training, and from a devil of a termagant, converted into a most docile creature, as willing to do my bidding as the slave of the lamp was to obey Aladdin. I discovered her weak point. It was discovered in seven letters—W-H-I-S-K-E-Y. Her old master, of course, would indulge an old bed-ridden creature in no such luxury, and for a drop of it, I found I could mould her to anything.

Productivity and alcohol are here given an inventive linkage. Despite the fact that many slave states passed laws restricting the access of slaves to liquor, many masters occasionally encouraged slaves to drink copiously—as Frederick Douglass eloquently testifies in his memoirs—in order to "disgust them with their temporary freedom and make them as glad to return to their work as they were to leave it. By plunging them into exhausting depths of drunkenness and dissipation, this effect is almost certain to follow."[30] In addition to mirroring that function, Diddleum's repeated use of alcohol as a means of drowning Heth's resistance to her labor (or her "cantankerous" behavior, as Diddleum describes it) also has a complex relation to the readership of the story. As social historians have noted, drinking occupied a central position in the lives of many urban workers, but as the split between masters, journeymen, and apprentices widened with the industrial ethos of the 1830s, employers' crackdowns on what they perceived as excessive drinking became common. Coupled with the strenuous efforts of genteel temperance societies to clean up what they thought was the chief vice of the working classes and the poor, this antidrinking activity on the part of employers predictably only solidified much of the workers' interest in drinking. The saloon, in fact, became a central space for working-class political activity.[31] Charges of drunkenness touched a nerve, though, and white workers—as they did so often—deflected the charges onto blacks: the term "nigger drunk" began to catch hold in this era.[32] In this light, Heth's penchant for whiskey resonates ambiguously with discussions of alcohol in antebellum New York. On the one hand, it could be said that Barnum was helping redirect the charge of irresponsible drinking from working whites to blacks; on the other hand, the high-spirited tone of the story and Diddleum's clever use of alcohol to promote his own interests would have made it a natural anecdote to share over a few drinks at a neighborhood tavern.

It is worth bearing in mind here that despite the patent fictionality of "Adventures of an Adventurer" (the plantation scene and several others never happened, for instance, and a show monkey was substituted for Signor Vivalla), this is actually the writing of the man who exhibited Heth. In some ways, it cuts as close to the heart of the story as any documentation we have. Although many of its incidents are dubious, the casual, sadistic machismo of the narrative does not feel highly crafted or premeditated; this may be, in other words, the clearest picture of how P. T. Barnum would have liked the event to have proceeded—or an unleashing of the aggression he had to hide while promoting the exhibit as a "moral" entertainment. And it was by no means *all* a fantasy. The story carefully documents many of the verifiable sojourns of the "real" Barnum and Heth, down to accounts of Diddleum's business arrangements with Niblo, his publication of a pamphlet biography of Heth, and reprints of newspaper articles from various cities. So while we may (and should) distrust the veracity of any particular detail, it is still worth considering whether the overall picture—of Heth resisting, of Barnum using whatever mechanism was close at hand to quash that resistance and simulate her compliance—was accurate. Given his history of relations with black employees and slaves and his subsequent record of strenuous—even zealous—denials of abuse, and given the many newspaper reports of Heth's outbursts (demanding that overinquisitive children be taken from the room, complaining when her food was not good enough or when her pipe was withdrawn), the question gains strength. In the familiar hoaxes that follow—the duping of New York editors and physicians, the false claims of benefiting the abolitionist movement in Providence, and so on—Heth is portrayed as gradually warming to her act, enjoying her notoriety and eventually becoming "an excellent actress." Bluford Adams, the only critic of Barnum's career to have analyzed "Adventures" at length, concludes that in the story Heth "emerges less as her owner's pawn than as his boozy, profane accomplice" and "a willing partner in the swindle."[33] This does seem to be the manifest intent behind the portrayal, but that happy gloss does nothing to erase the origins of the partnership in coercion and physical control. Taken as a whole, the story does not so much dismiss the idea of a slave's resistance to her master; rather, by making the slave come to side laughingly with her abusive master, it methodically refuses to take her resistance seriously.

Once again there is no way of tracking this version of the story to its end, because no surviving copies of the *Atlas* issues containing the final installments of "Adventures of an Adventurer" exist. But Diddleum's portrayal of a resistant Heth was taken a step further in an 1855 pamphlet called *The Autobiography of Petite Bunkum.* In this comic companion piece to the first edition of Barnum's "official" autobiography (which A. H. Saxon concludes to have been written by Barnum himself or at least with his aid), the narrator puts a new spin on the connection between Heth's reluctance to perform for her exhibitors, her rebellious impulses, and her penchant for drink. The story of "Judy Heath" begins when "Petite Bunkum" overhears a conversation between Heath and her owner, leading up to their arrangement for this human property to tour with the would-be showman:

> "How are you today, aunty?" inquired Mr. Shelby [the owner] kindly.
>
> "Bless de Lord, massa," mumbled the old woman—"I is alive. When is massa goin' to let de poor ole nigger go to de free States, so dat she may die and go to glory a free woman?"
>
> "Well, well; we'll see about it soon," answered Mr. Shelby, carelessly; and then, turning to me, he continued, in a low tone—
>
> "The poor old creature has taken a strange fancy to die in the free States. She appears to believe that if she dies a slave, she can not go to heaven. I would instantly set her free and send her North, were it not on account of the certainty of her coming to suffering and want."

As in the newspaper reports of Heth's singing about "a land of pleasure / Where joy and peace forever roll," she is portrayed here as longing for a release from slavery, and implicitly linking the North with heaven. But Bunkum sees a possibility for exploiting this desire to go north. Playing to the kindly affections of the "good master," Bunkum offers to take the slave woman off his hands and fulfill her dreams of dying in a free state. In the story that follows, though, her dream is endlessly deferred; their life on the road becomes a battle of wills, in which the northern master always has the upper hand and always pockets the money. She is quickly disabused of her notions about northern "freedom," which turns out to consist solely of the ability to get as drunk as she pleases:

> It may be asked what benefit did Mademoiselle Judy Heath derive from this arrangement? I will tell you, most inquisitive reader. In the first place, she had her regular rum; and, in justice to her memory, I must say that she was rather fond of that article of refreshment. In fact, the old lady occasionally used to get drunk; and in one instance she bestowed upon me the compliment of a black eye, by a blow of her crutch, because I refused to "come down" with another half pint."[34]

The story of "Judy Heath" drunkenly braining "Bunkum" with her crutch serves as a mock uprising, one that accords with the dynamics of the story as a whole. The focus in *Petite Bunkum*—as in "The Joice Heth Hoax" and "Adventures of an Adventurer" before it—is on the ingenuity of the Barnum figure, while Heth herself is made a blank slate. This erasure of her will, however, is not achieved without some trouble: she is shown struggling, swearing, resisting, even lashing out in violence, and she must be broken, taught to voice her master's will. Also negating the urgency of this comic resistance is the fact that she is impelled not by an ongoing secret desire for freedom, but by her enslavement to a master stronger than Bunkum (or Diddleum)—whiskey. These aspects of the Heth story seem to have passed into received wisdom. In one retrospective account from 1850, the medical writer Edward Dixon claimed that on a day when Heth had not had enough to drink, she responded to a caller's question about whether she remembered "massa George" by saying: "No! debil take 'em all; don't know notin bout him! Dey make me say dat all de time: gimme drink!"[35] And when Walter Lang made his picture *The Mighty Barnum* in 1934, he depicted "Josie Heath" as a gin-slinging runaway slave.[36]

The portrait of Heth's violent tendencies and her easy submission before the whiskey bottle represents both an acknowledgment and a dismissal of her resistance to her regime, a dynamic that was common in popular discussion of the politics of slavery. The troubling notion of a slave's resistance to white control that these texts laughed off was a recurrent preoccupation for the penny papers and in much antebellum popular culture in the North. During the 1830s, in the wake of the Nat Turner rebellion,

newspapers across the region were fascinated by slave uprisings and con-
spiracies. The insatiable appetite of the penny press's readers even for rumors of such distant events reflects the ambiguous mixture of envy and
anxiety that, according to Eric Lott, also characterized the appeal of blackface minstrelsy. Lott shows that for working-class whites, the black insubordination on display on the minstrel stage (like a blackface character who
beats the master's coat while the master is still in it) could be read meta-
phorically—the idea of the slave's transgression was often made to articulate the resentments of "class difference, intentionally or not, by calling on
the insurrectionary resonances of black culture."[37]

Mirroring the relation of minstrel audience to performers, the scene of
white workers consuming images of black rebels during the volatile labor
situation of the 1830s and 1840s in New York has more than a whiff of "insurrectionary resonance." And just as the comforting filter of grease and
cork allowed minstrelsy's audiences to dismiss the transgressive behavior
of the minstrel-blacks as an evening's antic fun, the editors of the penny
press exploited the sensational aspects of slave uprisings, the supreme evidence of slaves' calculated fury, only to reveal them as hollow. The *Herald*—and, to a lesser degree, the *Sun*—pulled off an extraordinary trick in
this regard by reporting slave uprisings in a manner that completely undercut the motive and intelligence behind them, and they displaced that
intelligence and motive onto the figure of ingenious if dastardly white
men. In the seven months' run of the *Herald* and the *Sun* during the time
when Joice Heth's story was reported, there were four reports of uprisings. One of them, in Farmington, Tennessee, turned out to have been instigated by "some white man, who refused to tell [the rebel slaves] his
name"; the other three, readers would be relieved and intrigued to learn,
were not uprisings at all, but were elaborate hoaxes. One of these involved
a southern speculator who wanted to create panic in the markets so that
he could profit from the ruins.[38] In these reports, the papers allowed readers to cling—as Herman Melville's Captain Delano would two decades
later in the story "Benito Cereno"—to their sense of the ultimate tractabil-
ity of slaves, even in the face of their violent fury. In this way, the papers
performed the disciplinary function of exposing the fraud—and even
more comfortingly, revealing that the transgression was not instigated by
those who had the highest stake in upsetting the social order. If the penny

press openly addressed (and profited from) readers' nervousness about the manipulations of untrustworthy capitalist speculators above them, it also assured them that blacks, at least, were not autonomously capable of plotting from below.

The goal of the various exposures of the Heth hoax was not to discern how she had come to gull thousands of white viewers and readers, but to reveal who was behind her; and it was comforting to find that it was a Yankee, one whose own story of upward mobility white northern working-class readers could identify with. During Heth's exhibition, many of her visitors had delighted in her animation, her improvised responses to questions as well as her well-rehearsed routine; but in her recommodified afterlife, she was a drunken, swearing negro who spoke nothing but her master's words on stage, and whose attempts at resistance were laughable. In these recycled legends of the Heth story, Barnum was both a capitalist confidence man and a breaker of slaves, a trader in bogus commodities and an emblem of white mastery.

Barnum and Lyman would team up for one more act, which proved to be the last for the lesser-known member of the team that had brought Joice Heth such renown. In the summer of 1842—by which time Barnum was the proprietor of the American Museum in New York—Moses Kimball of the Boston Museum approached him with an object and a story. Apparently an ingeniously sewn-together assemblage of monkey bones, fur, fish bones, and scales, the object had been exhibited as "a preserved specimen of a mermaid" that had been obtained from Japanese sailors by a Boston merchant in Calcutta. Barnum took it, but before exhibiting what came to be known as the Fejee Mermaid in New York, he arranged for letters to be written to the *Herald* and other New York papers, postmarked from places in the South as far away as Montgomery, Alabama, and Charleston, South Carolina, containing local news and information on crops and commerce, which the papers were generally happy to print. Included in these circulars was always the mention of a "Dr. Griffin, agent of the Lyceum of Natural History in London, recently from Pernambuco, who had in his possession a most remarkable curiosity, being nothing less than a veritable mermaid taken among the Fejee Islands, and preserved in China, where the Doctor had bought it at a high figure for the Lyceum." After a few weeks, "Dr. Griffin" (who was, of course, none other than Levi Lyman) showed up in a New York hotel, and shortly arranged for several editors to view the creature, which—as Barnum described it—was "an ugly, dried-up, black-looking, and diminutive specimen, about three feet long." The language here is suspiciously similar to that used to advertise Heth during her tour, suggesting that Barnum was replaying old themes in this new exhibit, but with a submerged rather than overt manipulation of racial issues.[39] Indeed, the familiar routine of newspaper notices, woodcuts, lighted transparencies, posters, and planted stories all contributed to the sensational success of the two men's new exhibit, highlighted perhaps by their success in persuading the Universalist minister Edwin H. Chapin to preach a sermon attesting to the mermaid's possible authenticity: "It is not only an arrogant but a *shallow* philosophy that says 'the existence of this or that is impossible, it is *contrary to the laws of nature*,' " he argued.

After exhibiting the mermaid and sending it off on tours with and without Lyman for the next two years, Barnum eventually returned it to Kimball. Lyman, meanwhile, had proved himself increasingly "slow, moping [and] lazyboned," and fell out of contact with Barnum. He traveled for a time with the painting *Christ and the Last Supper*, found a job with Kimball in Boston, and then drifted from view. Barnum records in a footnote to his autobiography that Lyman converted to the new church of Mormon, and moved out with the followers of Joseph Smith to their settlement at Nauvoo, Illinois.[40] After such a promising early career trafficking in the inauthentic, he seems finally to have found something to believe in.

ERASURE

BARNUM NEVER AGAIN left the public eye, and neither did the story that first made him famous ever quite leave him. It may seem that he had no desire for anyone to forget his dealings with Joice Heth, for in his obsessive chronicling of his own life from the 1840s onward, he always devoted at least a few pages to the woman his alter-ego Diddleum referred to as "my black beauty." One might even suppose that his later, more confessional, and apparently more frank writings about himself and his exploits would paint a more accurate picture of the exhibit and its aftermath, and these writings do, in fact, solve a few of the mysteries left open by earlier texts. The candor is deceptive, however, for as regards Heth the later writings progressively conceal more than they reveal. Like Minister D—— in Poe's story "The Purloined Letter," Barnum tried to hide the thing by putting it in full view. What was he trying to hide? As Barnum repackaged himself as a purveyor of "moral" entertainments, he found that there was much in this raucous early episode to put behind him. So too his changing political affiliations—especially with regard to race and slavery after the Civil War—made the earlier versions of the story dangerous to him. These factors, however, do not entirely explain the shape of his later writings on Heth, which become increasingly contorted the further they are removed from the event they are concealing. In addition to reflecting the changing social circumstances of their composition, they also indicate a private disturbance—a kind of haunting—that was apparently touched off by the clash of the author's memory of Heth and his overwhelming desire to forget.

Shortly after he published "Adventures of an Adventurer," Barnum scraped together enough cash and credit to purchase the institution that would become the platform for his escalating fame. The American Museum, one of the largest collections of eclectic "wonders" in the country but now fallen on hard times, housed over 150,000 curious objects in a five-story building on the corner of Broadway and Ann Street in New York. Over the next few years, Barnum steadily augmented the collection by purchasing the holdings of rival museum-owner Reubens Peale as well as minor collections like that of the Chinese Museum, by swapping with other proprietors like Moses Kimball of Boston, by adding numerous exhibits, dramatic acts, lectures, and what can only be described as pieces of performance art (such as the man silently laying a line of bricks along Broadway that led a throng of curious spectators to the museum, or the advertised "free" band concert outside the museum that was so bad it drove listeners and passersby to buy tickets for entry as a means of escaping the noise). Barnum's list of some of the museum's holdings gives a sense of its diverse attractions: "Industrious fleas, educated dogs, jugglers, automatons, ventriloquists, living statuary, tableaux, gipsies, albinoes, fat boys, giants, dwarfs, rope-dancers, caricatures of phrenology, and 'live Yankees,' pantomime, instrumental music, singing and dancing in great variety, (including Ethiopians,) etc. Dioramas, panoramas, models of Dublin, Paris, Niagara, Jerusalem, etc., mechanical figures, fancy glassblowing, knitting machines and other triumphs in the mechanical arts, dissolving views, American Indians, including their warlike and religious ceremonies enacted on the stage, etc. etc."[1]

He did not entirely give up the traveling life, mounting a triumphant tour of Europe with Charles Stratton (a.k.a. Tom Thumb) and orchestrating the spectacularly successful American tour of Jenny Lind, the Swedish Nightingale. But much had changed from the itinerant days with Joice Heth, Signor Vivalla, and Aaron Turner's circus. In the 1830s Barnum had tirelessly puffed the arrival of his performers in new cities, but sometimes found them (and himself) referred to as vagabonds. In the 1840s and 1850s, though, Barnum's fame always preceded him and virtually ensured the success of the events, and the tours were designed as much to puff his

own name as those of the star attractions. Even the foreign tours en-
hanced his prestige at home: the *Atlas*, for instance, published for New
York readers hundreds of Barnum's letters about his exploits with Tom
Thumb (climaxing, perhaps, in the latter's duel with Queen Victoria's poo-
dle). And he always had a "permanent investment," the museum, to fall
back on.

Much had changed, too, in his status as an author. By 1854, when
Barnum wrote the first full edition of his autobiography, he was a central
fixture in the cultural scene of New York. As many have noted,
his own self-presentation grew increasingly conservative as his social
position rose. His earliest published writings, from his days as editor of
the *Herald of Freedom,* positioned him squarely in opposition to the
"purse-proud overbearing lordlings" and in sympathy with commoners;
"Adventures of an Adventurer," while not as overtly political or class
conscious as the earlier editorials, certainly reveled in its hero's triumph
over the moneyed elites and spoke in the rowdy accents of Jacksonian
popular culture. But in *The Life of P. T. Barnum, Written by Himself,*
those class cues are subtly shifted. He does dwell for five chapters on
his youth and adolescence in Bethel, and exaggerates—perhaps even
invents—his humble origins; but as Bluford Adams notes, the tone
is overarchingly nostalgic, stressing the social harmony of small-town
life. And if he addresses working-class readers, he implicitly encourages
them "to identify with his climb up the U.S. social ladder."[2] In narrating
his early newspaper years, he dismisses his fiercely partisan attacks on
the Connecticut elite as "the vehemence of youth," episodes of which
the sober author wishes "to wipe out all unpleasant recollections."[3] Instead
he focuses on his rise to riches and wealth, stressing the underlying
morality behind even his most apparently shady transactions. If he had deceived anyone, it was only to teach his audience valuable lessons
about making choices or placing confidence in a democratic society;
and every deception was offset by a temperance drama or a scientific
demonstration in the lecture room of his museum. Popular culture, in
this new model, was not an agonistic struggle to dupe or be duped, to be
a master or be mastered, but a set of "innocent and rational amusements"—code words that signaled Barnum's courting of high-brow reformers.[4]

To mark this shift is not to suggest that Barnum's early acts were truly antagonistic to the upper classes or representative of working-class interests. After all, beginning with the Heth act, he had exhibited a remarkable opportunism—marketing her as a freak in New York, as a refined and tidy entertainment in New England, and as a sensation to be gobbled by the penny press. Nor is it to suggest that his later writings position him entirely on the other side of the fence, as an upper-middle-brow cultural paternalist. Instead, beginning with this 1854 autobiography, we can see a new kind of tension in Barnum's writing, in which he tells the old raucous stories and tries to squeeze them into a moralistic frame. These increasingly "clean" portrayals of himself as a purveyor of wholesome if somewhat mischievous entertainments reflect his ongoing alignment with the developing currents of nineteenth-century culture, and thus mark his engagement with a new cultural formation that was taking shape around him— that of the urban middle class. As Paul Boyer and Paul Johnson have written, this newly conceived social grouping was shaped crucially by the work of temperance activists, advocates of industrial morality, and other moral reformers in the mid-nineteenth century.[5]

It was not just Barnum, among the purveyors of mass culture, who shaped his productions to fit the ethos of this "embryonic middle class" during the 1850s. As the culture industry expanded, those other staples of mid-century entertainment—the penny press and the minstrel show—followed a similar route. They, too, had found their initial success by appealing strongly to workers' sentiments in the 1830s, but by the late 1840s and 1850s they, like Barnum, found themselves veering closer to the status of mainstream rather than oppositional culture, in part by virtue of their own success. The penny papers—most of which were now selling for at least two cents—moved away from their radical roots and rowdy populism in favor of a more "respectable" style. This development did not come about without a struggle: after a "moral war" launched on the *Herald* by six-penny sheets that reduced the circulation of Bennett's paper by approximately 20 percent, the publisher subtly began to shift it toward a more subdued tone and subject matter.[6] And starting with the performances of the Virginia Minstrels in 1843, minstrel acts were increasingly packaged as "concerts" that were advertised as "Chaste, Pleasing, Elegant" affairs, rather than the loosely structured, noisy events of the 1830s, which often spilled over into street celebrations and violence.[7] Significantly, Barnum played a role in this last development. In the performing spaces of his American Museum, he contracted with numerous minstrel performers, whose acts were now meant to be suitable for a more sedate audience than the boisterous Bowery denizens.

Indeed, the American Museum, Adams notes, officially promoted those middle-class virtues of "entrepreneurialism, temperance, Christianity, and domesticity."[8] As opposed to his earlier delight in Joice Heth's backstage swearing, Barnum now wrote that "no vulgar word or gesture and not a profane expression was *ever* allowed on my stage. Even in Shakespeare's plays, I unflinchingly and invariably cut out vulgarity and profanity." Similarly, his views on alcohol had changed: rather than encouraging his readers to laugh along with accounts of Heth's backstage tippling, he was now firmly on the side of the temperance crowd. Not only did the museum house numerous "temperance" dramas, but he even hired detectives to enforce standards of sobriety by monitoring the behavior of patrons.[9] And although the museum did still house freak shows and other sensationalist exhibits, he claimed to use "whales, giants, dwarfs, Albinos, dog shows, et cetera" to draw audiences toward "the more moral productions" (dramas, lectures, and the like) that would serve to uplift and educate families in New York.

The similarity between Barnum's description of the moral calculus of his museum and contemporary discussions of minstrelsy and the penny press is striking. In an 1855 biography of James Gordon Bennett, a fellow journalist defended him as follows:

> The dark character of Journalism was necessary, fifteen or twenty years ago, to educate the people into the enjoyment of a higher style of art, just as Negro Minstrelsy and Negro plays are at twenty-five cents a head, this very day, to prepare the taste-lacking portion of the public for the refinement and elegancies of the Opera and of the Drama . . . If he would become a great man, situated as he was, with but a small capital, and unpaid by any political spoils, he must be a mountebank. He must blacken his face, or the public would not look at him, and could not find any music in him—precisely as they can discover no music or mirth,

beauty or wit, in white men and women to-day, until they are daubed over with burnt cork and lard, and show the darkest of dark skins to be attractive.[10]

With an admission of 25 cents in the mid-1850s, Barnum's American Museum, too, was cheap enough to provide entertainment to the working classes, but once they were inside its halls they were expected to behave according to the strictures of middle-class respectability. So if Barnum was to continue courting the working classes, it was with the overt aim of "uplifting" them, rather than boisterously presenting images of social upheaval.

It is in this context that, in 1854, he returned once again to the Joice Heth story in his autobiography.[11] In this new version of the event that launched his career, the author purports to undo his and Lyman's deliberate deceptions of the public in favor of a more mature and responsible version: "The story of Lyman has since been generally accredited as the true history of the old negress, and never, until the present writing, have I said or written a word by way of contradiction or correction." In truth, Barnum does finally abandon some of the outrageous claims of "The Joice Heth Hoax" and "Adventures of an Adventurer." In a relatively straightforward tone—with none of the arriviste crowing of Diddleum—he admits, for instance, that he did not discover Heth on a plantation in Kentucky and even gives the details of his transactions with R. W. Lindsay for the "purchase" of Heth; he leaves off the dramatic accounts of how he dreamed up the story, extracted Heth's teeth, and addicted her to whiskey; he reprints crucial documents pertaining to the exhibit, including a bill of sale for Heth and numerous newspaper accounts of her act; he gives credit to Lyman for authoring the pamphlet biography of Heth and "The Joice Heth Hoax" in the *Herald;* and he gives a fairly accurate version of the autopsy and its attendant controversies. The events he narrates are largely verifiable by external sources, many of which Barnum includes. It is all the more surprising, then, to find that this version of the Heth episode is probably the least accurate one yet, since by casting the episode in terms acceptable to a more "respectable" readership, Barnum glosses over and even hides much of its turbulent content.

To start with, there is the selectivity of the story. In "Adventures of an Adventurer," he had bragged about conning the ministers of Providence into supporting the exhibit by advertising it as an abolitionist fundraiser—an element of the tour that is corroborated by many supporting documents. But in *The Life of P. T. Barnum*, all we hear of Providence is that "the exhibition was highly successful." There is no mention of Heth's lingering and deepening illness, which was noted by observers from the beginning of Barnum's tour with her. He never mentions charging admission to the autopsy or advertising Heth's posthumous tour of Europe as a vial of ashes. And finally, Barnum closes the chapter on Heth by commenting "that the remains of Joice were removed to Bethel, and buried respectably." No records of her interment in Bethel exist.[12]

All of this serves to clean up some of the rough edges of the exhibit and to make it seem less exploitative (a charge that probably would have flattered the author of "Adventures"). It also performs another function that Barnum apparently found important during a time of intense political fractiousness: by omitting reference to the antiabolitionist shenanigans in Providence, he attempted to remove the Heth story (and his life history in general) from the sphere of political controversy. An illustration of this tendency comes in an interlude to the Heth tour, when Barnum is exhibiting Vivalla in Washington and takes an afternoon off to watch the Senate in action. On the floor that day is John C. Calhoun, the South Carolina senator who was the nation's most prominent political defender of slavery. Calhoun reads from a New England newspaper "a violent and bitter attack upon southern slaveholders, denouncing them as man-stealers, pirates, robbers, murderers, men who set at nought every requirement of the decalogue, and who richly deserved to be butchered by their own slaves." As a climax to this inflammatory reading, Calhoun makes sure to turn the article against Martin Van Buren, the Democratic vice president who was then running for the presidency, by noting that the paper in question had endorsed Van Buren's candidacy. What is striking is that in 1845, when Barnum was traveling to Europe, he wrote a letter to the *Atlas* in which he voiced anxieties about slave violence similar to those that Calhoun gave vent to on the Senate floor. Describing a heated argument with two Scotsmen aboard a steamer bound for Glasgow, he reported: "After the contro-

versy had been continued a couple of hours, I happened to remark that in
a slave state or country where there were ten blacks to a white, I believed
'if the blacks were unceremoniously set free, and there was no army to
protect the whites, the blacks would murder them and take possession of
their property . . .'"[13] But ten years after that voyage to Scotland, his memory of Van Buren's response to Calhoun—or lack of one—earns Barnum's
highest regard and is presented retrospectively as solidifying his decision
to vote for the man known as "the little magician." What appeals to him is
Van Buren's ability to remain outside the fray, not to be sucked into the
great controversial issue of his day:

> The Senate was convulsed with laughter at this palpable hit. Meanwhile
> Mr. Van Buren maintained a countenance that was placid as a May
> morning, and the keenest eye could not have detected the slightest evi-
> dence that he was any more interested in the speech of Mr. Calhoun
> than an infant. Mr. Calhoun continued for twenty minutes to denounce
> the administration in the most scathing language. Van Buren manifested
> the utmost unconcern, and when the speech was finished, he beckoned
> to Mr. King, of Alabama, who took the chair, while "little Matty" quietly
> walked about among the Senators, shaking hands and smilingly convers-
> ing with them.

Since this story comes in the middle of a chapter on Barnum's own
management of a slave woman—a woman he had previously written about
(if laughingly) as violently angry about the terms of her labor—it is tempt-
ing to look to it for clues of his own thinking about where the Heth tour
stood in relation to the politics of slavery. Twenty years after Calhoun's reported attack on Van Buren, Barnum's memoir was published at a time
when controversies over slavery and abolition were raging. The passage of
the Fugitive Slave Act in 1850 and the Kansas-Nebraska Act of 1854
would have made the monumental disregard that Barnum saw in Van
Buren impossible. Barnum seems, then, to be looking back nostalgically
on a time when one could simply ignore the politics of slavery. It is implausible to think that, in 1854, his earlier rollicking descriptions of Heth's
ordeal could have escaped ideological scrutiny, and so they are rubbed
out. Juxtaposing the story of Joice Heth with this implied story of growing
political discord, Barnum is attempting to transport his early career onto

an imaginary politically neutral ground, to practice, like Van Buren, an Olympian public indifference to the supreme conflict of his age.[14]

Which brings us to the big humbug of this rendition of the events of 1835 and 1836. In the process of distancing himself from his previous claims to have practically invented Heth—dreaming up her story and her act, "improving" her appearance, subjecting her to harsh regimes of discipline and diet—Barnum diminishes his role in the exhibit to a point at which he could no longer be said to be truly responsible for it:

> The question naturally arises, if Joice Heth was an impostor, *who* taught her these things? and how happened it that she was so familiar, not only with ancient psalmody, but also with the minute details of the Washington family? To all this, I unhesitatingly answer, *I do not know.* I taught her none of these things. She was perfectly familiar with them all before I ever saw her, and she taught me many facts in relation to the Washington family with which I was not before acquainted.

The struggle of wills enthusiastically recorded in the earlier texts is here entirely discarded in favor of a portrait of the slave woman—or some unnamed tutor—as the author of her own exhibit. Barnum thus minimizes his own involvement in the politics and practice of mastery, casting himself as a manager who arranges for the production of an unusual entertainer rather than as a clever exploiter of a slave's labor. He even goes so far as to suggest that he actually believed the story she told him. As Barnum now has it, when Dr. Rogers informs him after the autopsy "that instead of being 161 years old, she was probably not over eighty," he responds:

> I stated to him, in reply, what was strictly true, that I had hired Joice in perfect good faith, and relied upon her appearance and the documents as evidence of the truth of her story. The same gentleman had examined her when alive on exhibition at Niblo's. He rejoined that he had no doubt I had been deceived in the matter, that her personal appearance really did indicate extreme longevity, but that the documents must either have been forged, or else they applied to some other individual . . .
>
> Here let me say a word in reply to the captious who may claim that I was over-credulous in accepting the story of Joice and her exhibitor, as a matter of fact. I assert, then, that when Joice Heth was living, I never met with six persons out of the many thousands who visited her, who

seemed to doubt the claim of her age and history. Hundreds of medical men assured me that they thought the statement of her age was correct, and Dr. Rogers himself . . . remarked to me that he expected to have spoiled half a dozen knives in severing the ossification in the arteries around the region of the heart and chest. Indeed, Mr. Locke plainly indicated his belief in her story, by the following remarks found in the editorial from which I make the above extract:

"We were half inclined to question the propriety of the scientific curiosity which prompted it," (the dissection.) "We felt as though the person of poor old Joice Heth should have been saved from exposure and mutilation, not so much on account of her extreme old age, and the public curiosity which she had already gratified for the gain of others, *as for the high honor with which she was endowed in being the nurse of the immortal Washington.*"

Barnum is using language carefully here, never stating outright his belief in the Heth story. To say, in strict truth, that he had hired Heth "in good faith" did not necessarily mean that he had faith in her identity; and that he "relied upon her appearance and the documents as evidence of the truth of her story" does not necessarily mean that he believed the story to be true—merely that he relied on her appearance and the documents to serve as evidence of that truth. It is then *Rogers* who claims that Barnum has been deceived in the matter, which of course Barnum the author does not dispute. He goes on, in the next two paragraphs, not precisely to defend his belief in her against those who claim that such belief would be "over-credulous," but to rehearse the story of others who "seemed" to believe.

If the point is simply to suggest that he believed in Heth's story and was deceived like so many others, then why go to the trouble of crafting such evasive language? Part of the answer—leaving aside political considerations—is that there were two competing pressures on Barnum: one to fess up, and one to deny. On the one hand, James Gordon Bennett, who had never forgiven Barnum for making such a fool of him, was continually mocking his every career move as another "humbug" in the *Herald,* and so Barnum took some pains to present his writing as scrupulously forthright. On the other, there was R. W. Lindsay, who was still hovering on the margins of Barnum's life, trying to extort money from him. The autobiography was published only two years after Barnum had sent Lindsay one hundred dollars, apparently to ward off further charges that the broken-down but still litigious former showman and tavern owner was considering bringing against him. As we have seen, Barnum sent a check to Lindsay, accompanied by a letter stating that he "honestly *believed*" in Heth's authenticity and regretted the "stigma of *originating*" her imposture.[15]

A possible explanation for all this posturing of credulity is that as fraud law was becoming increasingly sophisticated during this period, Barnum was trying to position himself as one who was duped by a swindling agent rather than the agent of fraud or forgery himself.[16] Perhaps Lindsay had a legitimate claim on some of the profits from Heth's exhibit—it is clear, from the paper trail of original contracts, that he could only have sold Barnum half of the exhibit, to begin with. At any rate, Barnum's defensive but slightly vague language in the autobiography certainly has a legalistic ring to it, and the one hundred dollars paid to Lindsay appears less like disinterested benevolence than self-protection against some sort of legal action. Overall, this rendition of the Heth story is one not of increased candor, but of increasing evasiveness—against moral, political, and perhaps even legal arguments to be made against his handling of Heth.

To interpret Barnum's own writings in this way is to portray a purely social Barnum, and to present a picture of the showman/author carefully inserting himself into the crevices of popular, political, and legal culture, minimizing the story's potential to harm his reputation, maximizing its congruence with his current pose. This is certainly a plausible interpretation; after all, the dominant picture we have had of Barnum since his own heyday has been, as A. H. Saxon notes, that of the entirely "public" man, the man whose private life was sealed off, rather than exposed, by his numerous autobiographies.[17] Constance Rourke has tied the problem of imagining a "private" Barnum to the fact that "his life was most often interwoven with mean or humble lives, which have left behind them no trace."[18] Figures like Joice Heth, it seems, could not offer their perspective on the personality of their employer to posterity, lacking, as they did, access to the tools of representation. The present study, too, contributes to this inter-

pretation of Barnum; I have been seeking primarily social meanings behind different aspects of Barnum's early career and leaving his psychology
to the side.

But there is something in these later writings about Heth—and particularly in his next autobiographical act, *Struggles and Triumphs* (1869)—that
presents a chink in the armor, that begs, if not a purely psychological interpretation, at least an interpretation that bridges Barnum's positioning
in the social world with some sort of negotiation of private anxieties. For as
he grew older, his defense against his involvement with Heth exceeded—
while it still responded to—the demands of popularity, morality, legality,
or ideology. In narrating the chapter of *Struggles and Triumphs* called
"My Start as a Showman," the author begins with a strangely passive account of his "destined" entry into the amusement line: "I did not seek the
position or the character. The business finally came in my way; I fell into
the occupation, and far beyond any of my predecessors on this continent, I
have succeeded." Then follows an extended assessment of the benefits of
wholesome amusement in brightening the busy world of commerce, and
an assertion that despite the ubiquity of "shameful . . . theatrical sensations," he has "sought to make amusement harmless." Then, in finishing
his wind-up to the story of his beginnings as a showman, he writes, "But I
shall by no means claim entire faultlessness in my history as a showman,"
and finally introduces the Heth story as follows:

> The least deserving of all my efforts in the show line was the one which
> introduced me to the business; a scheme in no sense of my own devis-
> ing; one which had been sometime before the public and which had so
> many vouchers for its genuineness that at the time of taking possession
> of it I honestly believed it to be genuine; something, too, which, as I
> have said, I did not seek, but which by accident came in my way and
> seemed almost to compel my agency—such was the "Joice Heth" exhi-
> bition which first brought me forward as a showman.[19]

In this rather breathless sentence, Barnum takes blame for the exhibit (or
at least declines to claim "faultlessness"); but then he claims that he did
not devise it, that he believed in it, that others believed in it, that he did
not seek it out, that it was an accident, that it "seemed almost to compel
my agency," that it brought him forward rather than the other way around.

This is reminiscent of a joke told by Freud in *The Interpretation of Dreams* in which a man is tried in court for the crime of borrowing a neighbor's pan and returning it with a hole in it. He defends himself by asserting "first, that he had given it back undamaged; secondly, that the kettle had a hole in it when he borrowed it; and thirdly, that he had never borrowed a kettle from his neighbor at all."[20] In Barnum's writing as in this anecdote, the claims of defense tend to cancel one another out, indicating a sense of guilt that is careening out of the author's control. But guilt about what? Of what does Barnum imagine himself accused? Again, a contextual answer will help, but it will not solve the riddle.

Struggles and Triumphs was printed in 1869, by which time Barnum had maintained his hold on the popular imagination for twenty-five years and was now entering a new career as a political figure in the postbellum North. In a changing world, Barnum's politics were changing, too; as he tells it, the Kansas-Nebraska Act of 1854, the increasing threat of southern secession, and a dawning realization of the evils of slavery caused him to switch his party affiliation from Democrat to Republican. This indicates that he, like so many other Americans of his time, was beginning to think of slavery as *the* defining political issue, displacing labor, immigration, territorial acquisition, and so many other issues that burned while conflicts over slavery simmered. No longer could one calmly ignore the subject and attempt a Van Buren–like apolitical pose as Barnum had in his 1854 autobiography.

Still, if he was adopting an antislavery stance, his feelings about racial difference were rather ill defined. An exhibit in his American Museum from the period just before the Civil War indicates—and gives objective shape to—his unsettled attitudes, as well as those of curiosity-seekers who came to visit. In this he displayed to the public, under the heading of "What Is It?," an African American man named William Henry Johnson who was apparently mentally retarded and afflicted with microcephaly. Dressed in a fur suit and usually crawling about the stage, "What Is It?" was given "lessons" by a white trainer, who would help Johnson to walk, to eat properly, and gradually to be fit for civilization. The central question, as James W. Cook, Jr., has put it in his study of this exhibition, was whether the "What Is It?" was a man, a monkey, or a Darwinian "missing link" between the species—precisely the questions that the "American

school" of ethnologists was asking about the African race in general. As
Barnum wrote about the exhibition in a letter, "The thing is not to be
called *anything* by the exhibitor. We know not & therefore do not assert
whether it is human or animal. We leave that all to the sagacious public to
decide."[21] Eventually, though, he did settle on a term—"nondescript"—to
describe that ambiguous, liminal position of the creature. The question
that he asked the public to decide about Johnson became a question that
he asked, and incoherently answered, about all blacks as he launched his
political career after the Civil War.

Barnum's antislavery stance appears to have hardened during the war.
Responding to his public railings against slaveholders, a group of southern
saboteurs who were attempting to set fire to central institutions in New
York placed their first incendiary devices in the American Museum.
Barnum's support for the Union became so strong that he decided to enter politics in order (as he later wrote) to have the honor of voting "for the
then proposed amendment to the Constitution of the United States to
abolish slavery forever from the land." Shortly after the war, as a member
of the Connecticut General Assembly, Barnum made an impassioned
speech before the state House and the Senate in favor of extending the
vote to the state's black population. Rather than portraying freed blacks as
a threat to the safety of whites—as he had done twenty years earlier—now
he asked, rhetorically, whether blacks had "seize[d] the 'opportunity,'
when their masters were engaged with a powerful foe, to break out in insurrection, and massacre those tyrants who had so long held them in the
most cruel bondage." The explanation he gave to his negative answer was
that "the poor black man is like a lamb in his nature when compared with
the white man . . . [He] possesses a confiding disposition, thoroughly tinc-
tured with religious enthusiasm, and not characterized by a spirit of revenge."[22] He was not exactly asserting the meaninglessness of race as a
cornerstone of identity here, since blacks as a group could still be differen-
tiated by their innate behavioral and spiritual qualities from whites. Instead, he was voicing a common form of Romantic racialism, which
George Fredrickson has defined as "concepts of inbred national character
and genius."[23] These were not necessarily tied to a natural hierarchy of the
races—as Harriet Beecher Stowe argued passionately. "The negro race,"
she explained, "is confessedly more simple, docile, child-like and affec-

tionate, than other races; and hence the divine graces of love and faith, when in-breathed by the Holy Spirit, find in their natural temperament a more congenial atmosphere."[24] Barnum's portrait of the lamb-like black man accords with this nonhierarchical natural difference, and he attributes any inferiority of blacks to their lack of education and opportunity.

The speech goes on, however, to complicate that claim. In discussing recent ethnological studies purporting to show that "the negroes are not human," Barnum at first seems to agree with their conclusions. "You look at their low foreheads, their thick skulls and lips, their woolly heads, their flat noses, their dull, lazy eyes, and you may be tempted to adopt the language [of the reports] and exclaim: Surely these people have 'no inventive faculties, no genius for the arts, or for any of those occupations requiring intellect and wisdom.'" But it turns out, in Barnum's analysis, that the centuries of "ignorance and barbarism" in Africa, compounded by the demoralizing effects of chattel slavery in America, have created these physical differences. If blacks are given education and Christianity, over succeeding generations their brains will be stimulated, and "the low foreheads will be raised and widened by an active and expanded brain; the vacant eye of barbarism, ignorance and idleness will light up with the fire of intelligence, education, ambition, and Christian civilization."

We have here a picture of moral influence actually changing the shape of William Henry Johnson's head. As loopy as this sounds, it is an idea that had at one point a respectable pedigree. Samuel Stanhope Smith, the leading proponent of the environmentalist explanation for racial difference, had argued about the negro skull in 1810 that "climate, modes of living, national customs, ideas, and the degree of civilization to which a people have arrived, all have an influence on the figure of this bony substratum of the head" and therefore contribute to vary the shape of the brain, "pressing upon it in some points, and giving it scope in others." As a result, "these causes must . . . assist, impede, or vary the operation of the mind, and affect the character of the national genius, or of the whole race of men placed in a particular climate, or existing in a particular state of society."[25] Through the 1830s and 1840s, phrenologists made the argument that all brains could expand given the proper exercise and atmosphere; antiracists in the antebellum period seized on this as proof of the potential equality of races.[26] Fittingly, Barnum's American Museum provided an opportunity for this kind of speculation. In 1843 Lydia Maria Child closely examined the skulls of fifteen living Native Americans exhibited in the museum and concluded: "The facial angle and shape of the head, is various in races and nations; but these are the *effects* of spiritual influences, long operating on character, and in their turn becoming *causes;* thus intertwining, as Past and Future ever do." Accordingly, bringing moral influences to bear on "Indians or Africans, as a race, would gradually change the structure of their skulls, and enlarge their perceptions of moral and intellectual truth."[27]

Was Barnum thinking of Joice Heth as he delivered his speech about the reformation of black character that would go along with the reshaping of black skulls? Not consciously, perhaps, but his dawning sense that blacks were human beings with physical and mental capacities equal to whites must have struck even him as a contrast to his decades-long efforts to exhibit the garish opposite before the public—an effort beginning, in many ways, with the Joice Heth exhibit. In this light, a question must have occurred to him: was Joice Heth a human being or not? He seems not quite to have made up his mind. Responding to questions about the beginning of his career in an 1877 interview, for instance, Barnum alternately referred to Heth as "the wonderful woman" and "the critter."[28] It is a sense of this ambivalence, I think, that disrupts his final writings and pronouncements about blacks in general and Joice Heth in particular, even as he tries to rush past his memory of her. And the continuation of the speech about the possibilities for uplifting blacks signals his consciousness of her somewhere in the back regions of his mind. Referring to a Wallingford legislator who opposed extending the vote to blacks on grounds of their supposed mental inferiority, Barnum tells of a young American man who has traveled to Europe and returns to find that nothing in America can compare with anything found in Europe—mountains, rivers, trees, parks, streets, and buildings all pale in comparison.

> "They have introduced a couple of Venetian gondolas on the large pond in Central park," remarked a friend.
> "All very well," replied the verdant traveller, "but between you and me, these birds can't stand our cold climate more than one season." The gentleman from Wallingford evidently had as little idea of the true na-

ture of the African as the young swell had of the pleasure-boats of
Europe.[29]

This rather out-of-place anecdote, apparently spontaneously ad-libbed in
an otherwise set speech, seems an irruption of unconscious associations,
linking the political scene of 1869 to an event thirty-three years earlier.
Barnum's first exhibit, after all, was a "critter" who was often described as
having long "talons," and was portrayed in at least one caricature as a
shriveled old bird (Figure 11). And her demise and death, as we saw, generated a swirl of reports that "the true nature of the African" was ill suited
to the coldness of the northern climate.

One final piece of oratory cements the linkage between Barnum's
postbellum political position and a spontaneous burst of guilt over his past.
Barnum was occasionally pilloried by his political and business opponents
for his dubious exploits in the past, but no one of importance seems to
have taken him to task for his treatment of blacks. However, in a rare moment of self-criticism (this time wisely not reprinted in his autobiography),
he beat his critics to the punch. As he was running (unsuccessfully) for a
seat in the U.S. Congress in 1867, he gave an ad-lib coda to a campaign
speech while waiting for another speaker to arrive. Here he again attacks
the behavior of the southern "rebels" and advocates strong punishment of
the South, but in a surprising rhetorical turn—surprising, perhaps, even to
Barnum as he spoke—he includes himself in the punishment: "I lived
among them myself, and owned slaves. I did more. I whipped my slaves. I
ought to have been whipped a thousand times for this myself. But then I
was a Democrat—one of those nondescript Democrats, who are Northern
men with Southern principles."[30] The echo of the term "nondescript" from
the "What Is It?" exhibit marks another small disturbance in Barnum's
self-presentation, a confusion not only about the relation between his exhibits and his politics, but about what he was or had been, about his commitment to the ideal he was now supporting, about his responsibility for
his past actions. Should he have been whipped, as he had whipped black
slaves, for the crime of whipping blacks, who themselves were nondescripts straddling the line between human and nonhuman, or did his
own nondescript status exonerate him?

Judy Heath, dressed up to receive company.

11. Caricature of "Judy Heath" as a shriveled old bird
in Revolutionary get-up, 1855.

It was only about a year after he uttered these words that he claimed in
Struggles and Triumphs that the exhibit of Joice Heth in Philadelphia
"seemed almost to compel my agency," and "brought me forth a showman," the position "for which I was destined" but "never sought out." It
was "the least deserving of all my efforts," but also the one that showed
him who he was, what he was destined to be. In some sense, in stumbling
upon Heth, he realized (and hated realizing) that he had stumbled upon
himself, so that she *was* him (compelling his agency, initiating the career

in which he had realized his true calling), even as he tried desperately to throw off his association with her. In this light, a favorite gibe of his antagonist James Gordon Bennett during this period must have stung: Barnum was nothing other than "Joyce Heth in breeches."[31]

The story Barnum gives of her exhibit in 1869 is a bare-bones four pages, down from eighteen in his 1854 autobiography. Three and a half of these pages concern his interview with R. W. Lindsay, his description of Heth's act under Lindsay's management, his assessment of the surrounding documents ("the evidence seemed authentic"), and the terms of his transaction with the original exhibitor. His own management of the exhibit is compressed to five sentences:

> At the outset of my career I saw that everything depended upon getting people to think, and talk, and become curious and excited over and about the "rare spectacle." Accordingly, posters, transparencies, advertisements, newspaper paragraphs—all calculated to extort attention— were employed regardless of expense. My exhibition rooms in New York, Boston, Philadelphia, Albany and in other large and small cities, were continually thronged and much money was made. In the following February, Joice Heth died, literally of old age, and her remains received a respectable burial in the town of Bethel.
>
> At a post-mortem examination of Joice Heth by Dr. David L. Rogers, in the presence of some medical students, it was thought that the absence of ossification indicated considerably less age than had been assumed for her; but the doctors disagreed, and this "dark subject" will probably always continue to be shrouded in mystery.[32]

How did his career as a showman begin? His new version is: I made posters, advertisements, and transparencies, my exhibition rooms were full, I made money, she died, there was a postmortem, a new thought "was thought," nothing was clear or will ever be. The last phrase, in particular, seems a self-fulfilling prophecy in such a deliberately mystifying "explanation." With this joyless recital over, he jumps on to Signor Vivalla, whose exhibit, "whatever it may have been in other respects, had the merit of being, in every essential, unmistakably genuine." He is trying here to make it seem as if the problem with Heth's exhibit is that her authenticity was murky, but he is also avoiding the human dimensions of his relationship with a black person, an issue that he was at the same time presenting as so central to his political and moral identity.

Barnum's multiple disavowals suggest that he was struck at this point by something like the pangs of conscience. But that conscience, implying a deep interiority which his writings are so loath to reveal, seems to have been produced by a clash of surfaces: a tendency to recount incidents of one's life that were at odds with the social position one was seeking, a desire to support a traumatizing war that was fought in the name of a cause one had actively opposed. Barnum was shrewd enough to see the dangers of recounting what now seemed "the least deserving" moment of his life and to try to minimize its impact on him. But he was not willing to ask of himself how this moment had come about through his own volitional actions or to reflect on his ethical treatment of another "critter" whom he now, somewhat imperfectly, recognized as belonging to the human species. Instead, he "did not seek" her, she "by accident came in my way," it was she who "brought me forward," she who "compelled my agency." It is not a far leap to say that in Barnum's final account of the Joice Heth affair, he was the slave and she was the master.

"To be haunted," writes Avery Gordon in a sociological study of ghosts, "is to be tied to historical and social effects."[33] Barnum's torturous language (what, after all, does it mean to "*seem almost* to compel" something?) appears to be an effort to repress an inchoate association that is struggling to find a way out in spite of the author. This desire to block access to and expression of his own interior represents a fundamental irony of his writing: the man who added so much to the nation's stock of public fantasies about race here refuses to allow those fantasies to take root within himself, to become private again. But Barnum's haunted language marks his ties to the past that he wished to evade, and it also ties him to a mode of dealing with the unfinished business of the past that was common in his own day. His language in this final narration of the Heth affair borrows much from the spiritualist displays and writings that were so popular during the second half of the nineteenth century. Typically, a young woman would be led to the stage and placed in a trance, at which point she would become a medium for the spirit of a dead person to voice itself. (Predictably, George Washington was a favorite spirit to channel; on at least one occasion, he came back to voice his regret for participating in slavery during "the time I was in active bodily life.")[34] In casting himself as

a medium through which Heth exerted a supernatural agency, Barnum allowed himself, for a moment, to be merely a vessel. His own actions surely
originated within him but, with the passage of time, he has located their
origin somewhere else, turning not only Heth but himself into some un-
knowable Other. The "dark subject" that he declared would be a permanent mystery, then, was not only Heth's identity but his own, and in order
to erase her, he had to erase himself.

Twenty years later, after serving a term as mayor of Bridgeport, returning to his museum and the production of ever-greater cultural spectacles
including The Greatest Show on Earth, and finally retiring to his new
home in Bridgeport, Barnum himself lay dying. In his final newspaper interview, he expressed a wish that his funeral would go off according to
"English custom"—that is, with no one allowed to visit the corpse but
close relatives. Opposed to this was what he referred to as the "old hea-
thenish way" of allowing random spectators to gape and remark on "a
black streak on the side of his nose, a discolored spot near the ear, or the
expression of his face." He preferred instead to be cremated, he said, but
there was no crematory in Bridgeport. Then he launched into a joke about
the widower who has his wife cremated and preserves her ashes in a glass
jar, but who upon remarrying uses the ashes to sprinkle the front steps of
his house to prevent his new wife from slipping on the ice. Barnum eventually got his wish for a closed coffin, and in addition got a respectful service and a widely reprinted eulogy. His loss was felt so deeply that businesses in Bridgeport shut down for the day. He did not, however, escape
all of the ravages of death, for in the following month, two suspicious characters were discovered trying to steal his corpse from the grave, presumably in order to hold it for ransom. Many newspapers picked up the story,
and some pronounced it an "advertising dodge."[35] Barnum was here subject to the indignity of his past coming back to haunt him, but this was not
the haunting he had imagined at his deathbed. Picturing his own dead
body, he was troubled by images of desecration involving a corpse with
black marks on the skin being subjected to the gaze of strangers, a fantasy
in which he avoids the fate of the "dark subject" by turning himself into a
vial of ashes.

Apart from the writings of Barnum, what sort of afterlife has Joice Heth
lived? Over the years, she has popped up in several interesting contexts.

Herman Melville had an enduring interest in Barnum, taking the showman's scams as an inspiration for his late novel *The Confidence-Man*. But it is in an 1847 short story, "Authentic Anecdotes of 'Old Zack,'" that he makes a direct reference to the nurse of Washington. In this story, a simultaneous satire on Zachary Taylor's growing fame as a hero of the Mexican War and on the star-struck tendencies of his public, Melville has a character named Peter Tamerlane B——m; this showman plans to exhibit in his museum first an unexploded Mexican shell that Taylor calmly picked up during battle, then the pants through which a tack had pierced his hindquarters, and, finally, General Taylor himself. In order to convince Taylor to go along with this last scheme, B——m writes the general a letter, assuring him that he will treat his new exhibit "no worse than he has the venerable nurse of our beloved Washington and the illustrious General Tom Thumb."[36] A few years later, the noted medical authority and editor of *The Scalpel,* Edward Dixon, published a brief remembrance of the Heth affair. Dixon here seems to have forgotten how the autopsy played out, and—despite his journal's focus on "the Exposure of Quackery"—he appears to celebrate the event as a great entertainment rather than as an act of medical obfuscation. Dr. Rogers, he wrote, gave her "a clean ticket for any period short of 200 years. What a spectacle it must have been! We are a great people, and there is but one Barnum."[37] There are a few references to Heth in popular "comic histories" of the second half of the nineteenth century. In one, she is remembered as "the first negro wench" who landed at Jamestown; in another she is featured in a cartoon lineup of "the crop of persons who have nursed and otherwise remember Washington" (the lineup is followed by a ridiculously mustachioed old man who is famous for "*not* remember[ing] Washington to any great extent").[38] And not surprisingly, Mark Twain remembered Heth. In a speech he delivered before the Correspondents Club in 1868 (and which was reprinted in Elizabeth Cady Stanton's journal *The Revolution*), he gave a toast to "Woman," whom he claimed to love "irrespective of age or color." After declaring that "wheresoever you place woman . . .—in whatever position or estate— she is an ornament to that place she occupies, and a treasure to the world," he asked his audience to "look at Joyce Heth!" And then, for the punch line: "You need not look unless you want to." And one last zinger: "As a wet nurse she has no equal among men."[39]

Joice Heth truly had become an "ornament" in these writings—a harmless anecdote about fame, humbug, history, memory, age, and sex. In Dixon's account, she is "usually shrewd and tractable," but she does scowl and swear when she's out of whiskey or tobacco. In the others, though, the story has all its rough or even human edges sanded down, and becomes simply an agreeable and uncontroversial quip that creates an instant sense of "insider" community between writer (or speaker) and knowing audience, in the way that talk-show hosts' references to popular culture or academic presenters' literary allusions stroke their audiences' sense of "getting it." Enough potential volatility resides in the anecdote so that, in 1872, a magazine editor disputing new Hemings family testimony in the case of Thomas Jefferson and Sally Hemings could comment that claiming "illustrious parentage" is "a well known peculiarity of the colored race. The children of Jefferson and Madison, Calhoun and Clay far out-number Washington's body servants when Barnum was in his prosperity."[40] Over time, though, as Heth slipped into the vernacular, she was denuded of any particular significance, and with the help of Barnum's gradual erasures, dropped out of the public eye altogether.

Contemporary scholarship has not done Heth much better. She is, in all biographies of Barnum, presented in much the way he would have liked to present her—as a first stop on the road to something higher, a perhaps regrettable but essentially minor opening to a glorious if rambunctious career. Each biographer successively adds a few documents to the puzzle of her identity and relationship with Barnum, but most prefer Barnum's late-period assessment of his relationship with her. Irving Wallace considers Barnum from this first instance a hero who "saved . . . America from its acute solemnity," and finds that the Joice Heth exhibit was "strange fun and even patriotic." He does, however, hint at a darker element by noting that Barnum's career as a showman coincided with his becoming a slaveholder.[41] Neil Harris—who, like Wallace and earlier commentators, was working without the benefit of Barnum's earliest published newspaper writings—stresses that Heth was not Barnum's invention, and that he never claimed to have fabricated the episode. In reading the Heth episode as a template for "the operational aesthetic," Harris stresses the connections between the puzzle of Heth's identity and the epistemological uncertainties facing audiences in an urbanizing, modern-

izing community, a reading that he gives to other hoaxing enterprises of
Barnum's.[42] Insightful as this formulation is, it tends to flatten out distinctions between the presentation of woolly horses and of representations of
slaves' bodies, and the ethical aspects of the human relationship between
Heth and Barnum are nowhere to be found.

Finally, A. H. Saxon, in his monumental 1989 biography, examines issues of race, power, and manipulation more forthrightly than any previous
biographer of Barnum. But he does so mainly to foreclose any possibility
of harsh judgment against the showman. After writing of Barnum's purchase of and disciplinary actions against slaves, Saxon writes: "Let us be
candid and have done with it: Barnum's opinion of blacks during the pre–
Civil War era was no higher than that of most of his countrymen, whether
Southerners or Northerners." As in Barnum's own self-portraits, the
showman's regrettable actions are simply a product of the times or are beyond his control, whereas all of his more agreeable features are innovations. Absent is the possibility that Barnum innovated in racism, as in so
much else. As for Heth, Saxon concludes that Barnum did not "own" her,
as previous commentators assumed. Instead he argues that Barnum had
purchased from Lindsay (and Lindsay from Bowling) merely "the right to
exhibit her," thus absolving Barnum from the most grievous charge of exploiting Heth. He quotes some of Barnum's early, sadistic writings about
Heth, but these, for Saxon, are merely "youthful bravado." The real relationship between the two was unfailingly chummy, one professional humbug to another. With a profound disregard for the social circumstances
facing blacks in the antebellum "free" North, Saxon writes, "One suspects
old Joice would have felt right at home in Connecticut." And after giving
the main outlines of the Heth tour, including the most thorough account
yet of Heth's autopsy, Saxon writes: "Let there be no crocodile tears shed
over the fate of Joice Heth. Her managers appear to have treated her decently enough, and for months she had been at the center of public attention, basking in her role of Washington's 'nurse.'"[43]

Saxon's manifest uneasiness in handling this material ("let us be candid
and have done with it," "let there be no crocodile tears") in an otherwise
clear-headed and judicious book was one of my first clues that something
was still bubbling beneath the surface of the story; some other voice, to
use the spiritualistic idiom that Barnum invoked, was still waiting to be re-

leased from beneath the usual narratives of Barnum's "struggles and triumphs" as an entertainer. Barnum's pronouncement about the eternal
mystery of the "dark subject" seemed to close off for future investigators
not only the central question of her identity but the possibility that her life
and death could mean something radically different from what Barnum
wanted them to mean. Finally, it seems to have closed off an investigation
into Heth's own subjective experience of the exhibit. It has proved impossible to recover this with any degree of certainty, but I submit that the attempt to do so will suggest how Barnum's early career, so important in
shaping the commercial culture we still inhabit, itself took shape out of a
dynamic relationship between a few particular white men (Lindsay,
Lyman, Bennett, Locke, and Rogers as well as Barnum), thousands
of (mainly white) readers and visitors, and a particular black woman, each
of whom responded very differently to the politics of race, the culture of
slavery, the history of the country, and the possibilities for public self-
expression.

III
LIFE

A SPECULATIVE
BIOGRAPHY

"Who the devil's old aunt Joyce?" asks Barnaby Diddleum of his acquaintance in Paris, Kentucky. After two years of thinking about her public role, I had the same question, and have been to Paris, Kentucky—as well as Frankfort, Louisville, Lexington, Clarksville, Washington, D.C., Mount Vernon, Salt Lake City, and various sites in cyberspace—to see if I could find the answer. Along the way, I hit many of the snags that routinely confront even professional genealogists, including missing legal documents, bad or smudged handwriting, and promising leads that turn into monumental digressions. My task was made more difficult yet by something that virtually every African American who has tried to trace a family history knows: that the standard genealogical archives (composed of things like birth certificates, marriage licenses, court records, land deeds, and wills) have little to say about the lives of slaves. The best one can hope for in many cases is the mention of a Betsy, a Tom, or a Joice in some white person's diary, or listed alongside furniture, cows, and lots of land in the valuation of some white person's property.

What I was looking for was not exactly Joice Heth herself, as if some archival record could animate her bones, or even point to their location. I could not hope to find that elusive "truth" that eluded so many doctors, editors, readers, and visitors during Heth's own last days of life and first days of death. What I wanted, and what I found, was the only type of connection to past lives we have anyway: a story, one that fills a gap in other

stories whose veracity is commonly agreed upon. The shape of such stories, contemporary critics have taught us, is always determined as much by
the subjective view of the historian as by some irrefutable essence of the
people and events that are sought. The private Joice Heth's peculiar inaccessibility was, in this sense, an extreme version of the inaccessibility of
anything that is gone, anything that can be connected to us only by frayed
documents, oral histories, totemic objects, and our own longing. In much
the same way that Heth became a site of memory—or of longing for memory—for her visitors, she became for me a marker of the pastness of the
past. My time in the archives did finally yield a story that gave shape to her
life before Barnum, but then I also got a lucky break, perhaps even a
smoking gun, with a name on a page that unlocked a swirl of compatible
narratives. My only doubts came from a patch of bad handwriting and the
distorting force of my own desire for certainty.

It is important to remember in trying to picture Joice Heth that despite all
the deliberate falsifications and distortions, a real person was being exhibited, and that some fragmentary accounts of her presence—some of those
bits of distorted glass—must have given a clearer picture than others.
What I started with were the documents surrounding the exhibit itself that
Barnum and Lyman made public in one form or another, and those that
Barnumologists have gathered over the years. Some of these are manifestly bogus (Lyman's pamphlet biography of Heth) and some (the bill of
sale from Lindsay to Barnum) appear authentic (see Figure 1 above). But
my assumption—here as with every aspect of this study—was that none
could be trusted absolutely, and none could be distrusted absolutely.
Carlo Ginzburg notes that "the fact that a source is not 'objective' . . . does
not mean that it is useless."[1] Every document, he shows, is evidence of
something; the trick is to understand what it is evidence *of.*[2] The Joice
Heth display and its associated fictions were compelling, after all, because
of their fantastical transmutation of elements of the factual and the facti-
tious into an absorbing fiction that itself had an aura of authenticity. This
was done, in part, by hewing to as many verifiable truths as possible, so
that audience members would have trouble knowing where to direct their
skepticism: every lie contained a truth, and every explanation deepened
the mystery. The first task, then, was to grind those fictions down into

their component parts, and to try to weigh the promising bits against external sources not involved in the construction of Heth's public persona. And then there were the documents that did not emanate from the exhibitors themselves: some of the newspaper accounts, the diaries and memoirs of visitors. Surely this record can tell us something about Heth as well as about those who put her on display or came to visit.

The story told in the documents that accompanied the traveling Heth exhibit is that after Heth had been captured from Madagascar at the age of fifteen in 1689, she was "imported to America, and sold as a slave to Thomas Buckner, an extensive planter of Virginia." After several years, the story goes, she became the property of Augustine Washington, who would in 1732 become the father of "little Georgy, as she now calls him." She then married Peter, a slave of Mrs. Elizabeth Atwood, who was a sister-in-law of Augustine Washington. Heth bore this Peter fifteen children and was eventually sold for thirty-three pounds to Mrs. Atwood, for whom she became a trusted nurse and kitchen slave. When Mrs. Atwood died, the estate was said to have fallen into the hands of the Bowling (or Boling or Bolen) family, in whose service Joice Heth remained until her engagement with R. W. Lindsay.[3]

Checking the claims of this narrative against the public record, I have been able to establish that Lindsay really did acquire the right to exhibit Heth from a man named John S. Bowling, who passed through the actual town of Paris, Kentucky, for at least long enough to get married, but who was apparently based in Louisville and Cincinnati.[4] Who this Bowling was and what sort of lives any of his slaves may have led remains obscure—there were apparently thirty or forty John Bowlings running around the country at the time, and this one seems to have been running more than most. He may well have been an itinerant salesman or showman who exhibited his slave—with an act that already seems well established by early 1835—in taverns and public houses in frontier Kentucky. It would make sense for Heth to have come from this area. Lexington had a strong African American Baptist community, led since 1801 by Peter "Brother Captain" Durrett, a slave whose master looked on his religious leanings favorably. Durrett proselytized widely among both slaves and free blacks in surrounding areas, and by 1823 the First Baptist Church of Coloured Persons had more than three hundred members.[5]

If we work backward in the narrative, however, the story breaks down at the point of transfer from "Mrs. Atwood" to Bowling. Many of the Bowlings did have significant contact with the Washington family, but as far as I can tell, no Bowling ever came into possession of properties from an Atwood estate.[6] Another problem with the story is that it does not account for Joice Heth's last name, which is spelled the same way in every document going back to the scrawled contract between Bowling and Lindsay, in which they agree "to equally participate in the gains and losses in exhibiting the African woman Joice Heth in and amongst the cities of the United States." In the line from Buckner to Washington to Atwood to Bowling, where would "Heth" have come from?

Interestingly, there was a prominent Heth family in the Louisville area at the time, one with substantial ties to both the Washington *and* the Bowling families. Andrew Heth was a Revolutionary War captain, who, after the war, received a land grant of four hundred acres in Clarksville in the territory that would become Indiana, just across the river from Louisville, Kentucky, where he kept his main residence. His brother William and his father, Henry, were both founding members of the Society of the Cincinnati, an organization of Revolutionary War officers and their male descendants, whose first president was George Washington. Andrew Heth's land grant is a testament to the strength of the family connection to circles of power in the new nation, as is the fact that, after the war, President Washington appointed William collector of the ports of Richmond, Petersburg, and Bermuda. William was proud—perhaps a bit too proud— of this association with Washington, as a copy of his diary (held in the Library of Congress's Special Collections) attests. A high point of his life seems to have been a private visit to Mount Vernon on February 21, 1788:

> I was fortunate enough to find the general without any other company than Colo. Humphreys who has been here some months. Dined & Spent an agreeable day; find that the General is very anxious to see the proposed Federal Constitution adopted by all the states . . .
>
> Friday, 22d February. Took my leave of the Gen'l (and family after breakfast) who sent with me a servant & pr. Horses. Maj'r Geo. Washington was polite enough to accompany me two or three miles.[7]

Once he had received his commission—which left him plenty of time to indulge in his favorite activity of theatergoing—he continued to record his visits with Washington. The diary is, among other things, the record of a growing sycophancy. The following are typical entries from a three-week period in March 1788: "Went to the play yesterday evening in company with the President & two or three other Members of Congress . . . Spent a few minutes with the President in the evening & ret. with him to my lodgings, where he let me down— . . . A fine day—walked out after breakfast, visited the President . . . Dined at the President's with 8 or 10 gentlemen . . . Find myself somewhat indisposed with gripings [?]—dined in a family way with the President—but very abstemiously—no Company . . . A pleasant day—walked a good deal in the forenoon—Dined at the President's with a small Company—indulged myself a little more."

When Thomas Jefferson was elected to the presidency in 1801, many of the old families of Virginia who had parlayed their connections into land grants, petty administrative fiefdoms in the new federal government, and other perquisites saw a reversal of fortunes. William Heth, who was always fond of a good joke, let his resentment of the new, less aristocratic order get in the way of his official duties. As the son of one of William's "comrades-in-arms" later wrote, "the election of Jefferson to the Presidency betrayed the impulsive veteran into some asperities of speech and the perpetration of a rhyming pasquinade [a lampoon posted in a public space], in which he dealt very freely with some alleged frailties of the President."[8] The result was the loss of his post. William Heth died a few years later of apoplexy.

My proposal is that Joice Heth was the property of this William through at least the early 1790s and made her way to the Louisville area with his brother Andrew (who raised tobacco on his nearby plantation). At some point after Andrew died in 1803—when she would have been approximately fifty, if Rogers's autopsy report is to be believed—she became the property of John S. Bowling. William's estate contained many slaves,[9] and although the name "Joice" does not appear in the wills or property records of any members of the Heth family, few slaves' names do appear. Furthermore, family members did loan one another slaves on occasion, and for William to send Andrew a slave to help with the homestead in Kentucky was not without precedent.[10] Finally, although Heth and Bowling were common names in this period, I found it striking that one of the few family friends mentioned by name consistently in William's diary is that of a man named "Bolling"—sometimes spelled "Bowling"—who visited the Heths' plantation frequently.

And then there is the smoking gun: William's description of one visit from the Bollings/Bowlings to his plantation home. On March 2, 1793, as William's wife lay ill during a pregnancy, he recorded an incident that hints at the presence of a woman who was trusted with intimate details of the family of a man who obsessively measured his worth by the strength of his connection to George Washington. And that woman's name, it turns out, was "Joice." Or perhaps I had been reading too long. Here is how I read the relevant passage (see Figure 12):

> Eliza taken ill abt. 10 of last night—threatened with a miscarriage in consequence of neglecting in spite of every advice, to be bled.

The next sentence is the one apparently containing the word "Joice," but either the syntax or the handwriting becomes maddeningly opaque at the crucial moment. Writing on the bottom of a crammed page below a somewhat sloping line, William uncharacteristically compressed his letters. My initial reading was

> I wish our Joice . . .

but it could have been

> I wish our I did . . .

neither of which makes perfect sense either internally or with the rest of the sentence as it continues on the next page:

> that none, but a more skillful Surgeon, could perform the operation. Yet, her father was now, as her case was critical, obliged to do it—with difficulty we took away [illegible]—and this fore noon I went down and brought up Doctor L——[illegible name] who did nothing more than approve of what had been done, and advised great temperance in eating & not to put her feet out of bed for three or four days, & to give her from 35 to 50 drops of [illegible] tonight. Found on our Return [name illegible] Bowling Lady & daughter to dine [illegible] that night . . .

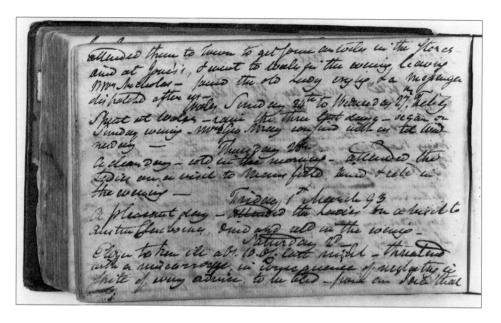

12. The diary of William Heth, Saturday, March 2, 1793, appears to refer to the presence of someone named "Joice" at the miscarriage of his wife, Eliza. The penultimate word may be "Joice," although the tail of the "J" is uncharacteristically squashed.

This is the writing of a man in a state of emotional and physical exhaustion, so perhaps it shouldn't all parse. Is he saying that he wished for a more skillful surgeon than "Joice" to attend his wife's threatened miscarriage and had to settle for Eliza's father? This is the most plausible reading that either I or the manuscripts specialist at the Library of Congress could work out, and certainly superior to anything that could come of: "I wish our I did that none, but a more skillful Surgeon . . ."

Having spent weeks in cheap motels across Kentucky and Virginia (and even Utah, where I scoured the Church of Latter Day Saints' remarkable genealogical archives for records of the Heths, Bowlings, Lindsays, and others), having pored over scores of court records, old newspapers, and diaries in vain, and having nearly run out of time and grant money, I liked the first, admittedly slightly forced reading for the period it would put on my research, for the sense it offered me of having outwitted Barnum and Lyman and Lindsay and Bowling and maybe Heth herself in finally getting to the bottom of the story, and for the dramatic picture of Heth that it enables: one that posits her—and not some enterprising master—as the originator of the Washington's nurse hoax. In this picture, there is a well-to-do master, made somewhat foolish by his incessant bootlicking of the war hero and new president. This master is an enthusiast of theatrical entertainments and other amusements, commenting favorably at one point in his diary on "the performances of a Negro man & small white boy" whose "feats of balancing & c . . . are equal to any thing within the powers of strength & activity";[11] he might therefore encourage or at least indulge the occasional wry comment from a histrionic slave who has earned the family's trust. And such a slave, in this picture, lived close enough to this man to have been mentioned as a possible "surgeon" during a most intimate family crisis. A midwife? A sick nurse? A wet nurse? Could an enslaved woman whose life was so intertwined with that of such a master *not* have heard his undoubtedly pompous and by now ridiculous stories of fighting with, strategizing with, dining with, riding with, walking with the man whom whites already referred to as their mythical "father"? And so hearing, could she not have laughed? Assume this woman to have been in her forties or fifties at the time of the diary entry. Could she have assumed, forty-two years later, the form of the wizened, emaciated, paralytic, blind, toothless old woman who so captivated (and occasionally disgusted or saddened) audiences? Could the career of the greatest entertainer of the nineteenth century have originated with a slave's subtle mockery of her master?

The story fits not only with what is known about the cultural dynamics of slavery but with the larger rhythms of American popular culture. In Ann Douglas's words: "Blacks imitating and fooling whites, whites imitating and stealing from blacks, blacks reappropriating and transforming what has been stolen, whites making yet another foray on black styles, and on and on: this *is* American popular culture."[12] The Heth story, then, could be one of the first such acts in a long line stretching through minstrelsy to Elvis, white rappers, and beyond. In my somewhat wishful reading of the diary, Barnum's career begins as an unwitting appropriation of the routine that developed from Joice's one-upping of William Heth, a self-informing flunky of George Washington. At its origin, perhaps there were two performances on the plantation. One would have been for the amusement of the master, or perhaps his family, in which Joice trumped all of William's stories by claiming not simply to have dined with Washington but to have diapered him. And another, behind closed doors or in the slaves' quarters, in which she elaborated this story until it became a full-throttled satire, her own performed "pasquinade" of her over-proud master. This accords with the outlines of the African American practice of "Signifyin(g)" as outlined by Henry Louis Gates, Jr. According to Gates, this African-derived process of "repetition and revision" of a commonly told story became under American slavery a potent tool for the creation of a semiautonomous black culture. Often under the noses of the masters, slaves "created unique vernacular structures and reveled in the double play that these forms bore to white forms."[13]

Such "Signifyin(g)" or double-voiced storytelling often involved revising stories about major historical figures and incidents. In his story "The Heroic Slave," for instance, Frederick Douglass invokes the story of the American Revolution in narrating a slave-ship revolt, appropriately led by a black man named Madison Washington.[14] Less somberly, slaves on the field or at a dance often poked fun at white politicians and historical figures. As one slave ditty went: "Polk and Clay went to war, / Polk came back with a broken jaw."[15] And one South Carolina planter recorded in his diary that slaves who were "of the country born could tell the wonderful stories of the old war—of the 'red coats' whom they had seen (when the State was overrun by British troops), of the hair-breadth escapes of old master from the British . . . With these and like marvelous stories they fed my childish credulity, and impressed me with a respect and veneration for their stately forms which I yet retain."[16] It is easy to imagine those same slaves repeating the stories of Washington and the redcoats in a somewhat less "stately" tone out of the earshot of the young master, and easy to imagine that the "inveterate antipathy" of Joice toward redcoats that struck one observer as so amusing originated as a plantation tale for either white children, for other slaves, or—with different inflections—for both.

Moreover, although Joice Heth's Washington's-nurse routine struck northern observers as altogether singular, it was not a particularly original role for an elderly early nineteenth-century slave to play. Joice Heth, it seems, was not the only African American during this period to trade on flimsy or spurious connections to Washington. An 1841 visitor to Mount

Vernon wrote of meeting a "black gardner . . . a good-natured, happy-looking negro, full of pompous pride, and grotesque vanity." Inquiring into his history, she found that he was born a slave of Washington, "and though his remembrance of the great man was very imperfect, to have *seen* Washington, seemed to have ennobled him in his own estimation, as it certainly did in ours."[17] Several other former slaves of Washington played cannily on white visitors' nostalgia for the Father of the Nation—and particularly his childhood. Sambo Anderson, a former house servant, told a visitor around the same time that one of his duties was "to keep his master's hatchet in good order . . . I don't know whether it was the same little hatchet that the General used in hacking his father's cherry tree with, as Sambo did not inform me."[18] This man, like Heth, was apparently familiar with the Mason Weems legend about the cherry tree, and signified on the story in order to make himself an actor in it, doing a sort of whiteface minstrelsy to promote himself above any position an ordinary black man could otherwise hold in his society or in the mythic history of the nation. As the nineteenth century drew on, several other elderly African Americans posed cleverly as "living relics" of the Washington family. Some of the connections were authentic, but one man, Richard Stanup (or Stanhope), concocted a fabulous tale that made him a local hero in southern Ohio. His story was that he had been Washington's chief of servants in Mount Vernon, and became his personal valet during the Revolutionary War, where he was slashed in the face by a British saber. He further claimed that he was present at the time of Washington's death, and that the likeness of a tall black man standing at the foot of Washington's deathbed in a well-known painting was his own. Researchers at the Mount Vernon Ladies' Association of the Union have concluded that he made up the story; but a testament to its success lies in the fact that the Urbana, Ohio, chapter of the Daughters of the American Revolution erected a plaque in his memory when he died. The plaque still stands.[19]

In looking for the "private" Joice Heth, I find that I have simply reenvisioned yet another "public" Heth—but with a different audience, a different set of performing conditions, and a different stock of materials to work from. Her act may have registered profoundly with the northern worlds of itinerant entertainers and oddities, journalists and barkers, scientists and clergy, refined men and women of leisure and boisterous work-

ing classes, but in this picture, it takes shape in relation to the cultural dynamics of the plantation. Paul Gilroy has noted that slaves were often
granted a certain amount of expressive license within the cultural field as a
substitute for the political freedoms they were denied on the plantation.[20]
Heth's act may have taken shape as just such a "safety valve"—an allow-
able trespass against hierarchy that was safely contained within the storytelling frame. Speaking to her masters and behind their backs, she deflects
the beams of mythical history that fall on her masters, and styles herself, in
hilarious but essentially harmless fashion, "Lady Washington." I imagine
that this routine, once it was viewed by enough whites, paradoxically
stoked her master's sense of worthiness: in allowing himself publicly to
take a "hit" from a slave, he was demonstrating his own psychological security, the fact that he could take it. From there the idea of expansion and
capitalization sets in. Perhaps on Washington's birthday—celebrated boisterously around the South shortly after Washington's death—William
Heth, his Kentucky brother Andrew, or a subsequent master exhibits her
for money or drink at a local tavern, while outside, in the streets of, say,
Louisville, there is the sound of "musketry and our artillery accompanied
by a fine choice of martial . . . stamping and prancing thro' the streets with
stiff legs and high heads equipped and dressed as much like butterflies."[21]
As in the North, her performance is a blend of the private and the public,
the ordinary and the exceptional, the invented and the real—but all of
these terms have different, and local, meanings within their original context. Hers is the intimate story of the private origins of the South's (and
the nation's) most public man, told to an admiring or at least amused public by a woman who had navigated the private spaces of her master's inner
life and the concealed byways of a transplanted African culture of storytelling and Signifyin(g).

But what could Heth have been thinking, years later, as she faced her
new public, who gazed at her with such a different type of interest—this
public of white people who held no slaves and yet were so reluctant to be
seen in the company of blacks? What passed through her mind as they approached to shake hands, their palms made sweaty from the palpitations
of disgust and excitement? And how did she react as they peered, pried,
asked, sang, laughed, offered food, filled her pipe, checked her pulse, inquired into her bowel movements, prayed, sneered, and scribbled notes?

To survive such an ordeal with even a shred of dignity, without publicly breaking down or acting out, one would need an extraordinarily thick wall separating oneself from one's own subjection, a wall that I imagine might have been provided by dementia. After performing her role so long and so steadily for white people, it seems to me that Heth—clearly infirm and sometimes disoriented (with no knowledge of the identity of Andrew Jackson or, apparently, the heights to which her former master "Georgy" had risen)—must actually have come to believe the story herself, or at least partially. One of the only visitors on record who seems to have asked himself what Heth thought of her display reached the same conclusion. This was a Presbyterian clergyman who recorded his thoughts about "Washington's nurse" many years later, as a metaphor for how one can come to believe in a false creed:

> I saw the old woman, and I saw *the documents* by which her pretensions were verified; thousands saw and also believed. In fact, the poor old creature had heard the story so long, and told it so often herself, and had heard so much about *the documents,* that she verily believed that she was a hundred and sixty years old, and had been the veritable nurse of General Washington![22]

In support of this suggestion, there is no record of her having dropped out of role, and she seems to have repeated elements of the story in a sincere and sometimes indignant way that suggests a realm of identification beyond conscious role-playing. A Heth who believed would be a shell of some former Heth, one whose dreams had been shattered and who retreated utterly into an identity-effacing delusion.

This loss of identity would, in an ironic way, complete the work of social- and self-alienation already done by slavery, which Orlando Patterson defines as a state of "social death." Slaves, he writes, are "not allowed freely to integrate the experience of their ancestors into their lives, to inform their understanding of social reality with the inherited meanings of their natural forebears, or to anchor the living present in any conscious community of memory."[23] Could Heth's "real" community—comprising a mother and a father, a family of her own, a name and identity anchored in a social reality that accounted for her unique human identity—have been any more available to her than the one she invented and seems so thoroughly to have inhabited? No matter where Heth's act came from, it was a public erasure of herself and a subordination of her new, fabricated self to the memory of a white man. Clearly some mixture of the volitional and the compelled, perhaps also a combination of the consciously invented and the delusional, her self-negation—by an odd twist of historical circumstance—became transformed into that which gave her an identity, a commodity of which she had been robbed by slavery. To suggest this interpretation may seem once again to convert Heth's troubling and uncanny performance into a medical condition, to disempower her in just the way that Barnum and the editors did. I think, though, that given the circumstances Heth faced, a retreat into delusion may well have been the most rational choice available: what advantages did reality offer?

And even in delusion there is some shaping force, some motivation for the performance, some self beyond the self who is longing for a reward: for stability, for love, for wholeness. After searching for the elusive facts held out by genealogy and orthography, after reviewing the hundreds of pages written about Heth in Barnum's memoirs and in the pages of newspapers, magazines, and journals, I find only one clue for the shape of this motivational force—and that, fittingly, comes from the most dubious source. In the version of the events of 1835 as narrated in *The Autobiography of Petite Bunkum* (the 1855 mock autobiography of Barnum that may or may not have been written by the showman himself, in which the drunken old woman brains her master with a crutch), Bunkum is conversing with Judy Heath's master, who informs him that his slave "has taken a fancy to die in the free states. She appears to believe that if she dies a slave, she can not go to heaven."

If this sentiment is in any way attributable to Heth, it suggests a woman who had clearly observed much of white Americans' longing for connection with the glorious figures of the past, and who found in their longing a bridge that might take her out of that past and into a better place. Scholars of slave culture have written that slaves' sense of time differed from that of whites; the West African conception of time from which it was derived is "two-dimensional," focusing on "present and past, not future." Additionally, slave spirituality often featured a conception of heaven and hell not as "concepts but as places that could be experienced during one's lifetime."[24] In becoming the nurse of George Washington, Heth found, somehow, an expressive mode that spoke both to her audiences' sense of the glorious past as slipping perilously away and a slave's sense of the possibilities of finding the future in the here and now. In seeking the "free states," she imagined an intermediate terrain between the bondage of the South and the absolute freedom of heaven, between the burdens of the past and a future that might materialize in a hazily pictured third dimension—an abstraction that might be reached through some combination of travel, spirituality, delusion, and imagination. She got her wish, but in the deathly embrace of the northern public, she found a captivity that was perhaps even more cruel than the one she had left behind.

NOTES / INDEX

NOTES

INTRODUCTION

1. Edward H. Dixon, M.D., "Barnum and Joice Heth," *The Scalpel: A Journal of Health, Adapted to Popular and Professional Reading, and the Exposure of Quackery* 9 (November 1850): 58–59.

2. "Longevity," *New York Baptist,* repr. *Springfield Gazette,* September 16, 1835.

3. This claim is made by, among others, Leo Braudy, in *The Frenzy of Renown: Fame and Its History* (New York: Oxford University Press, 1986), 500.

4. This is the conclusion of Carl Bode, in his introduction to P. T. Barnum, *Struggles and Triumphs, or, Forty Years' Recollections of P. T. Barnum,* ed. Carl Bode (New York: Penguin Books, 1981), 23.

5. P. T. Barnum, "The Adventures of an Adventurer, Being Some Passages in the Life of Barnaby Diddleum," *New York Atlas.* "Adventures" was serialized weekly or biweekly beginning April 11, 1841, through at least June of that year—the precise ending date is unknown because no issues of the *Atlas* from June through August 7 have survived.

6. P. T. Barnum, *Struggles and Triumphs, or, Forty Years' Recollections of P. T. Barnum* (Buffalo: Warren, Johnson & Co., 1873), 73, 76. *Struggles* was initially published in 1869, but Barnum regularly updated it over the next two decades. The chapter on Joice Heth, however, remained unchanged after the 1869 printing. The best source on Barnum's publishing history is Bluford Adams, *E Pluribus Barnum: The Great Showman and the Making of U.S. Popular Culture* (Minneapolis: University of Minnesota Press, 1997), 1–40.

7. Carlo Ginzburg, "Checking the Evidence: The Judge and the Historian," in *Questions of Evidence: Proof, Practice, and Persuasion across the Disciplines,* ed.

James Chandler, Arnold I. Davidson, and Harry Harootunian (Chicago: University of Chicago Press, 1994), 295.

8. Ginzburg gives a brilliant account of how to read historical documents for signs of competing social interests in "The Inquisitor as Anthropologist," in *Clues, Myths, and the Historical Method,* trans. John and Anne C. Tedeschi (Baltimore: Johns Hopkins University Press, 1989), 156–164. In a wider sense, my understanding of culture as a field of socially contested meanings is derived largely from the Birmingham school of cultural studies, especially Stuart Hall, "Notes on Deconstructing 'The Popular,'" in *People's History and Socialist Theory,* ed. Raphael Samuel (London: Routledge and Kegan Paul, 1981), 227–240, and "Encoding, Decoding," in *The Cultural Studies Reader,* ed. Simon During (London: Routledge, 1993), 90–103. For its attention to the symbolism of the human body in social struggle, Peter Stallybrass and Allon White's *Politics and Poetics of Transgression* (Ithaca, N.Y.: Cornell University Press, 1986) has also proved enormously suggestive. At a more local level, my conception of the interpenetration of antebellum popular and political realms owes much to Eric Lott, *Love and Theft: Blackface Minstrelsy and the American Working Class* (New York: Oxford University Press, 1993); David R. Roediger, *The Wages of Whiteness: Race and the Making of the American Working Class* (London: Verso, 1991); Alexander Saxton, *The Rise and Fall of the White Republic: Class Politics and Mass Culture in Nineteenth-Century America* (London: Verso, 1990); and Susan G. Davis, *Parades and Power: Street Theatre in Nineteenth-Century Philadelphia* (Philadelphia: Temple University Press, 1986). Adams's *E Pluribus Barnum* offered me a powerful model for understanding Barnum's career in relation to wider cultural formations, as well as much information and several leads.

9. Lorraine Daston and Katharine Park, *Wonders and the Order of Nature, 1150–1750* (New York: Zone Books, 1998), 20.

10. David Grimsted, *American Mobbing, 1828–1861: Toward Civil War* (New York: Oxford University Press, 1998), 4. This figure depends, admittedly, on Grimsted's rather capacious definition of a "mob" as an incident in which "six or more people band together to enforce their will publicly by threatening or perpetrating physical injury to persons or property extralegally, ostensibly to correct problems or injustices within their society without challenging its basic structures" (xii). On antebellum mobs, see also Leonard L. Richards, *"Gentlemen of Property and Standing": Anti-Abolition Mobs in Jacksonian America* (New York: Oxford University Press, 1970).

11. Grimsted, *American Mobbing, 1828–1861,* 1–32; Winthrop Jordan, *White over Black: American Attitudes toward the Negro, 1550–1812* (Chapel Hill: University of North Carolina Press, 1968), 331, 342–374.

12. Leon F. Litwack, *North of Slavery: The Negro in the Free States, 1790–1860* (Chicago: University of Chicago Press, 1961), 97.

13. Quoted in James Oliver Horton and Lois E. Horton, *In Hope of Liberty: Culture, Community, and Protest among Northern Free Blacks, 1700–1860* (New York: Oxford University Press, 1997), 243.

14. David Grimsted, *Melodrama Unveiled: American Theater and Culture, 1800–1850* (Chicago: University of Chicago Press, 1968). On the connections between riots and the contest over the meaning of the Revolution, see Alfred F. Young, *The Shoemaker and the Tea Party: Memory and the American Revolution* (Boston: Beacon Press, 1999); Davis, *Parades and Power;* and Chapter 3.

15. Jordan, *White over Black,* 269–311, 483–541; Reginald Horsman, *Race and Manifest Destiny: The Origins of American Racial Anglo-Saxonism* (Cambridge, Mass.: Harvard University Press, 1981), 98–115.

16. See Roediger, *Wages of Whiteness;* Horsman, *Race and Manifest Destiny;* Saxton, *Rise and Fall of the White Republic;* and Horton and Horton, *In Hope of Liberty,* 167–176.

17. See Horsman, *Race and Manifest Destiny,* 116–138; Stephen J. Gould, *The Mismeasure of Man* (New York: W. W. Norton, 1981), 30–72; Sander L. Gilman, *Difference and Pathology: Stereotypes of Sexuality, Race, and Madness* (Ithaca, N.Y.: Cornell University Press, 1985); and William Ragan Stanton, *The Leopard's Spots: Scientific Attitudes toward Race in America, 1815–1859* (Chicago: University of Chicago Press, 1960). On the development of racial science in the mid-nineteenth century, see George M. Fredrickson, *The Black Image in the White Mind: The Debate on Afro-American Character and Destiny, 1817–1914* (New York: Harper & Row, 1971), 71–96. See also James Brewer Stewart, "The Emergence of Racial Modernity and the Rise of the White North, 1790–1840," *Journal of the Early Republic* 18 (Spring 1998): 181–217.

18. See Lott, *Love and Theft;* Saxton, *Rise and Fall of the White Republic;* and Michael Denning, *Mechanic Accents: Dime Novels and Working-Class Culture in America* (London: Verso, 1987).

1. POSSESSION

1. P. T. Barnum, *The Life of P. T. Barnum, Written by Himself* (New York: Redfield, 1854), 91.

2. A. H. Saxon, *P. T. Barnum: The Legend and the Man* (New York: Columbia University Press, 1989), 34.

3. Quoted in Bluford Adams, *E Pluribus Barnum: The Great Showman and the Making of U.S. Popular Culture* (Minneapolis: University of Minnesota Press, 1997), 24.

4. Peter Benes, "Itinerant Entertainers in New England and New York, 1687–1830," in *Itinerancy in New England and New York: The Dublin Seminar for New England Folklife Annual Proceedings* (Boston University, 1984), 113.

5. Barnum, *Life of P. T. Barnum,* 98.

6. Saxon, *P. T. Barnum*, 37–38. The story of Barnum's secret marriage to Fish is told in Philip W. Kunhardt, Jr., Philip B. Kunhardt III, and Peter B. Kunhardt, *P. T. Barnum: America's Greatest Showman* (New York: Alfred A. Knopf, 1995), 237–239.

7. Barnum, *Life of P. T. Barnum*, 138; Saxon, *P. T. Barnum*, 41–43.

8. Fisk would go on to deliver an address called "Capital against Labor" to unruly workers petitioning for a reduction in their work weeks in Boston in 1835. See Alfred F. Young, *The Shoemaker and the Tea Party: Memory and the American Revolution* (Boston: Beacon Press, 1999), 149–150.

9. Quoted in Irving Wallace, *The Fabulous Showman: The Life and Times of P. T. Barnum* (New York: Alfred A. Knopf, 1959), 46.

10. Barnum, *Life of P. T. Barnum*, 140.

11. Leon F. Litwack, *North of Slavery: The Negro in the Free States, 1790–1860* (Chicago: University of Chicago Press, 1961), 94–95.

12. *The Record of Crimes in the United States* (1833), cited in David S. Reynolds, *Beneath the American Renaissance: The Subversive Imagination in the Age of Emerson and Melville* (Cambridge, Mass.: Harvard University Press, 1988), 263.

13. On the public executions of blacks, see Shane White, "The Death of James Johnson," *American Quarterly* 51, no. 4 (December 1999): 753–795. On public executions as street theater, see Susan G. Davis, *Parades and Power: Street Theatre in Nineteenth-Century Philadelphia* (Philadelphia: Temple University Press, 1986), 27, 32, 74, 76, and Peter Burke, *Popular Culture in Early Modern Europe* (Hants, England: Wildwood House, 1978, repr. 1988), 196–197. On penal reform see David J. Rothman, *The Discovery of the Asylum: Social Order and Disorder in the New Republic* (Boston: Little, Brown, 1971); and Michel Foucault, *Discipline and Punish: The Birth of the Prison*, trans. Alan Sheridan (New York: Vintage Books, 1979).

14. Saxon, *P. T. Barnum*, 32.

15. Isabelle Lehuu, *Carnival on the Page: Popular Print Media in Antebellum America* (Chapel Hill: University of North Carolina Press, 2000), 56.

16. P. T. Barnum, *Struggles and Triumphs, or, Forty Years' Recollections of P. T. Barnum* (Buffalo: Warren, Johnson & Co., 1873), 71.

17. Hugh Lindsay, *History of the Life, Travels, and Incidents of Col. Hugh Lindsay* (Macungie, Pa.: O. P. Knauss, 1883), 46.

18. Ricky Jay, *Learned Pigs and Fireproof Women* (New York: Villard Books, 1986), 10.

19. James W. Cook, Jr., "From the Age of Reason to the Age of Barnum: The Great Automaton Chess-Player and the Emergence of Victorian Cultural Illusionism," *Winterthur Portfolio* 30, no. 4 (Winter 1995): 234. Vaucanson's automaton duck also makes an appearance as a character in Thomas Pynchon's novel *Mason and Dixon* (New York: Henry Holt, 1997). It is described as having "a

Digestionary Process, whose end result could not be distinguish'd from that found in Nature" (372). The elephant is mentioned in Reed Benhamou, "From *Curiosité* to *Utilité:* The Automaton in Eighteenth-Century France," *Studies in Eighteenth-Century Culture* 17 (1987): 91.

20. Barnum, *Life of P. T. Barnum,* 148–149.

21. John Brown, *Slave Life in Georgia: A Narrative of the Life, Sufferings, and Escape of John Brown,* ed. L. A. Chamerovzow (London: W. M. Watts, 1855), 112, 118.

22. Robert C. Toll succinctly sums up Barnum's influence on the minstrel show in *Blacking Up: The Minstrel Show in Nineteenth-Century America* (New York: Oxford University Press, 1974), 18–20.

23. Barnum, *Life of P. T. Barnum,* 148–150.

24. "A Chat with Barnum," *The Era,* July 29, 1877.

25. Saxon, *P. T. Barnum,* 73. Saxon writes of Barnum's post-1854 disclaimers that, having fashioned a reputation as "a shrewd Yankee 'humbug' . . . it would have done him little harm, and possibly even some good, had he chosen to continue the lie [of having invented Heth's identity] when he came to write the first edition of his autobiography." His protestations never to have known of Heth's identity constituted leaning "a little too far in the opposite direction," for was it plausible, Saxon writes, that Barnum "never once suspect[ed] the truth about Joice Heth during all those months he was exhibiting and . . . publicizing her?"

26. *Boston Evening Transcript,* July 6, 1835; *Hempstead Inquirer* (Hempstead, N.Y.), July 8, 1835.

27. The consensus among Barnum's biographers prior to Saxon in 1989 was that first Lindsay and then Barnum did own Heth, but Saxon argues that both men possessed only the "right to exhibit her." Saxon, *P. T. Barnum,* 21.

28. Barnum, *Life of P. T. Barnum,* 150; Barnum, *Struggles and Triumphs,* 75.

29. Rhoda Golden Freeman, *The Free Negro in New York City in the Era before the Civil War* (New York: Garland, 1994), 56.

30. The original of this document is in the Fred D. Pfening III Collection, Columbus, Ohio.

31. *New York Atlas,* April 20, 1845; quoted in Saxon, *P. T. Barnum,* 84.

32. "A Chat with Barnum."

33. Jefferson County (Kentucky) Records, July 1837.

34. Barnum, *The Life of P. T. Barnum,* 213.

35. P. T. Barnum to Mr. Baker, c. March 1853, quoted in *Selected Letters of P. T. Barnum,* ed. A. H. Saxon (New York: Columbia University Press, 1983), 8.

2. THE CELEBRATED CURIOSITY

1. Richardson Little Wright, *Hawkers and Walkers in Early America: Strolling Peddlers, Preachers, Lawyers, Doctors, Players, and Others, from the Beginning to*

the Civil War (Philadelphia: J. B. Lippincott, 1927), 184–190; Richard W. Flint, "Entrepreneurial and Cultural Aspects of the Early-Nineteenth-Century Circus and Menagerie Business," in *Itinerancy in New England and New York: The Dublin Seminar for New England Folklife Annual Proceedings,* ed. Peter Benes (Boston University, 1984), 131–149; Charles Colbert, *A Measure of Perfection: Phrenology and the Fine Arts in America* (Chapel Hill: University of North Carolina Press, 1997), 21.

2. Mary Kupiec Cayton, "The Making of an American Prophet: Emerson, His Audiences, and the Rise of the Culture Industry in Nineteenth-Century America," in *Ralph Waldo Emerson: A Collection of Critical Essays,* ed. Lawrence Buell (Englewood Cliffs, N.J.: Prentice-Hall, 1993), 87.

3. Peter Burke notes that in early modern culture, the "little tradition" of popular culture was available to the elite as well as to the disempowered, whereas the "great tradition" was not available to the lower orders. See Burke, *Popular Culture in Early Modern Europe* (Hants, England: Wildwood House, 1978, repr. 1988), 23–64.

4. Donald M. Scott, "Itinerant Lecturers and Lecturing in New England, 1800–1850," in *Itinerancy in New England and New York,* 65–75; Jay Fliegelman, *Declaring Independence: Jefferson, Natural Language, and the Culture of Performance* (Stanford, Calif.: Stanford University Press, 1993).

5. "The Joice Heth Hoax," *New York Herald,* September 24, 1836.

6. Lawrence W. Levine's argument that the Astor Place Riot of 1849 marked the emergence of a "highbrow/lowbrow" cultural fission can be taken as a rough template; the story of Barnum and Heth, though, shows that signs of an emerging cultural hierarchy were already in place. See Levine, *Highbrow/Lowbrow: The Emergence of Cultural Hierarchy in America* (Cambridge, Mass.: Harvard University Press, 1988). See also Chapter 5.

7. Thomas M. Garrett, "A History of Pleasure Gardens in New York City, 1700–1865" (Ph.D. diss., New York University, 1978), 389, 492; Abram C. Dayton, *The Last Days of Knickerbocker Life in New York* (New York: Knickerbocker Press, 1880, repr. 1896), 303; Harry Lines, "Niblo's Garden," *Marquee* 13, no. 3 (1981): 3.

8. Carroll Smith-Rosenberg, *Religion and the Rise of the American City: The New York City Mission Movement, 1812–1870* (Ithaca, N.Y.: Cornell University Press, 1971), 30.

9. Peter George Buckley, "To the Opera House: Culture and Society in New York City, 1820–1860" (Ph.D. diss., State University of New York at Stony Brook, 1984), 145.

10. See Rosemarie K. Bank, "Hustlers in the House: The Bowery Theatre as a Mode of Historical Information," in *The American Stage: Social and Economic Issues from the Colonial Period to the Present,* ed. Ron Engle and Tice L. Miller (Cambridge: Cambridge University Press, 1993), 47–64.

11. P. T. Barnum, "The Adventures of an Adventurer, Being Some Passages in the Life of Barnaby Diddleum," *New York Atlas*, May 16, 1841.

12. George W. Foster, *New York by Gas-Light, and Other Urban Sketches*, ed. Stuart M. Blumin (Berkeley: University of California Press, 1990), 156–157.

13. *U.S. Gazette* (Philadelphia), July 22, 1835.

14. *New York Evening Star*, August 7, 1835.

15. Barnum, "Adventures of an Adventurer."

16. Barnum, *The Life of P. T. Barnum, Written by Himself* (New York: Redfield, 1854), 153.

17. Barnum, "Adventures of an Adventurer."

18. James L. Crouthamel, *Bennett's New York Herald and the Rise of the Popular Press* (Syracuse, N.Y.: Syracuse University Press, 1989), 43–44.

19. *The Diary of Philip Hone*, ed. Allan Nevins (New York: Dodd, Mead and Co., 1927), 195. On the penny press, see Andie Tucher, *Froth and Scum: Truth, Beauty, Goodness, and the Ax Murder in America's First Mass Medium* (Chapel Hill: University of North Carolina Press, 1994); Michael Schudson, *Discovering the News: A Social History of American Newspapers* (New York: Basic Books, 1978), 12–60; Frank M. O'Brien, *The Story of The Sun* (New York: D. Appleton and Co., 1928); and Alexander Saxton, *The Rise and Fall of the White Republic: Class Politics and Mass Culture in Nineteenth-Century America* (London: Verso, 1990), 95–108.

20. On the penny press's role in the history of antebellum publicity, see David M. Henkin, *City Reading: Written Words and Public Spaces in Antebellum New York* (New York: Columbia University Press, 1998), 101–135. Henkin also makes the connection between Barnum's use of handbills and advertisements and the broader development of a network of public reading in New York, 80–83.

21. See J. Paul Hunter, *Before Novels: The Cultural Contexts of Eighteenth-Century English Fiction* (New York: Norton, 1990), 197; Lorraine Daston and Katharine Park, *Wonders and the Order of Nature, 1150–1750* (New York: Zone Books, 1998), 191.

22. "The Joice Heth Hoax," *New York Herald*, September 24, 1836.

23. Quoted in Henkin, *City Reading*, 116.

24. Don C. Seitz, *The James Gordon Bennetts, Father and Son: Proprietors of the New York Herald* (Indianapolis: Bobbs-Merrill, 1928), 41.

25. Barnum, "Adventures of an Adventurer," May 16.

26. Barnum, *Life of P. T. Barnum*, 152.

27. *New York Sun*, August 21, 1835.

28. *Commercial Advertiser* (New York), repr. *Boston Evening Transcript*, August 15, 1835.

29. *New York Transcript*, August 22, 1835.

30. *New York Evening Star*, August 22, 1835.

31. "Joice Heth, Aged 161," *The Family Magazine, or, General Abstract of Useful Knowledge* 3 (1835): 155–157.

32. Rosemarie Garland Thomson, "Introduction: From Wonder to Error—A Genealogy of Freak Discourse in Modernity," in *Freakery: Cultural Spectacles of the Extraordinary Body*, ed. Rosemarie Garland Thomson (New York: New York University Press, 1996), 1–19; Rosemarie Garland Thomson, *Extraordinary Bodies: Figuring Physical Disability in American Culture and Literature* (New York: Columbia University Press, 1997), 56–80.

33. Daston and Park, *Wonders and the Order of Nature*, 173–214.

34. Robert Bogdan, *Freak Show: Presenting Human Oddities for Amusement and Profit* (Chicago: University of Chicago Press, 1988).

35. Wright, *Hawkers and Walkers*, 181.

36. Winthrop D. Jordan, *White over Black: American Attitudes toward the Negro, 1550–1812* (Chapel Hill: University of North Carolina Press, 1968), 418–423.

37. See Reginald Horsman, *Race and Manifest Destiny: The Origins of American Racial Anglo-Saxonism* (Cambridge, Mass.: Harvard University Press, 1981), esp. 116–138. See also James W. Cook, Jr., "Of Men, Missing Links, and Nondescripts: The Strange Career of P. T. Barnum's 'What Is It?' Exhibition," in Thomson, *Freakery*, 139–157. Cook sees the racial meanings of the "What Is It?" exhibit as open to different types of racism, including residual older models that still retained popular currency. Although this may be true, I believe that the very questioning of the exhibit's human status marks an abandonment of the egalitarian position dominant in the late eighteenth century.

38. *New York Evening Star*, August 22, 1835.

39. *New York Herald*, December 2, 1835.

40. Jordan, *White over Black*, 23, 387, 509–511, 514.

41. Quoted in Todd L. Savitt, *Medicine and Slavery: The Diseases and Health Care of Blacks in Antebellum Virginia* (Urbana: University of Illinois Press, 1978), 35–41.

42. Evelleen Richards, "The 'Moral Anatomy' of Robert Knox: The Interplay between Biological and Social Thought in Victorian Scientific Naturalism," *Journal of the History of Biology* 22 (1989): 393; Josiah C. Nott, "The Natural History of the Caucasian and Negro Races," in *The Ideology of Slavery: Pro-Slavery Thought in the Antebellum South, 1830–1860*, ed. Drew Gilpin Faust (Baton Rouge: Louisiana State University Press, 1981), 221.

43. *New York Evening Star*, September 20, 1835.

44. See Mary Poovey, "Figures of Arithmetic, Figures of Speech: The Discourse of Statistics in the 1830s," in *Questions of Evidence: Proof, Practice, and Persuasion across the Disciplines*, ed. James Chandler, Arnold I. Davidson, and Harry Harootunian (Chicago: University of Chicago Press, 1994), 401–421.

45. See John Galt, *Lawrie Todd* (London: R. Bentley, 1832). On Galt's use of Thorburn's life, see Elizabeth Mayer, ed., *Fanny Kemble: The American Journals* (London: Weidenfeld and Nicolson, 1990), 59–61.

46. Dayton, *Last Days,* 4.

47. Grant Thorburn, *Fifty Years' Reminiscences of New-York, or, Flowers from the Garden of Laurie Todd* (New York: Daniel Fanshaw, 1845), 145; *Life and Writings of Grant Thorburn* (New York: Edward Walker, 1852), 251; *American Magazine for Useful and Entertaining Knowledge* (July 1835): 496; *Boston Evening Transcript,* September 15, 1835.

48. Thomson, *Extraordinary Bodies,* 59.

49. Bogdan, *Freak Show,* chap. 4.

50. Mikhail Bakhtin, *Rabelais and His World,* trans. Hélène Iswolsky (Bloomington: Indiana University Press, 1984), 26.

51. Michael Holquist, "Prologue," in ibid., xiii–xxiii.

52. Ibid., 29.

53. Colbert, *A Measure of Perfection,* 3, 232–235.

54. O. S. and L. N. Fowler, *The Illustrated Self-Instructor in Phrenology and Physiology* (New York: Fowler and Wells, 1849), 26.

55. Barnum, *Life of P. T. Barnum,* 155.

56. Peter Stallybrass and Allon White, *The Politics and Poetics of Transgression* (Ithaca, N.Y.: Cornell University Press, 1986), 5, 58, 191–192.

3. Private Acts, Public Memories

1. "Joice Heth, Aged 161," *The Family Magazine, or, General Abstract of Useful Knowledge* 3 (1835): 155–157; "Joice Heth," *Providence Daily Journal,* August 30, 1835; *Sunday Morning News* (New York), December 6, 1836.

2. Captain Frederick Marryat, *Diary in America,* ed. Jules Zanger (Bloomington: Indiana University Press, 1960), 42.

3. "Joice Heth, Aged 161," 157.

4. John R. Gillis, "Introduction: Memory and Identity: The History of a Relationship," in *Commemorations: The Politics of National Identity,* ed. John R. Gillis (Princeton, N.J.: Princeton University Press, 1994), 3.

5. "Joice Heth, Aged 161," 156.

6. Jacques Le Goff, *History and Memory,* trans. Steven Rendall and Elizabeth Claman (New York: Columbia University Press, 1992), 3–4. The first quote is taken from Le Goff's citation of Fraisse. For a provocative but somewhat too sweeping critique of the recent wave of "memory studies," see Kerwin Klein, "On the Emergence of *Memory* in Historical Discourse," *Representations* 69 (Winter 2000): 127–150. Klein argues that the term "collective memory" has traditionally implied that racial, ethnic, or national groups have "natural" identities, and that

the vocabulary of "memory studies" functions as a "religious counterpart to historical discourse." Although his criticisms of individual studies are often persuasive, I see no reason to be suspicious—as Klein suggests we should be—of the critical enterprise of studying how groups make sense of the past in spiritual or ethnic rather than strictly historical terms. It is only the uncritical repetition of this practice by historians and critics that amounts to a problem.

7. The concept of "place in memory" is derived from Pierre Nora, "Between Memory and History: Les Lieux de Mémoire," trans. Marc Roudebush, *Representations* 26 (Spring 1989): 7–24.

8. Joseph Roach, *Cities of the Dead: Circum-Atlantic Performance* (New York: Columbia University Press, 1996), 36. At times I feel like an effigy myself, none more so than when I consider the fact that I am writing these lines in the very office at Tulane University that Joe Roach occupied when he wrote his book on memory, performance, race, and nation.

9. Gillis, "Introduction," 4.

10. *New York Herald,* November 25, 1835.

11. Walt Whitman, *I Sit and Look Out: Editorials from the Brooklyn Daily Times,* ed. Emory Holloway and Vernolian Schwarz (New York: Columbia University Press, 1932), 59.

12. Harriet Beecher Stowe, *Uncle Tom's Cabin, or, Life among the Lowly* (New York: Penguin Books, 1981), 68.

13. James Fenimore Cooper, *The Pioneers, or, The Sources of the Susquehanna* (New York: New American Library, 1980), 82.

14. Benedict Anderson, "Replica, Aura, and Late Nationalist Imaginings," *Qui Parle* 7, no. 1 (Fall 1993): 1–21. See also Anderson, *Imagined Communities: Reflections on the Origin and Spread of Nationalism* (London: Verso, 1983), esp. chap. 6.

15. Michael Kammen, *Mystic Chords of Memory: The Transformation of Tradition in American Culture* (New York: Alfred A. Knopf, 1991), 11, 55.

16. Barry Schwartz, *George Washington: The Making of an American Symbol* (New York: Free Press, 1987), 194.

17. George B. Forgie, *Patricide in the House Divided: A Psychological Interpretation of Lincoln and His Age* (New York: W. W. Norton, 1979). The quote is on pp. 28–29.

18. Schwartz, *George Washington,* 2.

19. See Michael Kammen, *A Season of Youth: The American Revolution and the Historical Imagination* (New York: Alfred A. Knopf, 1978); Susan G. Davis, *Parades and Power: Street Theatre in Nineteenth-Century Philadelphia* (Philadelphia: Temple University Press, 1986); and Alfred F. Young, *The Shoemaker and the Tea Party: Memory and the American Revolution* (Boston: Beacon Press, 1998).

20. Davis, *Parades and Power*, esp. chaps. 1–2.

21. Eric Hobsbawm, "Introduction: Inventing Traditions," in *The Invention of Tradition,* ed. Eric Hobsbawm and Terence Ranger (Cambridge: Cambridge University Press, 1983), 1–14.

22. Bruce Laurie, *Artisans into Workers: Labor in Nineteenth-Century America* (New York: Hill and Wang, 1989), 47–73.

23. Davis, *Parades and Power*, 42, 73–74; Young, *Shoemaker and the Tea Party,* xvi.

24. Quoted in Laurie, *Artisans into Workers,* 64.

25. *Boston Morning Post,* September 8, 1835.

26. Young, *Shoemaker and the Tea Party,* 7–8, 134–135.

27. The Abigail Adams and Elizabeth Cady Stanton citations are in *The Heath Anthology of American Literature,* 3d ed., vol. 1, ed. Paul Lauter (Boston: Houghton Mifflin, 1997), 905, 2035. On women's roles in Fourth of July celebrations as well as other civic ceremonies, see Mary P. Ryan, *Women in Public: Between Banners and Ballots, 1825–1880* (Baltimore: Johns Hopkins University Press, 1990), 19–57.

28. William Lloyd Garrison, "Declaration of the National Anti-Slavery Convention, December 14, 1833," reprinted in *William Lloyd Garrison and the Fight against Slavery: Selections from The Liberator,* ed. William E. Cain (Boston: Bedford Books/St. Martin's Press, 1995), 90.

29. David Walker, "Walker's Appeal in Four Articles . . . Written in Boston, September 28, 1829," reprinted in Herbert Aptheker, *One Continual Cry: David Walker's Appeal to the Colored Citizens of the World* (New York: Humanities Press, 1965).

30. Mason L. Weems, *The Life of Washington,* ed. Marcus Cunliffe (Cambridge, Mass.: Harvard University Press, 1962), 12.

31. Marcus Cunliffe, "Introduction," Weems, *Life of Washington,* xviii–xix.

32. Uncle Juvinell (Morrison Heady), *The Farmer Boy, and How He Became Commander-in-Chief* (1864), quoted in Cunliffe, "Introduction," xxii.

33. Russ Castronovo, *Fathering the Nation: American Genealogies of Slavery and Freedom* (Berkeley: University of California Press, 1995), 42, 27.

34. "The Joice Heth Hoax," *New York Herald,* September 13, 1836.

35. Cited in Castronovo, *Fathering the Nation,* 33.

36. See Dale Cockrell, *Demons of Disorder: Early Blackface Minstrels and Their World* (Cambridge: Cambridge University Press, 1997), 13.

37. Richard Moody, *America Takes the Stage: Romanticism in American Drama and Theatre, 1750–1900* (Bloomington: Indiana University Press, 1955), 68.

38. William L. Andrews, "Inter(racial)textuality in Nineteenth-Century Southern Literature," in *Influence and Intertextuality in Literary History,* ed. Jay Clayton and Eric Rothstein (Madison: University of Wisconsin Press, 1991), 304.

39. "The Joice Heth Hoax," *New York Herald,* September 17, 1836.

40. Nora, "Between Memory and History." The quote is on p. 13.

41. Robert C. Toll, *Blacking Up: The Minstrel Show in Nineteenth-Century America* (New York: Oxford University Press, 1974).

42. Dale Cockrell shows that minstrelsy—especially in its emergent stage before 1840—was a "creolized" form, taking shape from the social interactions of black and white lower-class urban dwellers; and that it sometimes expressed pro- as well as antiabolitionist sentiments. W. T. Lhamon (*Raising Cain: Blackface Performance from Jim Crow to Hip Hop* [Cambridge, Mass.: Harvard University Press, 1998]) has found in early blackface a serious working-class white interest in black culture, which he traces to learned and mimed gestures emerging from Catherine Slip in New York. Although, like Cockrell, he finds that minstrelsy's later formations were essentially racist, he argues that the subversive power of the early days was often smuggled into the later, more commercialized forms.

43. Nathan Irvin Huggins, *Harlem Renaissance* (New York: Oxford University Press, 1971).

44. Quoted in Eric Lott, *Love and Theft: Blackface Minstrelsy and the American Working Class* (New York: Oxford University Press, 1993), 112–113.

45. Charles Dickens, *American Notes for General Circulation* (New York: Harper & Bros., 1842), 36.

46. *New York Sun,* August 20, 1835.

47. Charles Colbert, *A Measure of Perfection: Phrenology and the Fine Arts in America* (Chapel Hill: University of North Carolina Press, 1997), 214–242.

48. Léon Beauvallet, *Rachel and the New World, a Trip to the United States and Cuba* (New York: Dix, Edward & Co., 1856), 244.

49. *New York Sun,* February 26, 1836.

50. Mary Kelley, *Private Woman, Public Stage: Literary Domesticity in Nineteenth-Century America* (New York: Oxford University Press, 1984); Mary P. Ryan, "Gender and Public Access: Women's Politics in Nineteenth-Century America," in *Habermas and the Public Sphere,* ed. Craig Calhoun (Cambridge, Mass.: MIT Press, 1992), 259–288. See also Ryan, *Women in Public.* For an interesting linkage of Barnum's career to the public meanings of women's "private" roles, see Richard H. Brodhead, "Veiled Ladies: Toward a History of Antebellum Entertainment," in *Cultures of Letters: Scenes of Reading and Writing in Nineteenth-Century America* (Chicago: University of Chicago Press, 1993), 48–68.

51. P. T. Barnum, "The Adventures of an Adventurer, Being Some Passages in the Life of Barnaby Diddleum," *New York Atlas,* May 16, 1841.

52. Rosemarie Garland Thomson, *Extraordinary Bodies: Figuring Physical Disability in American Culture and Literature* (New York: Columbia University Press, 1997), 61.

53. Quoted in John F. Kasson, *Rudeness and Civility: Manners in Nineteenth-Century Urban America* (New York: Hill and Wang, 1990), 142.

54. Peter Stallybrass and Allon White, *The Politics and Poetics of Transgression* (Ithaca, N.Y.: Cornell University Press, 1986), 25.

4. SACRED AND PROFANE

1. *New York Evening Star,* August 15, 1835.

2. *Albion* (New York), repr. *Boston Morning Post,* September 7, 1835.

3. *New York Baptist,* repr. *Springfield Gazette,* September 16, 1835.

4. *Boston Morning Post,* September 14, 1835.

5. See Eugene D. Genovese, *Roll, Jordan, Roll: The World the Slaves Made* (New York: Vintage Books, 1972, repr. 1976), 240, 246; and Lawrence W. Levine, *Black Culture and Black Consciousness: Afro-American Folk Thought from Slavery to Freedom* (New York: Oxford University Press, 1977), 33.

6. Frederick Douglass, *The Life and Times of Frederick Douglass,* quoted in Levine, *Black Culture and Black Consciousness,* 51.

7. Genovese, *Roll, Jordan, Roll,* 210.

8. Anonymous [Levi Lyman], "The Life of Joice Heth, the Nurse of Gen. George Washington" (New York: Printed for the Publisher, 1835), 7. A copy of this rare document is in the collection of the New-York Historical Society. See below for details of this text.

9. For a similar account of the problem of interpreting slaves' interiority, see Shane White, "'It Was a Proud Day': African Americans, Festivals, and Parades in the North, 1741–1834," *Journal of American History* 81, no. 1 (June 1994): 13–50.

10. "Rather a Tough Story," *Alexandria Gazette,* January 17, 1835; *U.S. Gazette* (Philadelphia), July 22, 1835.

11. *Providence Republican Herald,* August 30, 1835.

12. John S. Gilkeson, Jr., *Middle-Class Providence, 1820–1940* (Princeton, N.J.: Princeton University Press, 1986), 67.

13. Robert J. Cottrol, *The Afro-Yankees: Providence's Black Community in the Antebellum Era* (Westport, Conn.: Greenwood Press, 1982), 68–70.

14. P. T. Barnum, "Adventures of an Adventurer, Being Some Passages in the Life of Barnaby Diddleum," *New York Atlas,* May 30, 1841.

15. *Providence Daily Journal,* August 30, 1835.

16. Barnum, "Adventures of an Adventurer," May 30, 1841.

17. Bluford Adams, *E Pluribus Barnum: The Great Showman and the Making of U.S. Popular Culture* (Minneapolis: University of Minnesota Press, 1997), 20.

18. Sidney E. Ahlstrom, *A Religious History of the American People* (New Haven: Yale University Press, 1972), 438; Nathan O. Hatch, *The Democratization of American Christianity* (New Haven: Yale University Press, 1989), 5.

19. R. Laurence Moore, "Religion, Secularization, and the Shaping of the Culture Industry in Antebellum America," *American Quarterly* 41, no. 2 (June 1989): 216–242.

20. Hatch, *Democratization of American Christianity*, 142.

21. Carroll Smith-Rosenberg, *Religion and the Rise of the American City: The New York City Mission Movement, 1812–1870* (Ithaca, N.Y.: Cornell University Press, 1971), 30–35.

22. Carroll Smith-Rosenberg, *Disorderly Conduct: Visions of Gender in Victorian America* (New York: Knopf, 1985), 129.

23. Nell Irvin Painter, *Sojourner Truth: A Life, a Symbol* (New York: W. W. Norton, 1996), 72–73.

24. See William L. Andrews, "Introduction," in *Sisters of the Spirit: Three Black Women's Autobiographies of the Nineteenth Century* (Bloomington: Indiana University Press, 1986).

25. Painter, *Sojourner Truth*, 111.

26. Olive Gilbert, *Narrative of Sojourner Truth; A Bondswoman of Olden Time, with a History of Her Labors and Correspondence Drawn from Her "Book of Life"* (New York: Oxford University Press, 1991), xii.

27. Andrews, *Sisters of the Spirit*, 6.

28. P. T. Barnum, *The Life of P. T. Barnum, Written by Himself* (New York: Redfield, 1854), 153.

29. Olaudah Equiano, *The Interesting Narrative and Other Writings*, ed. Vincent Carretta (New York: Penguin Books, 1995); James Albert Ukawsaw Gronniosaw, "A Narrative of the Most Remarkable Particulars in the Life of James Albert Ukawsaw Gronniosaw, an African Prince," in *I Was Born a Slave: An Anthology of Classic Slave Narratives*, vol. 1, ed. Yuval Taylor (Chicago: Lawrence Hill Books, 1999), 1–28.

30. Phillis Wheatley, "On Being Brought from Africa to America," in *The Collected Works of Phillis Wheatley*, ed. John C. Shields (New York: Oxford University Press, 1988), 18.

31. See, for example, Katherine Clay Bassard, *Spiritual Interrogations: Culture, Gender, and Community in Early African American Women's Writing* (Princeton, N.J.: Princeton University Press, 1999).

32. Equiano, *The Interesting Narrative*, 112.

33. See *U.S. Gazette* (Philadelphia), July 29, 1835; *Boston Morning Post*, September 7, 1835.

34. Lyman, "The Life of Joice Heth, the Nurse of Gen. George Washington," 1–10.

35. Quoted in Carla Peterson, *Doers of the Word: African-American Women Speakers and Writers in the North (1830–1880)* (New York: Oxford University Press, 1995), 46.

36. Frederick Douglass, *My Bondage and My Freedom* (1855), in *Autobiographies* (New York: Library of America, 1994), 366.

37. Quoted in Henry Louis Gates, Jr., "From Wheatley to Douglass: The Politics of Displacement," *Frederick Douglass: New Literary and Historical Essays*, ed. Eric J. Sundquist (Cambridge: Cambridge University Press, 1990), 65n30.

38. Peterson, *Doers of the Word*, 75.

39. Painter, *Sojourner Truth*, 139.

40. "Imposition," *New York Herald*, October 26, 1835.

41. Gilbert, *Narrative of Sojourner Truth*, 138–139.

42. Leonard Cassuto, *The Inhuman Race: The Racial Grotesque in American Literature and Culture* (New York: Columbia University Press, 1997), 171.

43. Rosemarie Garland Thomson, "Introduction: From Wonder to Error—A Genealogy of Freak Discourse in Modernity," in *Freakery: Cultural Spectacles of the Extraordinary Body,* ed. Rosemarie Garland Thomson (New York: New York University Press, 1996), 12. See also Thomson's chapter, "The Cultural Work of American Freak Shows, 1835–1940," in her *Extraordinary Bodies: Figuring Physical Disability in American Culture and Literature* (New York: Columbia University Press, 1997), 57–102.

44. Michael Warner, "The Mass Public and the Mass Subject," in *Habermas and the Public Sphere,* ed. Craig Calhoun (Cambridge, Mass.: MIT Press, 1992), 388.

45. *Providence Daily Journal,* August 30, 1835.

46. *Providence Daily Journal,* September 2, 1835.

47. "Rich and Poor," *Providence Daily Journal,* July 28, 1835.

48. On Zip Coon, see Dale Cockrell, *Demons of Disorder: Early Blackface Minstrels and Their World* (Cambridge: Cambridge University Press, 1997), 92–139.

49. "Editor's Drawer," *Harper's New Monthly Magazine* 37 (September 1868): 363.

50. *Essex Gazette* (Haverhill, Mass.), September 29, 1835.

51. This version of the Heth story is developed most clearly in *The Autobiography of Petite Bunkum, the Yankee Showman* (New York: P. F. Harris, 1855), 22–26. For more on this text, see Chapter 9.

5. Culture Wars

1. P. T. Barnum, *The Life of P. T. Barnum, Written by Himself* (New York: Redfield, 1854), 156.

2. William W. Clapp, Jr., *A Record of the Boston Stage* (Boston: James Munroe and Company, 1853), 1–7.

3. Lawrence W. Levine, *Highbrow/Lowbrow: The Emergence of Cultural Hierarchy in America* (Cambridge, Massachusetts: Harvard University Press, 1988); Paul DiMaggio, "Cultural Entrepreneurship in Nineteenth-Century Boston: The Creation of an Organizational Base for High Culture in America," in *Cultural Theory and Popular Culture: A Reader,* 2d ed., ed. John Storey (Athens: University of Georgia Press, 1998), 454–475. The quote is from Levine, 9.

4. Roger Lane, *Policing the City: Boston, 1822–1885* (Cambridge, Mass.: Harvard University Press, 1967), 29–31.

5. Isabelle Lehuu, *Carnival on the Page: Popular Print Media in Antebellum America* (Chapel Hill: University of North Carolina Press, 2000), 131–132.

6. The exchange over Heth, which involved the editor of the *Boston Gazette,* was reported in the *Boston Morning Post,* September 30, 1835. The incident involving the Jim Crow singer was reported in the *Boston Atlas,* September 15, 1835.

7. *Boston Atlas,* September 16, 1835. On the politics of the *Atlas,* see Arthur M. Schlesinger, Jr., *The Age of Jackson* (Boston: Little, Brown, 1946), 163, 288–289.

8. On Buckingham and the *Courier,* see Schlesinger, *Age of Jackson,* 94, 271–272.

9. *Boston Courier,* September 8, 1835.

10. Quoted in David R. Roediger, *The Wages of Whiteness: Race and the Making of the American Working Class* (London: Verso, 1991), 102. On Negro Election Day, see also Joseph P. Reidy, "'Negro Election Day' and Black Community Life in New England, 1750–1860," *Marxist Perspectives* 3 (Fall 1978): 102–117; and Shane White, "'It Was a Proud Day': African Americans, Festivals, and Parades in the North, 1741–1834," *Journal of American History* 81, no. 1 (June 1994): 13–50.

11. This discussion of the ideological alignments of antebellum newspapers draws primarily from Alexander Saxton, *The Rise and Fall of the White Republic: Class Politics and Mass Culture in Nineteenth-Century America* (London: Verso, 1990), 53–76, 95–108. For more on the newspaper scene in antebellum Boston, see Gerald J. Baldasty, "The Boston Press and Politics in Jacksonian America," *Journalism History* 7, nos. 3–4 (Autumn–Winter 1980): 104–107. On the Whig idea of culture in Boston, see also Ronald Story, "Class and Culture in Boston: The Athenaeum, 1807–1860," *American Quarterly* 27, no. 2 (May 1975): 178–199.

12. See Saxton, *Rise and Fall of the White Republic,* 165–182; Roediger, *Wages of Whiteness;* Michael Denning, *Mechanic Accents: Dime Novels and Working-Class Culture in America* (London: Verso, 1987); and Eric Lott, *Love and Theft: Blackface Minstrelsy and the American Working Class* (New York: Oxford University Press, 1993).

13. Quoted in Schlesinger, *Age of Jackson,* 146.

14. Barnum, *Life of P. T. Barnum,* 157.

15. The calculation of wages comes from Bruce Laurie, *Artisans into Workers: Labor in Nineteenth-Century America* (New York: Hill and Wang, 1989), 58. For more on antebellum wages, see Stuart M. Blumin, *The Emergence of the Middle Class: Social Experience in the American City, 1760–1900* (Cambridge: Cambridge University Press, 1989), 343n6; Dale Cockrell, *Demons of Disorder: Early Blackface Minstrels and Their World* (Cambridge: Cambridge University Press, 1997), 180–181n111. On popular museums, see Andrea Stulman Dennett, *Weird and Wonderful: The Dime Museum in America* (New York: New York University Press, 1997).

16. *Lowell Courier,* September 24, 1835.

17. P. T. Barnum, "The Adventures of an Adventurer, Being Some Passages in the Life of Barnaby Diddleum," *New York Atlas,* May 30, 1841.

18. Laurie, *Artisans into Workers,* 63, 75–76.

19. Tom Ford, *A Peep behind the Curtain, by a Boston Supernumerary* (Boston: Redding and Company, 1850), 27–28.

20. Peter Stallybrass and Allon White, *The Politics and Poetics of Transgression* (Ithaca, N.Y.: Cornell University Press), 26.

21. On Greene, see Baldasty, "The Boston Press and Politics in Jacksonian America," 104; and Schlesinger, *Age of Jackson,* 102, 147.

22. *Boston Morning Post,* September 30, 1835.

23. Lane, *Policing the City,* 28–32; Leonard L. Richards, *"Gentlemen of Property and Standing": Anti-Abolition Mobs in Jacksonian America* (New York: Oxford University Press, 1970), 63–64.

24. David Grimsted, *American Mobbing, 1828–1861: Toward Civil War* (New York: Oxford University Press, 1998), 1–32. Grimsted persuasively argues against Richards's view that the social elite, rather than the adherents of Jackson, were behind much of the rioting.

25. P. T. B[arnum]., "European Correspondence," *New York Atlas,* February 16, 1845.

26. Saxton, *Rise and Fall of the White Republic,* 53–75, 127–161; Reginald Horsman, *Race and Manifest Destiny: The Origins of American Racial Anglo-Saxonism* (Cambridge, Mass.: Harvard University Press, 1981), 102.

27. For another case of ideological improvisation in the Boston press, see Daniel A. Cohen, "The Murder of Maria Bickford: Fashion, Passion, and the Birth of a Consumer Culture," *American Studies* 32, no. 2 (Fall 1990): 5–30.

28. *Boston Evening Gazette,* September 5, 28, 1835.

29. *Sunday Morning News* (New York), September 13, 1835.

30. Saidiya V. Hartman, *Scenes of Subjection: Terror, Slavery, and Self-Making in Nineteenth-Century America* (New York: Oxford University Press, 1997), 24–25.

31. David A. Gerber, "The 'Careers' of People Exhibited in Freak Shows: The Problem of Volition and Valorization," in *Freakery: Cultural Spectacles of the Extraordinary Body,* ed. Rosemarie Garland Thomson (New York: New York University Press, 1996), 40. Gerber is drawing on the investigation of "consent theory" developed in Don Herzog, *Happy Slaves: A Critique of Consent Theory* (Chicago: University of Chicago Press, 1989). I have also found this text useful for exploring issues of Heth's "enjoyment."

32. *Essex Gazette* (Haverhill, Mass.), September 29, 1835.

33. Frederick Douglass, *Narrative of the Life of Frederick Douglass, an American Slave* (New York: Anchor Books, 1989), 50; *Nineteenth-Century American Poetry,* ed. William C. Spengemann with Jessica F. Roberts (New York: Penguin Books, 1996), 76.

34. *Essex Gazette,* October 8, 1835.

35. Eugene D. Genovese, *Roll, Jordan, Roll: The World the Slaves Made* (New York: Vintage Books, 1972, repr. 1976), 165.

36. Barnum, *Life of P. T. Barnum,* 171.

37. *Hartford Times,* October 14, 1835.

38. My account of Maelzel's story comes largely from Stephen P. Rice, "Making Way for the Machine: Maelzel's Automaton Chess-Player and Antebellum American Culture," *Proceedings of the Massachusetts Historical Society* 56 (1994): 1–16; and James W. Cook, Jr., "From the Age of Reason to the Age of Barnum: The Great Automaton Chess-Player and the Emergence of Victorian Cultural Illusionism," *Winterthur Portfolio* 30, no. 4 (Winter 1995): 231–257. A notice for Maelzel's visit to Boston is in the *Boston Evening Post,* August 29, 1835.

39. This description of the Conflagration of Moscow comes from an advertisement for its earlier Philadelphia exhibit, published in the *Pennsylvanian,* July 27, 1835.

40. See Cook, "From the Age of Reason to the Age of Barnum." The Hoffmann story, "Die Automate," is translated as "Automata" in *The Best Tales of Hoffmann* (New York: Dover Books, 1967).

41. This is the argument of Stephen P. Rice, in "Making Way for the Machine." For a related argument on the fascination of antebellum Americans with obscurely operated machines, see Neil Harris, "The Operational Aesthetic," in *Humbug: The Art of P. T. Barnum* (Chicago: University of Chicago Press, 1973), 59–90.

42. Edgar Allan Poe, "Maelzel's Chess Player," *Complete Tales and Poems of Edgar Allan Poe* (New York: Random House, 1975), 421, 432–433.

43. Barnum, *Life of P. T. Barnum,* 156–157.

6. Love, Automata, and India Rubber

1. Quotes are from *Boston Evening Transcript,* September 5, 1835; *Worcester Republican,* October 7, 1835; *Boston Morning Post,* August 30, 1835; "Joice Heth," *Massachusetts Spy* (Worcester, Mass.), October 7, 1835; *Providence Daily Journal,* August 30, 1835; *New York Commercial Advertiser,* repr. *Boston Evening Gazette,* September 5, 1835; "Joice Heth," *Hartford Times,* October 14, 1835; "Joice Heth," *Boston Courier,* September 8, 1835; "Joice Heth," *Hartford Times,* October 17, 1835; *Lowell Courier,* September 24, 1835.

2. *Hartford Times,* October 14, 1835; *Sunday Morning News* (New York), November 15, 1835.

3. For more on the American Institute and its place within the labor struggles of New York, see Sean Wilentz, *Chants Democratic: New York City and the Rise of the American Working Class, 1788–1850* (New York: Oxford University Press, 1984), 151–152, 271–276.

4. See *New York Transcript,* October 22, 24, and 28, 1835.

5. P. T. Barnum, *The Life of P. T. Barnum, Written by Himself* (New York: Redfield, 1854), 159.

6. My account of the history of India rubber comes primarily from P. W. Barker's wonderful *Charles Goodyear: Connecticut Yankee and Rubber Pioneer* (Boston: Godfrey L. Cabot, 1940). The etymology of *caoutchouc* comes from M. de la Condamine, "Memoir Related to the Elastic Resin, Recently Discovered in Cayenne, by M. Fresneau," reprinted in *The American Magazine of Useful and Entertaining Knowledge* 3, no. 6 (March 1837): 233–235.

7. *Daily Herald* (New Haven, Conn.), November 14, 1835.

8. Ibid.

9. Edgar Allan Poe, "The Man of the Crowd," in *Complete Tales and Poems of Edgar Allan Poe* (New York: Vintage Books, 1975), 480; Francis Parkman, Jr., *The Oregon Trail* (Oxford: Oxford University Press, 1996), 43; Walt Whitman, "Song of Myself," in *Leaves of Grass* (Oxford: Oxford University Press, 1990), 73; Henry David Thoreau, "Civil Disobedience," in *Walden and Civil Disobedience* (New York: Penguin Books, 1986), 385–386; Ralph Waldo Emerson, "Experience," in *The Portable Emerson*, ed. Carl Bode (New York: Penguin Books, 1981), 269.

10. My account of Signor Antonio (or Signor Vivalla, as Barnum called him) is drawn mainly from Barnum, *Life of P. T. Barnum*, 92–99, and A. H. Saxon, *P. T. Barnum: The Legend and the Man* (New York: Columbia University Press, 1989), 72–75.

11. Lawrence W. Levine, *Highbrow/Lowbrow: The Emergence of Cultural Hierarchy in America* (Cambridge, Mass.: Harvard University Press, 1988), 146–168; Neil Harris, *Humbug: The Art of P. T. Barnum* (Chicago: University of Chicago Press, 1973). The quote is from Harris, *Humbug*, 78. See also Charles Coleman Sellers, *Mr. Peale's Museum: Charles Willson Peale and the First Popular Museum of Natural Science and Art* (New York: W. W. Norton, 1980).

12. Bruce A. McConachie, "Museum Theatre and the Problem of Respectability for Mid-Century Urban Americans," in *The American Stage: Social and Economic Issues from the Colonial Period to the Present*, ed. Ron Engle and Tice L. Miller (Cambridge: Cambridge University Press, 1993), 65–80.

13. Barnum, *Life of P. T. Barnum*, 160.

14. Alice Kessler-Harris, *Out to Work: A History of Wage-Earning Women in the United States* (New York: Oxford University Press, 1982), 59–60, 78.

15. See Peter George Buckley, "To the Opera House: Culture and Society in New York City, 1820–1860" (Ph.D. diss., State University of New York at Stony Brook, 1984), 141.

16. Wilentz, *Chants Democratic*, 257. See also Rosemarie K. Bank, *Theatre Culture in America, 1825–1860* (Cambridge: Cambridge University Press, 1997), 130–135.

17. George G. Foster, *New York by Gas-Light, and Other Urban Sketches*, ed. Stuart M. Blumin (Berkeley: University of California Press, 1990), 157.

18. Barnum, *Life of P. T. Barnum,* 161.

19. See Wilentz, *Chants Democratic,* 258.

20. Dale Cockrell, *Demons of Disorder: Early Blackface Minstrels and Their World* (Cambridge: Cambridge University Press, 1997), 58, 63.

21. *Boston Morning Post,* October 6, 1835.

22. "Imposition," *New York Herald,* October 26, 1835.

23. *New York Herald,* October 27, 1835.

24. *New Haven Daily Herald,* December 8–10, 1835.

25. Reprinted in "Joice Heth 'exflunctified,' " *Boston Morning Post,* December 15, 1835.

26. The lunatical observation was in fact the journalist Richard Adams Locke's 1834 perpetration of the "moon hoax," in which he reported the telescopic discovery that the moon was populated by a race of flying men. The resulting exposure of the hoax, defense of the original story, and counterexposures consumed the penny press for weeks. Locke would, in a few months, become an important figure in the Heth story. See Chapter 8.

27. *Sunday Morning News,* December 27, 1835.

28. The paper's coverage of the Heth autopsy states that "we have always been somewhat disposed to doubt the truth of her story, but from other circumstances than those which were developed at her post mortem examination" (*Sunday Morning News,* February 28, 1836). The only "other circumstances" generating doubt in the newspaper's coverage were the details of the automaton story. Prior to that account, the *News* had bought the story of her old age entirely (*Sunday Morning News,* September 13, 1835). Perhaps the best explanation for these wild swings in its position is that the newspaper never actually sent a correspondent to visit the exhibit, and reported exclusively from hearsay.

29. Barnum, *Life of P. T. Barnum,* 157.

30. See Reed Benhamou, "From *Curiosité* to *Utilité:* The Automaton in Eighteenth-Century France," *Studies in Eighteenth-Century Culture* 17 (1987): 91–105; Silvio Bedini, "The Role of Automata in the History of Technology," *Technology and Culture* 5, no. 1 (Winter 1964): 24–42.

31. Lorraine Daston and Katharine Park, *Wonders and the Order of Nature, 1150–1750* (New York: Zone Books, 1998), 91–94, 292–293.

32. Hillel Schwartz, *The Culture of the Copy: Striking Likenesses, Unreasonable Facsimiles* (New York: Zone Books, 1996), 134.

33. See Daston and Park, *Wonders and the Order of Nature,* 293.

34. Ibid., 260, 210.

35. Peter Benes, "Itinerant Entertainers in New England and New York, 1687–1830," in *Itinerancy in New England and New York: The Dublin Seminar for New England Folklife Annual Proceedings* (Boston University, 1984), 115–116.

36. Derek J. De Solla Price, "Automata and the Origins of Mechanism and Mechanistic Philosophy," *Technology and Culture* 5, no. 1 (Winter 1964): 20.

37. Bedini, "The Role of Automata in the History of Technology," 38, 39.

38. Michel Foucault, *Discipline and Punish: The Birth of the Prison,* trans. Alan Sheridan (New York: Vintage Books, 1979), 136.

39. *Strong on Music: The New York Music Scene in the Days of George Templeton Strong, 1836–1875,* vol. 1, *Resonances, 1836–1850,* ed. Vera Brodsky Laurence (New York: Oxford University Press, 1988), 232.

40. Harriet Beecher Stowe, *Uncle Tom's Cabin, or, Life among the Lowly* (New York: Penguin, 1981), 56.

41. On the New Haven riots, see Robert Austin Warner, *New Haven Negroes: A Social History* (New Haven: Yale University Press, 1940), 1–68; James Stewart Brewer, "The Emergence of Racial Modernity and the Rise of the White North, 1790–1840," *Journal of the Early Republic* 18 (Spring 1998): 203–204.

42. "Mix, Silas," *Obituary Record of Yale University, Deceased from June, 1880, to June, 1890* (New Haven: Tuttle, Morehouse & Taylor, 1890), 121; "Ample Satisfaction," *New Haven Daily Herald,* October 19, 1835.

43. "Ample Satisfaction"; "Hear Mr. Mix," *New Haven Daily Herald,* January 22, 1836.

44. *New Haven Daily Herald,* December 16, 1835.

45. On antebellum attitudes toward race and insanity, see William Ragan Stanton, *The Leopard's Spots: Scientific Attitudes toward Race in America, 1815–1859* (Chicago: University of Chicago Press, 1960); Sander L. Gilman, *Difference and Pathology: Stereotypes of Sexuality, Race, and Madness* (Ithaca, N.Y.: Cornell University Press, 1985), 131–149; Suman Fernando, *Race and Culture in Psychiatry* (London: Croom Helm, 1988); Lynn Gamwell and Nancy Tomes, *Madness in America: Cultural and Medical Perceptions of Mental Illness before 1914* (Ithaca, N.Y.: Cornell University Press, 1995); and Benjamin D. Reiss, "Madness and Mastery in Melville's 'Benito Cereno,' " *Criticism* 38, no. 1 (Winter 1996): 115–150.

46. *New Haven Daily Herald,* December 23, 1835.

47. "Monody on Joice Heth," *New Haven Daily Herald,* February 27, 1836.

48. "Mix, Silas," 121.

7. SPECTACLE

1. "Old Joice Heth Gone at Last," *New York Transcript,* February 23, 1836.

2. P. T. Barnum, *The Life of P. T. Barnum, Written by Himself* (New York: Redfield, 1854), 171.

3. Lorraine Daston and Katharine Park, *Wonders and the Order of Nature, 1150–1750* (New York: Zone Books, 1998), 146, 203–204.

4. Guy Debord, *The Society of the Spectacle,* trans. Donald Nicholson-Smith (New York: Zone Books, 1994), 16, 22. It could be said—following Michel Foucault—that the spectacular form of the autopsy had more to do with a premodern taste for public humiliation and punishment than with post-Enlight-

enment forms of social control, which emphasized surveillance rather than spectacle. Foucault, though, is charting the course of state-sponsored power (and its
handmaidens in the prisons, courts, schools, census bureaus, and so on) and has
relatively little to say about commercial culture, which seems to have taken over
the traffic in spectacle in the nineteenth century. See Michel Foucault, *Discipline
and Punish: The Birth of the Prison,* trans. Alan Sheridan (New York: Vintage
Books, 1979). On this point, see also Jonathan Crary, *Techniques of the Observer:
On Vision and Modernity in the Nineteenth Century* (Cambridge, Mass.: MIT
Press, 1990), 18.

5. Alexander Saxton, *The Rise and Fall of the White Republic: Class Politics
and Mass Culture in Nineteenth-Century America* (London: Verso, 1990), 77–108.

6. James Brewer Stewart, "The Emergence of Racial Modernity and the Rise
of the White North, 1790–1840," *Journal of the Early Republic* 18 (Spring 1998):
183.

7. "Longevity," *New York Baptist,* repr. *Springfield Gazette,* September 16,
1836.

8. "Dissection of Joice Heth.—Precious Humbug Exposed," *New York Sun,*
February 26, 1836.

9. "Death of Joice Heth," *New York Sun,* February 24, 1836.

10. Londa L. Schiebinger, *Nature's Body: Gender in the Making of Modern Sci-
ence* (Boston: Beacon Press, 1993), 160–172; Sander L. Gilman, "Black Bodies,
White Bodies: Toward an Iconography of Female Sexuality in Late Nineteenth-
Century Art, Medicine, and Literature," in *"Race," Writing, and Difference,* ed.
Henry Louis Gates, Jr. (Chicago: University of Chicago Press, 1985), 223.

11. William Ragan Stanton, *The Leopard's Spots: Scientific Attitudes toward
Race in America, 1815–1859* (Chicago: University of Chicago Press, 1960), 1–2.

12. Thomas Jefferson, *Notes on the State of Virginia* (New York: Harper &
Row, 1965), 22–72.

13. Ibid., 138.

14. "For the Transcript—Joice Heth," *New York Transcript,* March 1, 1836.

15. Ann Douglas, *The Feminization of American Culture* (New York: Anchor
Books, 1977, repr. 1988), 200–226.

16. Michel Foucault, *The Birth of the Clinic: An Archaeology of Medical Perception,* trans. A. M. Sheridan Smith (New York: Vintage Books, 1994), 124–148.

17. See Ruth Richardson, *Death, Dissection, and the Destitute* (London:
Routledge and Kegan Paul, 1987), 3–29; Gary Laderman, *The Sacred Remains:
American Attitudes toward Death, 1799–1883* (New Haven: Yale University Press,
1996), 73–85; and Robert L. Blakely and Judith M. Harrington, "Grave Conse-
quences: The Opportunistic Procurement of Cadavers at the Medical College of
Georgia," in *Bones in the Basement: Postmortem Racism in Nineteenth-Century
Medical Training,* ed. Robert L. Blakely and Judith M. Harrington (Washington,
D.C.: Smithsonian Institution Press, 1997), 162–183. See also Michael Sappol, *A

Traffic of Dead Bodies: Anatomy and Embodied Social Identity in Nineteenth-Century America (Princeton, N.J.: Princeton University Press, forthcoming). I thank Michael Sappol for making chapters of this book available to me in advance of publication and for his help generally in piecing together the scene of nineteenth-century American practices of and attitudes toward anatomical dissection.

18. See John B. Blake, "The Development of American Anatomy Acts," *Journal of Medical Education* 30, no. 8 (August 1955), 431–439; Harold Jackson, "Race and the Politics of Medicine in Nineteenth-Century Georgia," in Blakely and Harrington, *Bones in the Basement,* 184–205.

19. J. T. Headley, *The Great Riots of New York, 1712 to 1873* (New York: E. B. Treat, 1873), 57.

20. Sappol, *A Traffic of Dead Bodies,* chap. 1.

21. Todd L. Savitt, *Medicine and Slavery: The Diseases and Health Care of Blacks in Antebellum Virginia* (Urbana: University of Illinois Press, 1978), 281–282, 290–293.

22. William Wells Brown, *Clotel; or, The President's Daughter,* in *Three Classic African-American Novels,* ed. Henry Louis Gates, Jr. (New York: Random House, 1990), 108.

23. Cheryl Harris, "Whiteness as Property," *Harvard Law Review* 1106 (1993): 1709–1791; Priscilla Wald, "Terms of Assimilation: Legislating Subjectivity in the New Nation," in *Cultures of United States Imperialism,* ed. Donald E. Pease and Amy Kaplan (Durham, N.C.: Duke University Press, 1993), 59–84. Both Wald and Harris focus on the Dred Scott decision of 1854 as the moment in which this state of affairs was formalized; but clearly that decision, which held that no "persons of African descent" could become citizens because they held no inalienable right to self-possession, justified a preexisting racial stratification as much as it stipulated a new arrangement.

24. In *Death, Dissection, and the Destitute,* Ruth Richardson tells the story of the case of "The Irish Giant," a man well over seven feet tall who was exhibited in London and died in 1783. Despite his explicit arrangements to be buried at sea, his body was obtained by the body snatcher John Hunter, who bribed the undertaker approximately £500 to remove it from the coffin before the funeral (57–58).

25. Kenneth S. Greenberg, "Introduction: *The Confessions of Nat Turner:* Text and Context," in *The Confessions of Nat Turner and Related Documents,* ed. Kenneth S. Greenberg (Boston: Bedford Books/St. Martin's Press, 1996), 19–20. See also Henry Irving Tragle, *The Southampton Slave Revolt of 1831: A Compilation of Source Material* (Amherst: University of Massachusetts Press, 1971), 378.

26. See David L. Rogers, M.D., &c., *Surgical Essays and Cases in Surgery* (New York: John Westall, 1850).

27. "Dissection of Joice Heth."

28. Barnum, *Life of P. T. Barnum,* 171–172.

29. *The Autobiography of Petite Bunkum, the Yankee Showman* (New York: P. F. Harris, 1855), 26.

30. *The Diary of Philip Hone, 1828–1851,* vol. 1, ed. Allan Nevins (New York: Dodd, Mead and Co., 1927), February 26, 1836, entry.

31. See Sappol, *A Traffic of Dead Bodies,* chaps. 1 and 3; for the exclusion of women from dissecting and science generally, see Londa L. Schiebinger, *The Mind Has No Sex?: Women in the Origins of Modern Science* (Cambridge, Mass.: Harvard University Press, 1989).

32. Sappol, *A Traffic of Dead Bodies,* chap. 3.

33. J. N. Gannal, *History of Embalming, and of Preparations in Anatomy, Pathology, and Natural History,* trans., with notes and additions, R. Harlan, M.D. (Philadelphia: Judah Dobson, 1840), 146–147.

34. "Dissection of Joice Heth."

35. Saidiya V. Hartman, *Scenes of Subjection: Terror, Slavery, and Self-Making in Nineteenth-Century America* (New York: Oxford University Press, 1997), 3–4.

36. See James Allen, ed., *Without Sanctuary: Lynching Photography in America* (Santa Fe: Twin Palms, 2000).

37. On antebellum dissection techniques, see Shannon C. MacFarlin and Lawrence E. Wineski, "The Cutting Edge: Experimental Anatomy and the Reconstruction of Nineteenth-Century Dissection Techniques," in Blakely and Harrington, *Bones in the Basement,* 107–161.

38. "Dissection of Joice Heth."

39. "Old Joice Heth Gone at Last," *New York Transcript,* February 24, 1836.

8. AUTHENTICITY AND COMMODITY

1. David M. Henkin, *City Reading: Written Words and Public Spaces in Antebellum New York* (New York: Columbia University Press, 1998), 135.

2. Jean Baudrillard, *Simulations,* trans. Paul Foss, Paul Patton, and Philip Beitchman (New York: Semiotexte, 1983), 85–86.

3. Alexander Saxton, *The Rise and Fall of the White Republic: Class Politics and Mass Culture in Nineteenth-Century America* (London: Verso, 1990), 95. This section draws additionally on Andie Tucher, *Froth and Scum: Truth, Beauty, Goodness, and the Ax Murder in America's First Mass Medium* (Chapel Hill: University of North Carolina Press, 1994); and Michael Schudson, *Discovering the News: A Social History of American Newspapers* (New York: Basic Books, 1978).

4. *New York Herald,* January 9, 1836.

5. See Schudson, *Discovering the News,* 200n84.

6. *New York Herald,* November 28, 1835.

7. For the view of the penny press as a working-class–based institution, see Frank M. O'Brien, *The Story of The Sun* (New York: D. Appleton and Co., 1928); and Dan Schiller, *Objectivity and the News: The Public and the Rise of Commer-*

cial Journalism (Philadelphia: University of Pennsylvania Press, 1981). Saxton's revision of this idea is in *Rise and Fall of the White Republic*, 105.

8. Jonathan Crary, *Techniques of the Observer: On Vision and Modernity in the Nineteenth Century* (Cambridge, Mass.: MIT Press, 1990), 10.

9. On the solution of hoaxes and mysteries as a type of symbolic social mastery, see Neil Harris's classic chapter, "The Operational Aesthetic," in *Humbug: The Art of P. T. Barnum* (Chicago: University of Chicago Press, 1973), 59–90. For a study that emphasizes the class dynamics of exposing inauthenticity, see Karen Halttunen, *Confidence Men and Painted Women: A Study of Middle-Class Culture in America, 1830–1870* (New Haven: Yale University Press, 1982).

10. Quoted in O'Brien, *Story of The Sun*, 51–52.

11. "Dissection of Joice Heth.—Precious Humbug Exposed," *New York Sun,* February 26, 1836.

12. "Another Hoax," *New York Herald,* February 27, 1836.

13. "Joice Heth," *New York Sun,* February 27, 1836.

14. Susan Stewart, *On Longing: Narratives of the Miniature, the Gigantic, the Souvenir, the Collection* (Durham, N.C.: Duke University Press, 1993), 111.

15. On anxieties about social mobility and the legibility of character, see Halttunen, *Confidence Men and Painted Women;* and John F. Kasson, *Rudeness and Civility: Manners in Nineteenth-Century Urban America* (New York: Hill and Wang, 1990). For a study that links the rise in racial essentialism to rapid urbanization and the development of free-market liberalism, see Michael O'Malley, "Specie and Species: Race and the Money Question in Nineteenth-Century America," *American Historical Review* 9, no. 2 (April 1994): 369–395. O'Malley is writing about the second half of the nineteenth century, but many of his insights seem applicable to the world of the 1830s.

16. "The Joice Heth Hoax," *New York Herald,* February 29, 1836.

17. *New York Evening Star,* February 27, 29, 1836.

18. "The Heth Humbug," *New York Sun,* March 1, 1836.

19. Nickieann Fleener, "Benjamin Henry Day," in *Dictionary of Literary Biography,* vol. 43, *American Newspaper Journalists, 1690–1872,* ed. Perry J. Ashley (Detroit: Gale Research Company, 1985), 144.

20. "The Joice Heth Hoax," *New York Herald,* March 2, 1836.

21. "[For the Transcript] JOICE HETH," *New York Transcript,* March 1, 1836.

22. "Imposture Defended," *New York Sun,* March 2, 1836; "The Joice Heth Hoax," *New York Herald,* March 2, 1836; "Joice Heth," *Sunday Morning News,* February 28, 1836; "Joice Heth," *New Haven Daily Herald,* March 1, 1836.

23. This is a point made by Stephen Greenblatt in "Towards a Poetics of Culture," in *The New Historicism,* ed. H. Aram Veeser (New York: Routledge, 1989), 1–14.

24. See Ludmilla Jordanova, *Sexual Visions: Images of Gender in Science and Medicine between the Eighteenth and Twentieth Centuries* (Madison: University

of Wisconsin Press, 1989), 87–110; and Michael Sappol, *A Traffic of Dead Bodies: Anatomy and Embodied Social Identity in Nineteenth-Century America* (Princeton, N.J.: Princeton University Press, forthcoming), chap. 3

25. On the gender dynamics of the penny press, see Tucher, *Froth and Scum.* Two studies that touch on the penny press's treatment of women's bodies are Amy Gilman Srebnick, *The Mysterious Death of Mary Rogers: Sex and Culture in Nineteenth-Century New York* (New York: Oxford University Press, 1995); and Patricia Cline Cohen, *The Murder of Helen Jewett: The Life and Death of a Prostitute in Nineteenth-Century New York* (New York: Vintage Books, 1998).

26. *New York Herald,* October 24, 1836.

27. "The Negro Steaks (A Chapter from the Diary of a N.Y. Physician)" ["from the N.Y. Transcript"], *Thomsonian Manual* 1 (1835): 181–182, quoted in Sappol, *A Traffic of Dead Bodies.*

28. Geoffrey Sanborn, *The Sign of the Cannibal: Melville and the Making of a Postcolonial Reader* (Durham, N.C.: Duke University Press, 1998). The quote is from Reverend Josiah Priest, p. 27.

29. On mob attitudes toward interracial sex, see Timothy J. Gilfoyle, *City of Eros: New York City, Prostitution, and the Commercialization of Sex* (New York: W. W. Norton, 1992), 36–46. On the popularity of minstrelsy among the likely participants in mob action, see David R. Roediger, *The Wages of Whiteness: Race and the Making of the American Working Class* (London: Verso, 1991), chaps. 5–6.

30. *New York Herald,* October 11, 1836.

9. EXPOSURE AND MASTERY

1. P. T. Barnum, *The Life of P. T. Barnum, Written by Himself* (New York: Redfield, 1854), 177–179.

2. Richard M. Brown, "James Watson Webb," in *Dictionary of Literary Biography,* vol. 43, *American Newspaper Journalists, 1690–1872,* ed. Perry J. Ashley (Detroit: Gale Research Company, 1985), 436.

3. Barnum, *Life of P. T. Barnum,* 175.

4. "The Joice Heth Hoax," *New York Herald,* September 8, 1836. Subsequent installments of this story ran on September 13, 17, and 24. In the first edition of his autobiography, Barnum describes this as a story that "Lyman dictated while the editor took down the heads of what purported to be the history of Joice." See Barnum, *Life of P. T. Barnum,* 175.

5. The first woodcut, also in the *Herald,* depicted the great fire of New York City in December 1835. See Isabelle Lehuu, *Carnival on the Page: Popular Print Media in Antebellum America* (Chapel Hill: University of North Carolina Press, 2000), 40–41.

6. A similar point is made by Michael Schudson and David M. Henkin. See Schudson, *Discovering the News: A Social History of American Newspapers* (New York: Basic Books, 1978), 26–27; Henkin, *City Reading: Written Words and Public Spaces in Antebellum New York* (New York: Columbia University Press, 1998), 116.

7. Neil Harris, *Humbug: The Art of P. T. Barnum* (Chicago: University of Chicago Press, 1973), 78.

8. On Biddle and the Bank, see Robert V. Remini, *The Jacksonian Era* (Arlington Heights, Ill.: Harlan Davidson, 1989), 30–38.

9. "The Joice Heth Hoax," *New York Herald,* September 17, 1836.

10. This is David Grimsted's assessment in *American Mobbing, 1828–1861: Toward Civil War* (New York: Oxford University Press, 1998), 10. He is responding to Charles Sellers' critique of Marvin Meyers.

11. Timothy J. Gilfoyle, *City of Eros: New York City, Prostitution, and the Commercialization of Sex, 1790–1920* (New York: W. W. Norton, 1992), 36–46.

12. *New York Herald,* October 27, 1835.

13. Karen Halttunen, *Confidence Men and Painted Women: A Study of Middle-Class Culture in America, 1830–1870* (New Haven: Yale University Press, 1982), 7.

14. On the development of the figure of the confidence man, see Gary H. Lindberg, *The Confidence Man in American Literature* (New York: Oxford University Press, 1982).

15. Harriet A. Jacobs, *Incidents in the Life of a Slave Girl* (Cambridge, Mass.: Harvard University Press, 1987), 128.

16. "Ancient Families," *New York Herald,* October 19, 1836.

17. Barnum, *Life of P. T. Barnum,* 189.

18. Quoted in A. H. Saxon, *P. T. Barnum: The Legend and the Man* (New York: Columbia University Press, 1989), 84. Saxon concludes that the letter, like the novella "Adventures of an Adventurer," was the work of Barnum; the discussion of many private matters in both texts is virtually identical to their later narration in Barnum's autobiography. As for this *Atlas* article, Barnum subsequently "cheerfully acknowledged being familiar with the sketch and never contradicted or protested it."

19. Thomas Low Nichols, quoted in Eric Lott, *Love and Theft: Blackface Minstrelsy and the American Working Class* (New York: Oxford University Press, 1993), 112.

20. Barnum, *Life of P. T. Barnum,* 212–213.

21. Quoted in Bluford Adams, *E Pluribus Barnum: The Great Showman and the Making of U.S. Popular Culture* (Minneapolis: University of Minnesota Press, 1997), 1.

22. Ibid., 2.

23. On the Jacksonian vernacular, see Alexander Saxton, *The Rise and Fall of the White Republic: Class Politics and Mass Culture in Nineteenth-Century America* (London: Verso, 1990), 117–123. Adams also comments on the Jacksonian politics of "Adventures" in *E Pluribus Barnum,* 2–10.

24. "Adventures of an Adventurer, Being Some Passages in the Life of Barnaby Diddleum," *New York Atlas,* April 11, 1841.

25. "Adventures," April 25, 1841.

26. Orlando Patterson, *Slavery and Social Death: A Comparative Study* (Cambridge, Mass.: Harvard University Press, 1982), 337–338.

27. See Eugene D. Genovese, *Roll, Jordan, Roll: The World the Slaves Made* (New York: Vintage Books, 1972, repr. 1976), 285–309.

28. George Lipsitz, *Time Passages: Collective Memory and American Popular Culture* (Minneapolis: University of Minnesota Press, 1990), 64; and David R. Roediger, *The Wages of Whiteness: Race and the Making of the American Working Class* (London: Verso, 1991), 95–111. For a related argument, see E. P. Thompson, "Time, Work-Discipline, and Industrial Capitalism," *Past and Present* 38 (1967): 56–97.

29. Saidiya V. Hartman, *Scenes of Subjection: Terror, Slavery, and Self-Making in Nineteenth-Century America* (New York: Oxford University Press, 1997), 7.

30. Frederick Douglass, *My Bondage and My Freedom,* in *Autobiographies* (New York: Library of America, 1994), 291. On the regulation of slaves' access to liquor, see W. J. Rorabaugh, *The Alcoholic Republic: An American Tradition* (New York: Oxford University Press, 1979), 13–14.

31. See Sean Wilentz, *Chants Democratic: New York City and the Rise of the American Working Class, 1788–1850* (New York: Oxford University Press, 1984), 53–55.

32. Roediger, *The Wages of Whiteness,* 108.

33. Adams, *E Pluribus Barnum,* 7.

34. *The Autobiography of Petite Bunkum, the Yankee Showman* (New York: P. F. Harris, 1855), 24–26.

35. Edward H. Dixon, M.D., "Barnum and Joice Heth," *The Scalpel: A Journal of Health, Adapted to Popular and Professional Reading, and the Exposure of Quackery* 9 (November 1850): 59.

36. Gene Fowler and Bess Meredyth, *The Mighty Barnum: A Screen Play* (Hollywood, Calif.: Twentieth Century Pictures, 1934), 69, 83.

37. Lott, *Love and Theft,* 85. The episode of the coat beating is mentioned in Robert C. Toll, *Blacking Up: The Minstrel Show in Nineteenth-Century America* (New York: Oxford University Press, 1974), 75.

38. "Attempted Insurrection," *New York Herald,* September 2, 1835; "Negro Insurrection in Virginia," *New York Herald,* November 25–26, 1835; "Rumored Negro Insurrection at the South," *New York Sun,* July 25, 1835; "A Villainous Hoax," *New York Sun,* February 22, 1836.

39. I thank Bryan Wolf for this suggestion.

40. My account of the Fejee Mermaid hoax and the end of Lyman's career comes from Barnum, *Life of P. T. Barnum,* 231–241; Saxon, *P. T. Barnum,* 116–123; and Saxon, pers. comm., July 2, 1996.

10. ERASURE

1. P. T. Barnum, *The Life of P. T. Barnum, Written by Himself* (New York: Redfield, 1854), 214–246. The quote is on p. 225. For more on Barnum's management of the American Museum, see A. H. Saxon, *P. T. Barnum: The Legend and the Man* (New York: Columbia University Press, 1989), 89–90, 92–109, 113–116; and Bluford Adams, *E Pluribus Barnum: The Great Showman and the Making of U.S. Popular Culture* (Minneapolis: University of Minnesota Press, 1997), 75–115. See also the ambitious on-line "Lost Museum" project run by Joshua Brown of the Center for Media and Learning at the City University of New York at *http://web.gc.cuny.edu/ashp/lostmuseum.*

2. Adams, *E Pluribus Barnum,* 25.

3. Barnum, *Life of P. T. Barnum,* 138, 139.

4. Adams, *E Pluribus Barnum,* 22–23.

5. Paul E. Johnson, *A Shopkeeper's Millennium: Society and Revivals in Rochester, New York, 1815–1837* (New York: Hill and Wang, 1978); Paul S. Boyer, *Urban Masses and Moral Order in America, 1820–1920* (Cambridge, Mass.: Harvard University Press, 1978).

6. See Michael Schudson, *Discovering the News: A Social History of American Newspapers* (New York: Basic Books, 1978), 55–57.

7. Dale Cockrell, *Demons of Disorder: Early Blackface Minstrels and Their World* (Cambridge: Cambridge University Press, 1997), 147–152.

8. Adams, *E Pluribus Barnum,* 76.

9. Bruce A. McConachie, "Museum Theatre and the Problem of Respectability for Mid-Century Urban Americans," in *The American Stage: Social and Economic Issues from the Colonial Period to the Present,* ed. Ron Engle and Tice L. Miller (Cambridge: Cambridge University Press, 1993), 67.

10. Isaac C. Pray, *Memoirs of James Gordon Bennett and His Times, by a Journalist* (New York: Stringer and Townsend, 1855), 224.

11. Quotations from this text in the rest of this chapter are from Barnum, *Life of P. T. Barnum,* 142–176.

12. Saxon, *P. T. Barnum,* 74.

13. *New York Atlas,* February 16, 1845.

14. It is ironic that Van Buren was, in reality, no more neutral than Barnum ever was. The "little magician" may have had other reasons than Barnum suggests to be silent: the very week that Calhoun was attacking him in the Senate, at least four mobs, headed by prominent Democrats (including Van Buren's closest asso-

ciate in the House) would coordinate antiabolitionist actions across the North. That Van Buren knew about these actions seems likely; if so, they would certainly speak louder than words. See David Grimsted, *American Mobbing, 1828–1861: Toward Civil War* (New York: Oxford University Press, 1998), 22–27.

15. P. T. Barnum to Mr. Baker, c. March 1853, *Selected Letters of P. T. Barnum,* ed. A. H. Saxon (New York: Columbia University Press, 1983). See also Saxon, *P. T. Barnum,* 73.

16. See Morton J. Horwitz, *The Transformation of American Law, 1780–1860* (Cambridge, Mass.: Harvard University Press, 1977), 263. See also James W. Cook, *The Arts of Deception: Playing with Fraud in the Age of Barnum* (Cambridge, Mass.: Harvard University Press, 2001).

17. Saxon, *P. T. Barnum,* 5.

18. Constance Mayfield Rourke, *Trumpets of Jubilee: Henry Ward Beecher, Harriet Beecher Stowe, Lyman Beecher, Horace Greeley, P. T. Barnum* (New York: Harcourt, Brace, 1927), 370.

19. P. T. Barnum, *Struggles and Triumphs, or, Forty Years' Recollections of P. T. Barnum* (Buffalo: Warren, Johnson & Co., 1873), 73.

20. Sigmund Freud, *The Interpretation of Dreams,* trans. James Strachey (New York: Avon Books, 1965), 123.

21. James W. Cook, Jr., "Of Men, Missing Links, and Nondescripts: The Strange Career of P. T. Barnum's 'What Is It?' Exhibition," in *Freakery: Cultural Spectacles of the Extraordinary Body,* ed. Rosemarie Garland Thomson (New York: New York University Press, 1996), 139–157. The quote is on p. 145.

22. Barnum, *Struggles and Triumphs,* 623.

23. George M. Fredrickson, *The Black Image in the White Mind: The Debate on Afro-American Character and Destiny, 1817–1914* (N.Y.: Harper & Row, 1971), 97.

24. Harriet Beecher Stowe, "A Key to *Uncle Tom's Cabin*" in *The Oxford Harriet Beecher Stowe Reader,* ed. Joan D. Hedrick (New York: Oxford University Press, 1999), 418.

25. Samuel Stanhope Smith, *An Essay on the Causes of the Variety of Complexion and Figure in the Human Species* (New Brunswick, N.J.: J. Simpson, 1810), 263–264, 268.

26. Charles Colbert, *A Measure of Perfection: Phrenology and the Fine Arts in America* (Chapel Hill: University of North Carolina Press, 1997), 215.

27. Lydia Maria Child, *Letters from New-York,* ed. Bruce Mills (Athens: University of Georgia Press, 1998), 163.

28. "A Chat with Barnum," *The Era,* July 29, 1877.

29. Barnum, *Struggles and Triumphs,* 629.

30. Quoted in Saxon, *P. T. Barnum,* 223.

31. *New York Herald,* October 3, 1865.

32. Barnum, *Struggles and Triumphs,* 76.

33. Avery F. Gordon, *Ghostly Matters: Haunting and the Sociological Imagination* (Minneapolis: University of Minnesota Press, 1997), 195.

34. Isaac Post, *Voices from the Spirit World, Being Communications from Many Spirits. By the Hand of Isaac Post, Medium* (Rochester: Charles H. McDonnell, 1852), 39. See also Russ Castronovo, *Necro-America: Death and Citizenship in the United States* (Durham, N.C.: Duke University Press, forthcoming).

35. See Saxon, *P. T. Barnum,* 326–328.

36. Herman Melville, "Authentic Anecdotes of 'Old Zack,' " in *The Writings of Herman Melville: The Newberry-Northwestern Edition,* vol. 9, ed. Harrison Hayford, Hershel Parker, and G. Thomas Tanselle (Evanston: Northwestern University Press and The Newberry Library, 1987), 212–229.

37. Edward H. Dixon, M.D., "Barnum and Joice Heth," *The Scalpel: A Journal of Health, Adapted to Popular and Professional Reading, and the Exposure of Quackery* 9 (November 1850): 59.

38. Herold Otis, *Pictorial History of the United States* (New York: Leavitt & Allen, 1861), 15; Livingston Hopkins, *A Comic History of the United States* (New York: American Book Exchange, 1880), 151–152.

39. "A Eulogy on Woman, by 'Mark Twain,' " *The Revolution,* January 22, 1868.

40. Quoted in Dumas Malone and Steven H. Hochman, "A Note on Evidence: The Personal History of Madison Hemings," *Journal of Southern History* 41, no. 4 (November 1975): 527.

41. Irving Wallace, *The Fabulous Showman: The Life and Times of P. T. Barnum* (New York: Alfred A. Knopf, 1959), 33, 5, 10.

42. Neil Harris, *Humbug: The Art of P. T. Barnum* (Chicago: University of Chicago Press, 1973), 61–89.

43. Saxon, *P. T. Barnum,* 84–85, 20, 73, 74.

11. A SPECULATIVE BIOGRAPHY

1. Carlo Ginzburg, *The Cheese and the Worms: The Cosmos of a Sixteenth-Century Miller,* trans. John and Anne Tedeschi (Baltimore: Johns Hopkins University Press, 1980), xvii.

2. Arnold I. Davidson, "Carlo Ginzburg and the Renewal of Historiography," in *Questions of Evidence: Proof, Practice, and Persuasion across the Disciplines,* ed. James Chandler, Arnold I. Davidson, and Harry Harootunian (Chicago: University of Chicago Press, 1994), 304–320.

3. This account is taken from Lyman's "The Life of Joice Heth, the Nurse of Gen. George Washington" (New York: Printed for the Publisher, 1835), 3–5. Newspapers such as the *Sunday Morning News* and *Lowell Courier* followed this in outline, with minor changes—such as her husband's name.

4. The Bourbon County Clerk's Office of Kentucky has on file a certificate of his marriage to Jane Hughes in Paris on March 5, 1820. The handwriting of this marriage certificate more or less matches that of the older man who leased Heth to Lindsay fifteen years later.

5. *Essence of a Saga: A Complete History of the Oldest Black Baptist Congregation West of the Allegheny Mountains, Historic Pleasant Green Missionary Baptist Church,* ed. T. H. Peoples, Jr. (n.p., 1990), 1–15.

6. Todd Bolen, pers. comm., December 4, 1996; Major General A. R. ("Bud") Bolling, Jr., pers. comm., December 6, 1996. These two men are members of the Bolling Family Association, which has conducted extensive genealogical research into the family line of Bollings, Bowlings, and Bolens. I thank them for their assistance.

7. Diary of William Heth (unpublished, unpaginated) located in the Special Collections division of the Library of Congress. These extracts are also printed in Phillip Slaughter, "Introduction" to "Orderly Book of Major William Heth of the Third Virginia Regiment, May 15–July 1, 1777," *Collections of the Virginia Historical Society,* n.s., 11 (Richmond, Va., 1892): 323–324.

8. Slaughter, "Introduction," 328.

9. Ibid., 329.

10. William's diary entry for July 30, 1792, reports that he loaned a "mulatto girl Jenny" to Andrew.

11. Diary of William Heth, March 28, 1788.

12. Ann Douglas, *Terrible Honesty: Mongrel Manhattan in the 1920s* (New York: Farrar, Straus & Giroux, 1995), 76.

13. Henry Louis Gates, Jr., *The Signifying Monkey: A Theory of African-American Literary Criticism* (New York: Oxford University Press, 1988), xxiv.

14. Frederick Douglass, "The Heroic Slave," in *Violence in the Black Imagination: Essays and Documents,* ed. Ronald T. Takaki (New York: Oxford University Press, 1993), 37–77.

15. Quoted in John W. Blassingame, *The Slave Community: Plantation Life in the Antebellum South* (New York: Oxford University Press, 1972, rev. 1979), 121.

16. Quoted in Lawrence W. Levine, *Black Culture and Black Consciousness: Afro-American Folk Thought from Slavery to Freedom* (Oxford: Oxford University Press, 1977), 86.

17. This account, by Ann S. Stephens, was published in *Brother Jonathan,* April 10, 1841. I thank Mary V. Thompson, curatorial registrar of the Mount Vernon Ladies' Association of the Union, for showing me a transcript of this article as well as the following accounts of Sambo Anderson and Richard Stanhope.

18. "Mt. Vernon Reminiscences Continued," *Alexandria Gazette,* January 22, 1876.

19. Mary V. Thompson, pers. comm., May 4, 1995.

20. Paul Gilroy, *The Black Atlantic: Modernity and Double Consciousness* (Cambridge, Mass.: Harvard University Press, 1993), 56.

21. Diary of John Brown, February 22, 1822, held in the Filson Club, Louisville, Kentucky.

22. Flavel S. Mines, *A Presbyterian Clergyman Looking for the Church* (New York: Gen. Protestant Episcopal Sunday School Union, 1853), 311.

23. Orlando Patterson, *Slavery and Social Death: A Comparative Study* (Cambridge, Mass.: Harvard University Press, 1982), 8.

24. Eugene E. Genovese, *Roll, Jordan, Roll: The World the Slaves Made* (New York: Random House, 1972, repr. 1976), 289; Levine, *Black Culture and Black Consciousness*, 37.

INDEX

Abolitionism, 7–8, 26, 74–76, 79, 81, 84, 86, 96–97, 102, 122, 144–145, 157–158, 165–166

Adams, Abigail, 60

Adams, "Black Amos," 16

Adams, Bluford, 76, 171, 177, 185, 187, 227n6, 228n8

Adams, John, 57

"Adventures of an Adventurer" (Barnum), 4, 75, 171–178, 179, 183, 184, 188, 189, 227n5

African Americans: in antebellum North, 7–8, 16, 24, 42, 44, 76, 89, 93, 122–124, 145, 174–175, 196, 206; and antebellum politics, 8–9, 98; and capital punishment, 16–17; and freak shows, 41–42, 84–86; and phrenology, 48–50; and history, 58, 64; and American Revolution, 60–61; and theater, 63, 65, 66; and blackface minstrelsy, 66; as abolitionists, 76; and religion, 77–79, 84, 196–197, 213; social mobility of, 87–88, 150, 166, 220; as automata, 121–122; and prostitution, 122, 157, 166; and morbid anatomy, 130, 131–134, 156–157; and property rights, 133–134, 249n23; and work, 171–174; and alcohol, 176–177; and genealogy, 211; and "signifyin(g)," 219–221

Agassiz, Louis, 131

Albany Museum, 110

Alcohol, 176–177, 187

Alexandria Gazette, 22

American Institute, 106–109

American Museum (New York City), 3, 31, 41, 135, 181, 184, 187–188, 195, 196, 197–198

American school of ethnology, 131, 195–196

Anatomy, morbid, 129, 132; and freak shows, 127, 130, 249n24; and race, 130, 132–134, 155–157; and popular culture, 135–136, 156–157; and gender, 155–156; and sex, 156–157

Anderson, Benedict, 56

Anderson, Sambo, 220

Andrews, William, 64

Atwood, Elizabeth, 21, 23, 81, 82, 213, 214

"Autobiography of Petite Bunkum" (attrib. Barnum), 178–179, 223

Automata, 18, 104–105, 117–122, 184

Baartman, Sartje, 130, 131

Bacon, Francis, 119

Bailey, James A., 3

Bakhtin, Mikhail, 45–46

Barnum, Caroline, 111